Family Therapy Supervision:

Recent Developments in Practice

Family Therapy Supervision:
Recent Developments in Practice

Edited by

Rosemary Whiffen and John Byng-Hall
The Tavistock Clinic
120 Belsize Lane
London NW3

ACADEMIC PRESS, INC.
London   Toronto   Sydney   Tokyo
GRUNE & STRATTON, INC.
Orlando   New York   San Diego   Montreal
(Harcourt Brace Jovanovich, Publishers)

ACADEMIC PRESS INC. (LONDON) LTD.
24/28 Oval Road
London NW1 7DX

United States Edition published by
GRUNE & STRATTON INC.
Orlando, Florida 32887

British Library Cataloguing in Publication Data

Family therapy supervision.
1. Family psychology — Congresses
I. Whiffen, R.   II. Byng-Hall, J.
616.89′ 15   RC488.5

ISBN (Academic Press) 0-12-794815-5

ISBN (Grune & Stratton) 0-8089-1462-6

LCCCN 82-81692

84 85 86 87   10 9 8 7 6 5 4 3 2

Contributors

MAURIZIO ANDOLFI, Psychiatrist, Director, Family Therapy Institute of Rome, 00198 Roma, Via Reno 30, Italy.

LUIGI BOSCOLO, Psychiatrist, Co-Director of the Training Programme, Centro Per Lo Studio Della Famiglia, 20123 Milano, Via Leopardi 19, Italy.

ELSA A. BRODER, Assistant Professor, Department of Psychiatry, University of Toronto, C. M. Hincks Treatment Centre, 440 Jarvis Street, Toronto, Ontario M4Y 2HR, Canada.

JOHN BYNG-HALL, Consultant Psychiatrist, Co-Chairman, Family Therapy Programme, Tavistock Clinic, Department for Children and Parents, 120 Belsize Lane, London NW3 5BA, U.K.

BRIAN W. CADE, Family Therapist and Social Worker, The Family Institute, 105 Cathedral Road, Cardiff, Wales, U.K.

DAVID M. CAMPBELL, Clinical Psychologist, Family Therapy Programme, Tavistock Clinic, Department for Children and Parents, 120 Belsize Lane, London NW3 5BA, U.K.

ELIZABETH A. CARTER, Family Therapist and Social Worker, Director, Family Institute of Westchester, 147 Archer Avenue, Mount Vernon, New York 10550, U.S.A.

GIANFRANCO CECCHIN, Psychiatrist, Co-Director of the Training Programme, Centro Per Lo Studio Della Famiglia, 20123 Milano, Via Leopardi 19, Italy.

ALEC CLARK, Family Therapist and Social Worker, Formerly Family Therapy Trainee, Family Therapy Programme, Tavistock Clinic, Department for Children and Parents, 120 Belsize Lane, London NW3 5BA, U.K. At present: Kettering and District Child and Family Guidance Service, 41 Headlands, Kettering, Northamptonshire, U.K.

ALAN COOKLIN, Consultant Psychiatrist, Marlborough Hospital, 38 Marlborough Place, London NW8 0PJ, U.K.

JOHN de CARTERET, Psychiatrist, Formerly Family Therapy Trainee, Family Therapy Programme, Tavistock Clinic, Department for Children and Parents, 120 Belsize Lane, London NW3 5BA, U.K. At present: Department for Children and Parents, Tavistock Clinic.

ROSALIND DRAPER, Family Therapist and Social Worker, Family Therapy Programme, Tavistock Clinic, Department for Children and Parents, 120 Belsize Lane, London NW3 5BA, U.K.

SOPHIE FREUD LOEWENSTEIN, Professor of Social Work, Simmons School of Social Work, Boston, Massachusetts, U.S.A.; formerly Visiting Scientist, Family Therapy Programme, Tavistock Clinic, Department for Children and Parents, 120 Belsize Lane, London NW3 5BA, U.K.

GILL GORELL BARNES, Family Therapist and Social Worker, Family Therapy Programme, Tavistock Clinic, Department for Children and Parents, 120 Belsize Lane, London NW3 5BA, U.K.

CHRIS HATCHER, Associate Clinical Professor of Psychology, Director, Family Therapy Program, University of California, Langley Porter Neuropsychiatric Institute, San Francisco, California 94143, U.S.A.

CAROLINE LINDSEY, Consultant Psychiatrist, Family Therapy Programme, Tavistock Clinic, Department for Children and Parents, 120 Belsize Lane, London NW3 5BA, U.K.

JANE LLOYD, Family Therapist and Social Worker, formerly Family Therapy Trainee, Family Therapy Programme, Tavistock Clinic, Department for Children and Parents, 120 Belsize Lane, London NW3 5BA, U.K.

MONICA McGOLDRICK, Family Therapist and Social Worker, Director of Family Training, College of Medicine and Dentistry of New Jersey, Rutgers Medical School, University Heights, Piscataway, New Jersey 08854, U.S.A.

ANTHONY J. MANOCCHIO, Family Therapist and Director, Centre for Therapeutic Communication Ltd., 46 Antrim Mansions, Antrim Road, London NW3 4XU, U.K.

PAOLO MENGHI, Psychiatrist, Director of the Education Programme, Family Therapy Institute of Rome, 00198 Roma, Via Reno 30, Italy.

PATRICIA F. PEGG, Family Therapist, Programme Administrator, Centre for Therapeutic Communication Ltd., 46 Antrim Mansions, Antrim Road, London NW3 4XU, U.K.

PHOEBE PROSKY, Family Therapist and Social Worker, Ackerman Institute for Family Therapy, 149 East 78th Street, New York, N.Y. 10021, U.S.A.

PETER REDER, Psychiatrist, Family Therapy Trainee, Family Therapy Programme, Tavistock Clinic, Department for Children and Parents, 120 Belsize Lane, London NW3 5BA, U.K.

DAVID REEVES, Nurse-in-Charge, formerly Marlborough Hospital, 38 Marlborough Place, London NW8 0PJ, U.K. At present: North East London Polytechnic, Three Mills, Abbey Lane, London E.15, U.K.

PHILIPPA M. SELIGMAN, Family Therapist and Social Worker, The Family Institute, 105 Cathedral Road, Cardiff, Wales, U.K.

LEON L. SLOMAN, Associate Professor, Department of Psychiatry, University of Toronto, Clarke Institute of Psychiatry, 250 College Street, Toronto, Ontario M5T 1R8, Canada.

HELM STIERLIN, Professor of Psychiatry and Chief, Division of Psychoanalysis and Family Therapy, University of Heidelberg, Institut für Psychoanalytische Grundlagenforschung und Familientherapie, Mönchhofstr. 15a, 6900 Heidelberg, West Germany.

KARL TOMM, Psychiatrist, Director, Family Therapy Program, University of Calgary Medical Clinic, 3350 Hospital Drive N.W., Calgary, Alberta, 52N 4N1, Canada.

GUNTHARD WEBER, Psychiatrist, University of Heidelberg, Institut für Psychoanalytische Grundlagenforschung und Familientherapie, Mönchhofstr. 15a, 6900 Heidelberg, West Germany.

ROSEMARY WHIFFEN, Family Therapist and Social Worker, Co-Chairman Family Therapy Programme, Tavistock Clinic, Department for Children and Parents, 120 Belsize Lane, London NW3 5BA, U.K.

MICHAEL WIRSCHING, Lecturer in Psychosomatic Medicine and Psychotherapy, University of Heidelberg, Institut für Psychoanalytische Grundlagenforschung und Familientherapie, Mönchhofstr. 15a, 6900 Heidelberg, West Germany.

LORRAINE M. WRIGHT, Associate Professor, Faculty of Nursing, Consultant, Family Therapy Program, University of Calgary Medical Clinic, 3350 Hospital Drive N.W., Calgary, Alberta, Canada 52N 4N1.

Foreword

This important and timely book will be welcomed by teachers of family therapy from all backgrounds and orientations, and will be as useful to those working in isolated situations with limited resources as to teachers in prestigious settings blessed with lavish funds and equipment.

As the Preface indicates, it developed from a gathering of family therapy teachers at the Tavistock Clinic in London in 1979, to which had been invited, by the Editors of this volume, leading members of staff from major teaching centres in Europe and the United States. The aim had been to give an opportunity for extended and reasonably intimate discussion (the total group numbered less than fifty) of issues of general concern to trainers, which the size and wide range of topics in larger conferences does not usually permit.

This International Forum for Family Therapy Trainers, which I had the pleasure of attending, was successful and productive over a wide spectrum of topics. It revealed both a similarity in many of the problems faced, together with a great variety of approaches in attempting to cope with them. Despite strong differences of view about the theory and techniques employed in therapy, much experience was found to be widely shared, and in certain respects most participants were discovered to be in agreement or at least to be moving in a similar direction.

One shared view which emerged was the increasing importance given by teachers to learning by observation of therapy sessions, whether by videotape recording or direct vision, and by supervision of the students' work in the course of the session by the variety of means now available. Towards the end of the Forum, when it appeared worthwhile to share some of the interesting things we had learned from each other with a wider audience by means of a book, and thereby to continue the exchange and learning of the Forum experience, this central issue of observation of clinical work and live supervision was selected as the theme.

That enterprise has come to fruition; the Editors and Contributors have between them achieved a volume which avoids repetition, hangs together and reflects some of the taut, attentive interest of the original gathering; and though each reader will find different parts of it closest to his or her preoccupations, I believe all will find rich and stimulating ideas in most contributions which will further their own thought and practice. The Editors' request that Contributors should include a detailed description of an "event" which illustrates the practice of their training methods will be particularly helpful in enabling readers to translate the printed word into experiment with the different methods described.

Of the many new and interesting thoughts this book has given there is space to mention only one, which seems particularly relevant to its purpose. It is: that deprivation of resources can stimulate innovation and effective technique, as much as can wealth of equipment, staff and time. One comes away with the realization that there are assets to having supervisor and trainees in the room with the family and therapist, which are not available working with one-way screens and videotape equipment, as well as vice versa. In Heidelberg the need for a few trainers to deal with large numbers of students, and the consequent use of groups which meet part of the time without a trainer, appears to facilitate autonomy. In Milan the necessity for many students to travel long distances for their tuition has had to be solved by employing a parsimonious model for training as well as for therapy, which (like the therapy) may not necessarily be inferior to more leisurely, time-consuming approaches. Throughout Europe, there appears to be a more conscious and systematic use of the dynamics of group interaction in teaching, perhaps partly because the one-to-one ideal (and one-to-two actuality) of supervision to therapy time in San Francisco was so remote from possibility. Thus, though those less well endowed with funds and hardware will naturally strive to gain such advantages too—and there is much material here to guide those who are more fortunate—this excellent book will find practical application in small, isolated facilities as much as in the major teaching centres.

A.C. Robin Skynner
March, 1982   Institute of Psychiatry, London

Preface

As long as there are many and varied ways of treating families there will be many and varied ways of passing on these skills. In 1979 after four years of teaching an advanced training course in the Family Therapy Programme, Department for Children and Parents at the Tavistock Clinic, we found that we had a great curiosity about the training methods of other family therapists. We therefore decided to convene an International Forum for Family Therapy Trainers and sent invitations to leading Family Therapy Institutes and training courses in the U.K., Europe, U.S.A. and Canada. All, except one, were able to send two delegates and the Forum took place at the Tavistock Clinic in 1979. It was always intended that the rich and varied contributions to the Forum should one day find their way into a book. This book is the evidence that our expectations were well founded.

Although the aim of the Forum was to explore many training issues, it soon became apparent that the core of all training courses lay in direct supervision of clinical work. In the last plenary of the Forum it was therefore decided that the book should focus on supervision. The book is intended for trainers, supervisors and family therapy trainees as well as practitioners who hone up their skills in peer groups. In order to illustrate supervision of a number of different therapeutic methods, contributors were asked to explain how their style of supervision was congruent with their method of therapy and also to give a picture of the context in which they train. We asked that wherever possible "an event" occurring between supervisor and supervisee should be described, with a transcript of the supervisory intervention or discussion.

As the contributions from the Forum members began to arrive, together with one or two contributions from those who had not been at the Forum, we realized that there was a major problem in terminology, mainly around the usage of terms such as "structural", "strategic" and "systemic" as applied to methods of therapy. An editorial decision was taken to let each contributor speak for himself and to let the meaning emerge from the handling of the texts rather than to enforce a uniform usage.

It soon became apparent too that, like all authors, some responded to the precise requests of the editors while others "gang their own gait". Like many editors before us we let this ride, thereby widening the application and usefulness of the book.

Apart from the introductory overview of the evolution of supervision (Part I) the book falls into four sections. In Part II (Chapters 2-7) various techniques of supervision are described which illustrate the range of options available to the supervisor. In Part III (Chapters 8-12) the authors have addressed themselves to the way people learn, largely drawing on their own experience as consumers.

In Part IV (Chapters 13-16) authors who employ a specific model of therapy have described how they supervise their particular method. In Part V (Chapters 17-19) the impact of context on the methods and the organization of training and supervision is explored.

Our acknowledgements are due to our colleagues of the Family Therapy Programme, Department for Children and Parents at the Tavistock Clinic; David Campbell, Rosalind Draper, Gill Gorell Barnes, Caroline Lindsey, all of whom not only contributed to the book but are the group with whom we promulgate ideas and try out new methods; and to Gill Parker whose wide experience and wisdom allows her to preside over our thinking.

We are also indebted to Janet Clark, Training Officer, whose organizing ability made the International Forum for Trainers a reality and to Janice Uphill who has patiently and good humouredly typed and retyped numerous drafts. Thanks are also due to Oula Jones for her painstaking indexing.

We would also like to express our appreciation to the staff of Academic Press, for having steered and encouraged us through the procedures of publishing and who have done so much to promote Family Therapy publications during the past few years.

Finally we would like to thank our trainees over the past six years who have explored, experimented and developed ideas with us, and to all the contributors in this book who have shared their own experiences so openly and generously.

March, 1982   Rosemary Whiffen

Contents

To all our families

Videotape of Family Therapy Supervision

Title: "Closing the Gap"

A videotape is available for hire or sale which illustrates a range of supervisory techniques described in the book. Staff of the Tavistock Clinic demonstrate how to supervise through videotape; family sculpting; a one-way mirror using telephone or earphone or periodic consultations to communicate with trainees; or by remaining in the same room with the trainee during a session.

Distributed by: and   I.E.A. Productions Inc.
Concord Films   520 East 77 Street
Ipswich   Dept. B
Suffolk   New York
U.K.   N.Y. 10021
                                          U.S.A.

Part I
Evolution of Supervision:
An Overview

1. Evolution of Supervision: An Overview

John Byng-Hall, John de Carteret and Rosemary Whiffen

Closing the Gap

"He who rides the tiger cannot dismount." This Asian proverb quoted by Paul Watzlawick in his book "The Language of Change" (1978) at times resembles the dilemma of the family therapist at the beginning of training. From the first it is essential for the trainee to remain in charge of the session for, as in the proverb, to dismount could place him in danger of being swallowed up by the family system. From experience the supervisor has become aware of the precarious position of the family therapist trainee and for the need for help to be more available. He has become aware that supervisory techniques are required which are swift enough to be within the same time scale as interactions occurring in families. The main thrust of supervisory methods has, therefore, been to close the gap between the supervisor and his trainee and to move ever closer to "where the action is".

In the following chapters, notable family therapists from different countries, orientations and teaching institutions, have written about their theoretical stance and their related teaching methods. They describe where they stand at the moment but, whatever their conceptual orientation, it is noticeable how many have undergone a similar journey during the past ten years. The Family Therapy Programme in the Department for Children and Parents of the Tavistock Clinic is no exception. In the late 1960's and early 1970's supervision, conducted in groups rather than on an individual basis, consisted of case discussions in which a therapist reported on an interview, using written or verbal reports. Later audiotapes were used. At this time role play and exploration of the therapist's own family for teaching purposes, were also introduced. (See Stierlin *et al.*, Chapter 8 and McGoldrick, Chapter 2 this volume.)

Next, videotapes enabled the supervisor to observe the process of the interview as well as to hear the dialogue. While it has its own particular value (see Whiffen, Chapter 3) teaching from videotapes only allows the supervisor a retrospective view of the interview. There is a time gap. "Live" supervision from behind a one

3

FAMILY THERAPY SUPERVISION
ISBN 0-12-794815-5

way mirror followed. This enables the supervisor to observe at first hand the dynamics of the family and to give his own observations and directions to the therapist while he is still actively engaged with the family.

In order for the supervisor to have more immediate contact with the trainee, various techniques evolved. At first a consultation with the supervisor behind the screen was planned at a pre-arranged time in the session. Even then, the supervisor's contribution might be too late for the trainee to make use of in that interview. The telephone into the therapy room was next introduced for messages to be given to the trainee therapist while he was working with the family. However, a telephone call can interrupt the flow of an interview and so the "earphone" was used instead. This device, popularly known as the "bug in the ear", consists of an earpiece plugged into the ear of the trainee which allows the supervisor to speak directly to the trainee therapist without the family hearing (see Byng-Hall, Chapter 4, and Loewenstein *et al.*, Chapter 10). This allows direct, immediate and, when both trainee and supervisor are used to it, surprisingly unobtrusive input into the therapy session while it is in progress.

The last move to close the gap (although for some supervisors it is from where they started, see Pegg and Manocchio, Chapter 5) is for the supervisor to position himself even closer to the action and to join the therapist in the same room as the family (Gorell Barnes and Campbell, Chapter 12). The supervisor is sometimes accompanied by the supervisory group (see Carter, Chapter 6, and Pegg and Manocchio, Chapter 5), at other times the group remains behind the one way mirror and act as observers. Although this method brings the supervisor physically closest to the therapist and family it does not constitute the closest involvement with the therapeutic process. In our opinion, supervision with the earphone provides the most direct method of influencing the therapist's interaction with the family and therefore the most appropriate either for trainees early in their training, or for helping change established ways of working.

Whether or not the earphone is used as a means of communication between the supervisor and the therapist, the group behind the mirror or in the room with the family, until recently have remained predominantly observers. Now with the practice of writing "prescriptions" or giving messages from the group for the therapist to deliver to the family, the group is required to become part of the supervisory and hence therapeutic process (see Lindsey and Lloyd, Chapter 7). The group searches for hypotheses on which to base their prescriptions and all are involved in planning strategies (see Boscolo and Cecchin, Chapter 13, and Cade and Seligman, Chapter 14). The trainee therapist, the observing trainee group and the supervisor, are all part of one team.

Without doubt, supervisory methods have been influenced by the flow of conceptual thinking, which had arisen from and permeated the Family Therapy Programme over the past decade, as elaborated later in this chapter.

In the early 1970's most members of the programme were involved in the struggle to move from working with the individual, using a causal-linear model, to working with the family group using a cybernetic-circular model; a move essential to the systemic approach to family therapy.

From this point on, problem solving manoeuvres aimed at changing the process of family functioning in the present, gained in importance. Despite this shift, ways of constructing the past which still influenced the present day perceptions within the family, remained central to our thinking. Family sculpting, the use of genograms, role play with families and setting family tasks, were all innovations which influenced the programme. The Ackerman Family Institute played an important role in introducing these techniques. Jay Haley and Salvador Minuchin's work on the importance of family structure, sub-systems, triangles and cross-generational family ties, directed the programme to more detailed observation of process and to employ therapeutic techniques for changing the family system in the present, often within the family session. Their live supervision techniques influenced our own.

Theories of change, as developed in the writings by Watzlawick (1978) and Watzlawick *et al.* (1967, 1974), prepared the group for the impact of the approach formulated by Palazzoli (1974) and Palazzoli *et al.* (1978, 1980). Their formulation of systemic hypotheses and strategies of intervention delivered through a "prescription" to the family, frequently involving paradoxical injunctions aimed at procuring "second-order change" (Palazzoli *et al.*, 1978) are now included in the programme's repertoire of therapeutic techniques, particularly for certain "crazy" or highly resistant "homeostatic" situations. The Programme has attempted to produce conceptual formulations which enable therapists to decide which techniques are appropriate for which families and at what time (Byng-Hall and Campbell, 1981).

A Paradigm for Thinking about a System Which Learns: A Stochastic Process

We have developed a way of thinking about change and lack of change which we are finding useful. It draws on general systems theory, Russell and Whitehead's theory of logical types and Bateson's concept of stochastic processes (Bateson, 1979).

Let us think first in an abstract way about any collection of ideas, techniques and technologies. We will assume for the sake of argument that initially the elements in this collection are not related to each other in any specific way. They are brought into interaction with each other. This we call an exploratory phase. The interaction between them will result, however, in those which articulate with each other combining, while others drop out. Selection has occurred. At some point the interacting elements will have formed a system, that is a new whole with unique properties dependent on the *relationships* between the elements. This we will call a consolidation phase.

In order for this system to change further or in other words to learn, two components are needed. The first is exposure to fresh ideas, coming either from outside or generated by change in one or more of the elements within the system. The second is a selection process, which as we have seen, is created by interaction between elements in the system. For example, theories of change which involve changes in family processes, together with live supervision and the use of the earphone all come together to produce a new coherent method of supervising therapeutic process. The repeating cycle of interaction, selection and consolidation followed by further interaction, etc. is what Bateson calls a stochastic process.

Let us apply these ideas in general to the setting up and running of a training programme. At the beginning of the training programme the trainers responsible for setting it up provide the initial selective component according to their personal value system, current models of training and theories of change. The trainers, trainees, families, ideas and techniques which have been selected, all interact, which leads to further selection, as some elements combine or make sense while others do not. The tension produced may result in attempts to resolve difficulties by working it out within the group, or to stimulate the opening up of the external boundary to relevant outside ideas. These new ideas may resolve the impasse. This resolution leads to a consolidation phase where the external boundary is again closed and the integrated set of new ideas is in turn put into practice. Once again, practice will throw up a new set of tensions, but in this new phase the selective boundary has changed as a result of experience. If, for example, new external ideas have dramatically solved an impasse in the previous phase the system would tend to operate the concept that "new ideas solve problems". The result will be that the external boundary will be more permeable and less selective. The effect of the flood of new ideas may be to prolong the next exploratory phase before a new resolution or consolidation phase could be reached.

In the phase following this the system has the opportunity to integrate the experience of the two previous phases. This may lead to the formation of a new selective boundary which will only admit new ideas which relate specifically to outstanding problems in the programme.

We see from this example that the actual direction of change depends upon the nature of selection criteria operating at each phase and that these change from phase to phase. Let us examine the nature of selective criteria more closely.

At each exploratory phase of the learning process there are, as we have seen, two levels of selection; external and internal. External selection of what is allowed in from outside is relatively within the control of the trainers who plan the training scheme and its curriculum. This depends on the trainers' experience and tend to be organized around their theories of change even if these are not articulated clearly. On the other hand the selective criteria which are generated within the training scheme itself are much less under the control of the trainers, since they arise by interaction at each exploratory phase. As these supervisor/trainee/family experiences are allowed to interact with the theories of change held by the trainers, theories are adjusted to fit the experience and the selective characteristics of the external boundary are modified accordingly. A new set of supervision techniques are now seen as relevant. This is a description of co-evolution (Bateson, 1979) of therapy and supervision which is potentially highly creative because changes in each system provide new ideas for the other, e.g. the observing supervision group is found to be capable of providing an intervention in its own right. (See Lindsey and Lloyd, Chapter 7 and Boscolo and Cecchin, Chapter 13.)

All the selective processes have at least three elements which operate at both external and internal levels. The survival of a system is of course the basic element. If anxiety is too high in a supervisor-therapist-family system, the therapist, the family or the supervisor will leave the field and the system dies. Thus systems which keep anxiety within tolerable limits are selected. The two other main elements which interact with survival are rewards and effectiveness. These three elements of selective criteria have to relate to each other if a functional learning and teaching system is to emerge. First, a predominantly survival oriented system, operating for its own sake, is unlikely to be effective therapeutically. Secondly a system which selects new concepts or technology for the fun of exploration may easily accept ideas which could be damaging or ineffective. Thirdly a system oriented to effectiveness will only be successful if it also takes account of survival and rewards.

It is useful to examine ways in which these three elements within the selective criteria can interact creatively. For example, a technique which in other settings has been shown to be effective, may engender too much anxiety to survive if introduced by a supervisor into a group which is new and feeling unsafe. The same technique could be introduced successfully to a group which has first developed a sense of security by sharing rewarding activities.

The principles of the stochastic process will now be illustrated by describing briefly how one aspect of supervision unfolded in the Family Therapy Programme, Department for Children and Parents, Tavistock Clinic. Supervision of impasse in therapy is chosen to simplify issues. It also encompasses most of the principles of supervision. The aim is to help the reader consider the evolution of his own practice of supervision and in particular to think about selective processes as these can be adjusted and hence can influence the direction of evolution.

Evolution of Supervision of Impasse in Therapy

Techniques of supervision are required for therapy which is no longer producing change. The various theoretical explanations of this state of "no change", along with the reciprocal theories of change will influence how this problem is tackled. The experience of the supervision devised to meet this challenge will contribute to the stochastic process.

Many theories of therapy at the point of impasse involve the idea of an overlap between the family and therapeutic systems; that is certain aspects of the therapist's (or therapeutic team's) make up is already or becomes the same as that of the family. Therapists bear witness to this problem when they describe being inexorably sucked into the family system; becoming like a member of the family, powerless to change anything. Another simpler explanation is that the therapist's techniques are not adequate to the task. It is important to disentangle these two situations because, working on problems of lack of technique with theories of overlap will produce no change, just as increasing the range of techniques may not solve overlap difficulties.

In viewing an evolutionary process it is important to return to the original building blocks, although they may seem dated from the perspective of those inside the evolution. What usually happens in the stochastic process is that favoured aspects are retained but used in a much more specific way within a new synthesis. Ideas at each phase retain their validity in certain contexts. In the Tavistock Clinic theories developed in the 1950's and 1960's (Dicks, 1963; Bannister and Pincus, 1971; Ezriel, 1959; Bion, 1965) postulated that unchanging pathological relationships were based on mutual collusive defence against shared unconscious fears and phantasies. These ideas have now been extended by the Adolescent Department, Tavistock Clinic, to encompass psychotherapy with the family (Box et al., 1981).

When working with whole families increased in late 1960's and early 1970's cotherapy with a male/female pair was preferred. Briefly the theory of change went as follows, the cotherapy couple would be sucked into the family system, often reflecting the nature of the collusive marital relationship, change would then follow the resolution of the collusive cotherapy relationship in a new way, thus providing a model for the family of how to do the same. This resolution is achieved by the therapists' experiencing and then making conscious the unconscious fears and assumptions of the family, thus breaking the collusion. Supervision was mediated through reports or audiotapes of sessions and an exploration of how the family made the cotherapists feel and act towards each other (an aspect of countertransference). The dysfunctional pattern might also be shown in the presentation by the cotherapists to the supervision group. The supervision group helped the therapists to become aware of their collusions with the family and with each other, enabling them to reduce the overlap between family and therapists. This also freed the cotherapists to interpret the dynamics in the next session. The unconscious material was "worked through" via the transference. Interpreting the transference became the vehicle of change.

The phenomena of family dynamics and how these invade therapeutic systems had been learned. This phenomenon remains as a preoccupation within the field of family therapy and supervision as the rest of this book reveals, although it is often conceptualized in very different ways. A consolidation of the therapy undertaken from 1969–1972 was done in writing (an important consolidation technique) and published (Byng-Hall, 1973, 1975). Within that writing were seeds of many changes to come, in particular an attempt to integrate systems and psychoanalytic theory.

Videotape was used when it became available in 1972. This stimulated a lengthy exploratory process. First, it enabled the staff to examine the circular sequences described in systems theory. They became interested in reciprocal and circular processes. For example, a mother could be seen to be treating her own daughter as if she were a disapproving mother. The daughter in turn disapproved, father glanced approvingly at his daughter; mother, noticing this, was petulant, provoking another scolding from her daughter, etc. The realization of the obvious, that the most fundamental "transference" was not to the therapists but to other members of the family enabled the model of change to alter. The transference to the therapists did not have to be the primary route of change. Change could be wrought through altering the family's interpersonal perceptions. This theoretical shift freed the therapists to be more active. They did not have to passively wait for transference and counter-transference to develop. A repertoire of techniques from outside were now sought.

The selective process can only take in new ideas which "fit" at that point in time. Salvador Minuchin was at the Tavistock in 1972 for a sabbatical period and had demonstrated the use of live supervision with a one-way screen and telephone. It was not, however, until four years later that it was possible to properly incorporate this. Instead, as already mentioned, the Ackerman Family Institute of New York with its more psychodynamic tradition provided the main input. Running a jointly sponsored conference in 1974 enabled the staff to learn techniques such as family sculpting and use of genograms. These techniques meshed perfectly with the idea of exploring and changing interpersonal perceptions and tracing their historical origins within the family. In this way, as shown in the example above, mother could be helped to mourn her mother, which freed the daughter from this role. Father could be helped to understand why he used his daughter to express his own anger against the image of his irresponsible mother, and the daughter could be helped to understand the historical origins of what was happening, and how she was now helping to maintain it.

The trainee's family of origin was sculpted and his genogram drawn; keeping him experientially in touch with his client's therapy. Supervision was via videotape. When he became visibly "stuck", overlapping themes in his own family were sculpted or explored on a genogram and then understood in interactive circular form. One therapist became paralysed whenever the mother in the family became aggressive towards her husband. It emerged that his own father had left home after being nagged by his mother.

Consolidation of supervision using videotape and experiential techniques followed and the therapy was more successful and supervision was fun. New ideas were experienced as both exciting and effective. The evolutionary process speeded up. As has been discussed earlier, the supervisor needed to get closer to the process. The ideas from structural family therapy, available since 1972, showed that techniques could be used during the session to stop a mother treating her daughter as a mother, to help parents take back parental authority and to reduce the daughter/father coalition. It was no longer necessary to deal with the historical antecedents to this phenomenon. Interpersonal perceptions, it was argued, would be modified following a change in role rather than vice versa. Systems theory supported this view by conceptualizing the family homeostasis as being maintained by cybernetic feedback loops, not by perceptions from the past. Theory of change now centred on taking the family beyond their homeostatic boundaries.

The supervision of structural moves aimed at changing the process had to include the capacity to change the therapist's technique at the moment he became "stuck", not afterwards. This involved a one-way screen with telephone contact to give the trainee appropriate instructions. The immediate efficiency of this method proved startling. Families changed very rapidly.

The idea of therapeutic impasse being due to overlap phenomena almost disappeared. It was now considered to be due to lack of appropriate technique or through not pursuing goals with enough energy or tenacity. Exploration of the trainee's family of origin was reduced to a minimum and the supervision group became purposive, active and enthusiastic. The supervisor became more in charge of the group, which was congruent with a therapy which aimed to establish appropriate intergenerational boundaries.

A new exploratory phase started when it was found that while families frequently changed for several sessions, they then reached an impasse. It may be that the supervisor did not sufficiently press the supervisee beyond *his* homeostatic boundaries or the technique was not adequate. The technique of the supervisor entering the session to take over the therapy when stalemate was reached, provided experience of startling power. Some families, however, took flight and other families now treated their trainee therapists as insignificant. The supervisors in the programme following this experience reduced the frequency of their entry.

Perhaps if the power of the supervisory entry had been more congruent with the style of the staff, or if skill in handing power back to the trainee had been developed, the programme might have consolidated the use of structural techniques, without need to look for others. However, the concepts of defence and resistance provided another explanation for the impasse with structural techniques which occurred either early on in very disturbed "homeostatic" families or later in those having initially shown more readiness to change. Strategic family therapy techniques, however, seemed to be effective in this situation. A steady input of strategic ideas has come during the 1970's from the literature and from contact with the "Brief and strategic groups" at the Ackerman (Papp, 1976). Direct contrast with the Palazzoli group started a new interactive phase. The systems hypotheses elaborated by them (Palazzoli *et al.*, 1978) fitted well with concepts of mutual defence elaborated at the Tavistock previously (Byng-Hall, 1973). At the time that original paper was written (1971) the family defence was interpreted in "bits and pieces", and not via a complete systemic circular formulation. Also the way interpretations were given at that time implied that the defence should be changed because it was "bad", that is the defence was not given positive connotation. Naturally change had been slow because it had to be resisted.

The use of the one-way mirror and consultation with the supervisor behind the screen enabled the systemic formulation to be made outside the family/therapist system, and also provided sufficient time to elaborate a complete systemic hypothesis. The formulation or interpretation is made by the group, and hence is meta to the family/therapist system. Positive connotation of the symptom, with injunction not to change for the time being, removes the need for resistance. Techniques for supervising this procedure are discussed in Boscolo and Cecchin (Chapter 13).

The programme is moving into a new period of differentiation and integration. Current ideas about change and no change are that the family/therapist system potentially alternates between homeostatic and exploratory phases just as in any stochastic learning system. Strategic/paradoxical approaches may be indicated in the homeostatic phase, while structural, sculpting, historical or other direct approaches are appropriate in the exploratory phase. These phases can occur on a micro and or macro time scale, so that therapy ebbs and flows in the session itself as well as in different phases of treatment. Supervision through the earphone can track the ebb and flow during the session. The consultation with the Supervisory Group in the middle of the session relates better to the long-term issues. Either strategic or structural techniques can be planned then.

When for some reason live supervision or videotape is not possible, techniques which illustrate the system are usually used, rather than merely reported. Techniques such as sculpting or role play, using the supervision group, or drawing the family genogram and map of the family structure are used.

These represent the most useful remnants of previous supervisory techniques.

Differentiation comes from the use of different techniques to fit the type of family homeostasis. It also comes from the fact that different supervisors are developing their own theories and style of therapy and supervision. One group for instance is currently exploring strategic techniques in greater depth; another is elaborating a conceptual framework related to distance regulation (Byng-Hall and Campbell, 1981).

Implications of the Stochastic Process for Planning Supervisory Practice

Each trainee needs to experience at least one cycle of the stochastic process, exploration, selection, consolidation and back to exploration. In this way rules are taught about how and when to change rules about change: the trainee learns to learn. It must be remembered that the faculty is (or should be) going through a learning process themselves, and that each staff member may be at different points in the process. Coupled with this is the fact that family therapy is a world-wide system and an open one, also evolving and learning. Thus new ideas are continually exchanged in the literature, via videotape or through live demonstrations by travelling experts. Because of their visibility, backed up by the charisma of the visiting experts, these ideas carry more impact than those exchanged in traditional ways. This may sometimes lead either to an over permeable external boundary; no idea being consolidated before the next one takes its place, or in contrast to this may lead to the establishing of a "school" which protects itself by rejecting outside ideas and becomes a closed system. A proper balance must be found.

In considering how this balance is to be found trainers should think of (1) time scale (2) selective processes, both external and internal, and (3) evaluation.

Time scale

Short training courses require that only a few new ideas should be explored and much of the supervisory time available be given to their consolidation. Input should be from the staff's own repertoire.

Supervision within a training scheme, however, often covers one, two or three years. This may encompass one stochastic cycle within the staff group, in which case their "growing edge" can be taken into the supervision with advantage to trainer as well as trainee, although it is still the responsibility of the trainer to teach those areas which are well established in his own practice. This is particularly important when the staff of the programme are undergoing a long exploratory phase which may span the trainee's whole stay. It is also beholden on the trainee to do his own synthesis or consolidation. The staff faculty has to decide how much of their "growing edge" can be held in supervision and how much in mutual supervision by staff colleagues (Gorell Barnes and Campbell, Chapter 12) or within specially designed projects in which new ideas can be explored.

Selection processes

External

The trainer's response to outside ideas or to visitors largely determines the permeability of the external boundary. However polite and enthusiastic their responses are, if the trainee observes no change in his supervisor's practice, the message is clear: these ideas cannot be integrated. They can, however, be "parked" ready to be used at a later date either by trainer or trainee and to become part of the "stochastic storehouse" of the individual.

The strongest affirmative message comes if the supervisor is prepared to be supervised himself by a visiting expert, or to change his practice incorporating the new ideas, or to reinvite the visitor at a later date.

Internal

As has been suggested already, coevolution of supervision and therapy provides a particularly rich change potential. The supervision needs to be sensitive to the creative events which occur during supervision. Trainees, especially experienced ones, will be more creative if they realize that they are contributing to an exploratory process. Comments made by trainees behind the one-way screen, either during the session or in the break may be incorporated by the supervisor. At times, however, the supervisor needs to set a limit on the discussion and he must always take authority for the final supervisory intervention.

In order to remain creative, trainers are wise to mix the level of teaching; only to teach beginners for brief periods deprives them of an invaluable learning experience; on the other hand only to train very senior family therapists deprives them of having to continually re-evaluate the fundamental aspects of therapy.

Evaluation

As we have seen, the openness to change in response to ideas and techniques which appear to solve problems is of utmost importance. However, in order to avoid the danger of the self-validating closed system, effectiveness should be evaluated, both in a wider context and over a long time scale. This systematic follow up and evaluation of changes in both trainees and in families should be undertaken in a way which feeds the information back into the system. This should be an integral part of a training scheme. It is unfortunately all too often given low priority.

References

Bannister, K. and Pincus, L. (1971). *Shared Phantasy in Marital Problems: Therapy in a Four Person Relationship*. Tavistock Institute of Human Relations, Institute of Marital Studies, London.

Bateson, G. (1973). *Steps to an Ecology of Mind*. Paladin, St. Albans.

Bateson, G. (1979). *Mind and Nature: A Necessary Unity*. Wildwood House, London.

Bion, W. R. (1965). *Transformation, Change from Learning to Growth*. Heinemann Medical, London.

Box, S., Copley, B., Macagna, J. and Moustaki, E. (eds) (1981). *Psychotherapy With Families: An Analytic Approach*. Routledge and Kegan Paul, London.

Byng-Hall, J. (1973). Family myths used as defence in conjoint family therapy. *Br. J. Med. Psychol.* **46**, 239-250.

Byng-Hall, J. (1975). *Adolescence and Breakdown*. (S. Meyerson, ed.), 119-134. Allen and Unwin, London.

Byng-Hall, J. and Campbell, D. (1981). Resolving conflicts arising from distance-regulation: an integrative approach. *J. Marital Fam. Ther.* **7**, 321-330

Dicks, H. (1963). Object relations theory and marital studies. *Br. J. Med. Psychol.* **36**, 125-129.

Ezriel, H. (1959). The role of transference in psychoanalysis and other approaches to group treatment. *Acta Psychotherapeutica* **7**, 101-116.

Palazzoli, M. (1974). The treatment of children through brief therapy of their parents. *Family Process* **13**, 429.

Palazzoli, M., Boscolo, L., Cecchin, G. and Prata, G. (1978). *Paradox and Counter Paradox: A New Model in the Therapy of the Family in Schizophrenic Transition*. Jason Aronson, London and New York.

Palazzoli, M., Boscolo, L., Cecchin, G. and Prata, G. (1980) Hypothesizing, circularity, neutrality: Three guidelines for the conductor of the session. *Family Process* **19**, 3-18.

Papp, P. (1976). *Family Therapy, Theory and Practice* (P. J. Guerin, ed.). Gardner Press, New York and London.

Watzlawick, P. (1978). *The Language of Change*. Basic Books, New York.

Watzlawick, P. Beavin, J. and Weakland, J. (1967). *Pragmatics of Human Communication: A Study of Interactional Patterns, Pathologies and Paradoxes*. W. W. Norton, New York.

Watzlawick, P. Weakland, J. and Fisch, R. (1974). *Change: Principles of Problem Formation and Problem Resolution*. W. W. Norton, New York.

Part II
Special Techniques of Supervision

2. Through the Looking Glass: Supervision of a Trainee's "Trigger" Family

Monica McGoldrick

This chapter will describe a method of supervision in which the supervisor moves between the trainee's own family and the work with a clinical family. In the example discussed here, the trainee came to call the clinical family his "trigger" family, because their issues were so close to his own. It is our view that work focussed on the trainee's own family in relation to his clinical work enhances his/her development as a family therapist. Perhaps every student has a certain family or few families which take on special meaning in his/her training because of the ways their issues reflect his/her own. Successful work on their issues and clarifying the connections to the trainee's own, may produce a quantum leap in clinical development.

The Supervisory and Theoretical Context

The supervision model on which this paper is based was developed at a community mental health centre, where the author directs an inter-disciplinary inservice family training programme. Participants in the programme are staff and trainees of the Centre, which is also the primary teaching facility for the Psychiatry Department of Rutgers Medical School. Trainees include psychiatric residents, psychology interns, psychiatrists, psychologists, social workers and graduate nurses.

Although some trainees participate only in portions of the programme, the full training is designed for those who wish to use the family as the primary context of their work and is carried out over a three-year period as follows:

1st year: 2 hour didactic seminar (lectures, videotapes, etc.)
           1 hour individual supervision (primarily live or videotape)

17

FAMILY THERAPY SUPERVISION
ISBN 0-12-794815-5

(Optional) Group consultation seminar on the Therapist's own family
or clinical cases.

2nd year: 3 hour small group supervision seminar.

3rd year: 3 hour small group seminar devoted to supervision and special topics.

Constraints of the setting, which is oriented primarily toward service, mean
that time and equipment are often not as available for training as might be ideal.
How much trainees get from the programme depends largely on their motivation
and initiative. Periodic feedback is given to trainees on their progress, but they
are assumed to have the major responsibility for getting what they want from the
training, just as families are assumed to have the major responsibility for
making the changes they want in therapy, once their options have been
clarified.

While structural therapists maintain that the therapist's own family is
irrelevant to clinical training (Haley, 1976), and Bowen Systems therapists
de-emphasize training in clinical techniques (Bowen, 1978), the view presented
here is that these models are by no means mutually exclusive.

This approach integrates the use of varying models at difficult stages of
training. The Structural model focuses on the micro-system of the household
and carefully elaborates therapeutic moves designed to alter this structure
(Minuchin, 1974). The Bowen model provides a way to conceptualize the macro-
system of the entire family as it moves through time. The specificity of the
Structural model seems particularly useful for the initial stages of supervision in
family therapy. It teaches trainees to focus in on micro-shifts in the system and to
track the impact of their therapeutic interventions. Our initial supervision
emphasis is thus structural in nature, emphasizing live supervision aimed at
helping trainees to understand the immediate situation and to help families
overcome their presenting problems. We consider this type of supervision
important for developing the trainee's competence in relating to families and
helping families have success in resolving their presenting problems.

However, as a conceptual framework, we find Bowen's model the only
comprehensive family systems model yet developed. The Structural model
focuses on the household, the Strategic model on the context in which the
problem exists, and the Epstein model on the nuclear family. Of the major
models used in the field, the Bowen model is by far the most comprehensive and
at the same time succinct. It takes account of the specific relational bonds of all
family members in their natural system, and provides specific guidelines for
hypothesizing about family patterns as they flow over generations. While
therapists can learn something about this model through reading or didactic
presentations, it is our impression that they come to understand it best by
considering how the processes operate in their own families. Thus our training
moves between presentations of theory, the specifics of clinical work and the

patterns in the therapists' own families, particularly in the advanced stages of training.

Our training programme gives priority to both didactic training and to live and videotape supervision. The initial aims of the programme are to teach the trainee to:

(1) Establish a therapeutic alliance.

(2) Track family process.

(3) Gather adequate information to make a family definition of the problem and its context. This includes formulating problems in family systems terms and becoming able to ask system-oriented rather than intrapsychic questions. It also includes evaluating and analysing all systems involved in the problem, including other therapists or agencies which may be involved with the family or may have referred them for therapy.

(4) Establish a contract with the family to work together based on an evaluation of all levels of the system.

(5) Develop skill in intervening to help the family change dysfunctional patterns.

(6) Develop the ability to observe and gain feedback on one's effectiveness in order to shift strategies when necessary (to keep the therapeutic system open).

In the initial phase and theoretical training, emphasis is on teaching the basic elements of Bowen Systems theory (Bowen, 1978). Trainees at the start are taught to use this model as a framework within which to analyse family patterns and problems. Within this theoretical model, they are encouraged to develop a broad array of skills and techniques for intervening in different situations.

This teaching approach assumes that a relatively simple theoretical framework is crucial and sufficient for the beginning stages of clinical work. The major problem for beginning trainees is learning to filter the overload of information one gets in observing families. A simple model serves this purpose better than a complex one. As they move along, trainees can gradually integrate more complexity, while still maintaining a focus.

Trainees are encouraged to spend time applying systems concepts to the study of patterns in their own families as a major way of making the shift to systems thinking.

There is much need for research to determine the value of work on the therapist's own family in training. It is our impression that such work benefits the trainee's clinical work, and that it is particularly helpful in aiding trainees to shift from linear to systems thinking (Carter and Orfanidis, 1976). Structural therapists suggest that a person who has difficulty with, for example, a distant father, should overcome this by getting direct supervision on many families with distant fathers, where he or she learns techniques for dealing with them (Haley, 1976). It is my impression that even a small amount of time spent in defining and shifting patterns in one's own family is a much more efficient way of learning to deal with this. Understanding one's functioning in his/her own most important system, his/her own family, seems to facilitate the ability to understand the operation of other natural systems and the ability to generate hypotheses about families on a systems level.

Many factors influence a trainee's willingness or interest in pursuing work on his/her own family, and such a pursuit cannot be dictated by a training programme. Obviously, working out a personal relationship with one's mother or father does not in itself make one a good family therapist. It is possible for therapists who have never paid attention in clinical supervision to their roles in their own families to function as very talented therapists. Nevertheless, it is my strong impression that one tends to get blocked with clinical families in the same ways one does in one's own family. In the long run, work on one's own family seems a valuable insurance against the difficulty of getting caught with clinical families. (In the short run, of course, the use of live supervision, a team approach, or short-term problem-focussed therapy are commonly used and helpful ways of keeping perspective and avoiding this difficulty.)

We emphasize strongly the trainee's evaluation of his/her work and openness to the family's feedback. We consider this an essential ingredient of learning, and of not coming to take one's theories or techniques too seriously. For this reason we have built into the programme the requirement of trainees doing at least informal evaluation, and follow-up of their cases.

We believe that trainees learn in many ways. Change can lead to insight and insight can lead to change. Thus, some aspects of the training, particularly the live supervision, encourage behavioural change, which is subsequently integrated as insight. Other aspects of training, didactic lectures, theoretical discussion, and analysis of videotapes are used as teaching tools on the assumption that modelling and imitation are also important ways to learn. Our model of change in therapy is similar to our model of change in learning. We believe that a family's behavioural change may lead to a conceptual change or to further behavioural change. On the other hand, some families change their behaviour when offered new concepts for viewing themselves. Thus we often employ educational techniques in treatment, especially with less disturbed families. Some families are able to change when they understand, while some families change and never understand why. When families are very rigid and their anxiety is very high, educational techniques do not appear to work. Such families may change through new perceptions of themselves brought about by strategic interventions, reframing their situation as in the Milan approach. We encourage trainees to modify techniques depending on the family context.

In our programme we combine small group and individual supervision using:

(1) Live interviews which supervisor (and group when available) observes behind a one-way mirror. A "bug in the ear", a small earphone is placed in one of the trainee's ears and connected to a microphone held by the supervisor, and

is used to offer supervision suggestions to the trainee from behind the one way mirror.

(2) Videotaped interviews, which the trainee reviews with the group and supervisor.

(3) Discussion of the therapist's own family (optional, but encouraged, and used by about half the trainees in any given year).

(4) Case discussion, planning strategies and developing hypotheses about families and the moves the therapist can make.

The initial supervision emphasis is on live supervision, because this format offers the best opportunity to teach the trainee new skills on the spot and thus promote success. Videotape supervision is used more often with advanced trainees, where microanalysis of their work and style become important aspects of their training. As mentioned, the initial supervision is focussed primarily on Structural interventions, (Minuchin, 1974; Haley, 1976), that is, on aiding trainees to help families shift their structure to resolve the presenting problem. While trainees are taught about other models of intervention, the use of such techniques as Strategic interventions (Palazzoli, 1978; Weakland *et al.*, 1974) and Coaching (Bowen, 1978) are reserved for more advanced trainees. The first year of supervision focuses more on engaging, evaluating and intervening to help families shift dysfunctional structures. Supervision of advanced trainees places more emphasis on difficult families, the complexities of family process and the interface between the therapist's own family and his or her clinical work.

The Trainee and his "Trigger" Family

The trainee's family

The following example indicates the shifting of modes in supervision. Peter B., during his first year of training had related in a rather distant way to his families. He tended to be eager to use "techniques" and "gimmicks", pushing behavioural or paradoxical strategies without developing adequate rapport and without awareness of issues his families were presenting. He avoided presenting material on his own family and tended to keep his distance in supervision.

Both of Peter's parents had survived the holocaust, while their first spouses had been killed. They had met and married in this country, but Peter's mother had died when he was eight, after a long cancer illness, contracted, Peter thought, when he was born. The mother's death was never dealt with openly by the family, and afterwards Peter withdrew more and more from his father and older sister. When his father remarried a few years later and took on two stepchildren, Peter did not accept his stepmother and felt further shut out of the family.

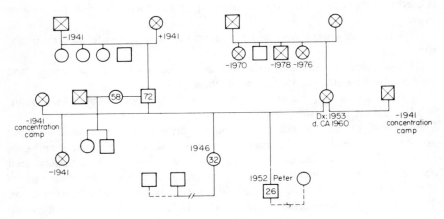

Fig. 1. Peter's family of origin.

At the start of his second year of training he requested to do a presentation of his own family, saying he had decided he wanted to overcome the distant standoff he had with his father. He said that supervisory feedback he had received during his first year of training made him aware that the pressure he felt to help clinical families derived from a sense of not having a family himself. He said his enjoyment of family work was partly a function of always looking for fathers and mothers, and for a chance to belong to a family in which things would work out well. As he later commented, "I think it just built up and eventually hit home that the only way I was going to stop looking for other families was if I made peace with my own family. After that I began to move gradually, step by step". At the time Peter was still reluctant to come to terms with his stepmother and had trouble seeing that this would be necessary in order to improve his relationship with his father to any great extent. He was also reluctant to learn more about his natural mother and her family, about whom he knew almost nothing. For the time being he decided to put this off.

Trigger family

Peter's clinical work began to develop well. He was becoming better able to develop rapport with his families and to tune into their issues sensitively, and no longer pushed them with "gimmicky" techniques. Then, after several months of good work, he presented one of his clinical families in a strikingly disorganized way. He could not define the family patterns, goals of treatment, or how he was getting "stuck", only that he found the family overwhelming. The Arthur case involved an enmeshed three-generational family, in which the eight-year-old boy, Billy, had been referred by the school because of hyperactivity and learning problems. Billy was apparently caught between his mother, Martha, who played the role of "black sheep" in her family, and Martha's mother, who was Billy's primary caretaker. Martha alternatively argued to have Billy for herself and when she felt overwhelmed, turned his care over to her mother. The grandmother was very critical of Martha's way of caring for Billy, while denying that she wanted to interfere. Martha's two siblings, George and Joan, were also actively involved in the family's debates over what was best for Billy, while the grandfather always took a back seat.

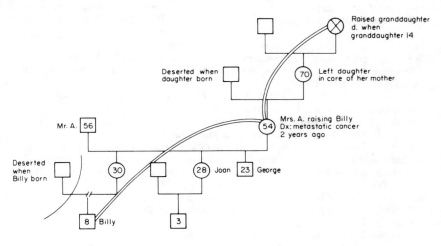

Fig. 2. Arthur family.

Peter brought in a videotape he felt demonstrated the family overwhelming him. In the tape we saw the family going from topic to topic while Peter remained relatively passive. He said he could find no way to set effective limits on their chaotic discussions or to help them develop functional generational boundaries.

I suggested a live supervision session. Peter said it would have to be postponed because the grandmother was ill. When questioned, he mentioned casually that she had had a "recurrence of her cancer". Here was a possible key to his difficulty. He had not thought that the family's emotional crisis might underlie Billy's school problems. Nor had he realized the way the problems paralleled his own childhood experience.

The next problem was how to deal with the family's resistance. We needed to determine how Peter could help the family with the issues that were upsetting them, rather than merely reacting to them. We scheduled the live supervision for soon after the grandmother came out of the hospital. From behind the one-way mirror, using the earphone, I encouraged Peter quite directly to ask family members about the impact of the grandmother's cancer, which they had never discussed. With supervisory suggestions through the earphone, Peter addressed Billy directly about his fears of his grandmother dying.

> (Transcript, after about ten minutes of family discussion of Billy's problems and Martha's incompetence. The family kept avoiding the therapist's attempts to focus on the grandmother's illness.)
>
> *George* (Martha's brother): Martha didn't even call the other day.
> *Grandmother:* I'm just worried about Billy. Martha doesn't even take care of him.
> (*Supervisor* (through earphone): Ask grandmother how worried she is about her cancer.)
> *Therapist:* Do you worry about what will happen to Billy if something happens to you?
> *George:* Martha just doesn't act responsibly. She makes. . . .
> (*Supervisor:* Push it about grandmother's worry about dying.)
> *Therapist:* Mrs. A., let me try to cut through this, do you worry about dying and what may happen to Billy?
> *Grandmother:* No. I'm not afraid of dying. I've never been afraid of dying. I just don't think about it. I just want to make sure Billy is taken care of.
> (*Supervisor:* That's very good. Support her concern for Billy's welfare.)
> *Therapist:* Billy, do you worry about your grandmother?
> *Billy:* Yes, I do. I just want to have one grandmother — her (points), and one mother — her (points), and one grandfather — him (points), and one aunt and one uncle.
> *Therapist:* So you'd like to see the relationships sorted out, would you?
> *Billy:* Yes.
> (*Supervisor:* Ask him if he's worried about his grandmother dying.)
> *Therapist:* Billy, do you worry about your grandmother dying?
> *Billy:* Yes, I do.
> *Therapist:* What do you do when you get worried?
> *Billy:* I go to see where she is and make sure she's alright. (Walks over to grandmother.) By the way, are you going to die soon?
> *Grandmother:* No, Billy, I hope I'm going to be around for a long while yet.
> *Billy:* That's good.

As the session continued the family discussed for the first time the seriousness of Mrs Arthur's cancer and the feelings family members had about the possibility of her dying. Interestingly, once Peter zeroed in on the significant issues, Billy and his young cousin, who was also present, went from being rambunctious and disruptive to being quiet and attentive. Having begun to deal with the issue of death with the family, Peter became more comfortable helping them deal with it in other sessions. He also became more interested in understanding his own family's fear of talking about death.

Trainee's Family

Peter spent several afternoons with his father, talking a good deal about the family background. He learned that there were many instances of early parent loss in his father's family, which had probably contributed to a family tendency to back away from emotional issues and to avoid dealing with loss.

Peter also began to shift his relationship with his stepmother. He found the occasion to talk to her and discovered that she was somehow not quite as "crass" as he had thought. He made several special efforts to be positive towards her, complimenting her on how good she had been to take on his sister and him, since they must have been quite a handful. He had also begun to make positive comments to his father about her. Probably the loosening up of his relationship with his father and the lessening of difficulty in dealing with loss made him now able to make use of earlier coaching suggestions to approach his stepmother. He brought up again in supervision his desire to open things up on his mother's side of the family, from whom he had been cut off since childhood. But again he put this off, deciding instead that his next family move would be a visit to his sister in California, whom he had not seen for five years, and with whom he had never discussed his mother's death.

Trigger family

Peter proceeded for several sessions with the Arthur family, but then he again said he was "stuck" with the family's resistance. We discussed the possibility of his telling the family about his own experience, to help lower their resistance to dealing with issues of death. I wondered with him whether he felt his own experiences were well enough integrated for him to use them in this way. He said he thought they were. We discussed the potential hazards of dealing with issues that are too "raw" in a therapist's experience to be presented constructively in a therapy session. It is, of course, crucial that personal references be brought up to further the family's aims and not to serve as an emotional outlet for the therapist.

Where appropriate, therapists' family stories can occasionally help family members deal with their own issues. Such displacement stories may get a point across more effectively than a direct comment on the family's situation. It can be a useful joining manoeuvre—helping a family see that the therapist has had struggles too, and may be useful in diminishing the aura of over-importance clients often place on a therapist. However, it is especially important in using this material that the therapist be clear about his/her own issues. In Peter's case, his own experience had mirrored the family's so closely that it seemed he might be able to help them overcome their fears of dealing with the grandmother's cancer. At the same time, Peter was just beginning to work out his own family issues, so there was some risk of his bringing in his own unresolved feelings. Because we could not work out a time for live supervision, we agreed that Peter would tell the Arthur's about his own experience, if appropriate, and would videotape the session for later review. In retrospect, although the self-disclosure session was an important point for the family and also for Peter, it would probably have been better to have made a greater effort to arrange live supervision.

Trainee's family

In the session, Peter recounted his own experience as a child whose mother was dying and whose family was not talking about it. This appeared especially helpful to the grandmother in dropping her coverup of the impact of her likely death. However, review of the tape also indicated Peter's pressure that the family resolve their problems, which carried an overlay of personal emotion from his own still-unresolved family issues:

> *Therapist:* When I was eight years old, my mother died of cancer. She was sick for a number of years, and I watched her die. My family acted for all those years as if that wasn't happening. They told me that my mother was sick, but that she wasn't going to die. They kept telling me that till the day she died. When everyone else was at the funeral they left me home and someone came to deliver a fruit basket. I asked the man who delivered the fruit what it was for. And that's how I found out about my mother dying. I know how it feels not to be prepared for that, and not to know what's happening. What happened to me was that for a long time I didn't trust anybody, because nobody squared with me, nobody was honest with me. And you have the opportunity and I can't let you, I can't sit here and let you not take it. And I know too well for myself what it means when you don't take it. And I can't for Billy, for all of you. You can do whatever you want, but for Billy I can't let you do that. You have the opportunity and you have the time, O.K.? What happened to me, it happened. I never had the time. He's got the time, you've got time now and that way it's a blessing because you know what's happening to you. You know what's coming and you've got the time. But if you pretend that it's not true, if you pretend, like my family did, that it's not going to happen, then you're wasting your time, like my family did. Even though there was nobody to replace my mother, my family could have at least used the time and gotten me ready and prepared me for what was going to happen, but they didn't. They chose to pretend. They kept saying: 'There will always be people around, you've got uncles, you've got aunts, and besides, she's not going to die.' So we didn't use the time.

Peter's move was effective in helping the family break through the resistance to dealing with death. The grandmother dropped her coverup of her feelings, but Peter's over-investment was evident in his saying, "I can't let you do that," "You must. . . ." and, "I can't let you not take the opportunity". In discussing the tape we reviewed again the issues in Peter's own family. He saw that his sense of not having had the opportunity to prepare for his mother's death led to an over-investment in the Arthurs' doing "right" for Billy. His own sense of not having had a family was clearly leading to an over-investment in other families working out their emotional issues.

Once again a clinical block led him to make further moves in his own family.

The following transcript of his discussion in supervision of his own family, conveys some of the difficulties he was struggling with:

> *Peter:* In those years I wasn't taking in a lot. It was almost as if I was experiencing, but not experiencing. Things were happening to me, but as a child I began to feel what it was like to be so detached. And even though I still have feelings, emotions are very difficult. You know, when I think about myself, I can picture a photograph of myself, but I can't even remember myself, and the same thing with my mother. I can picture a photograph I have of her, but I can't picture her. There's a real detachment there . . . I remember my mother getting progressively ill. I also remember becoming very angry with her and telling her to drop dead. And shortly afterwards she died, and that's really haunted me all these years.
> *Supervisor:* Have you made any contact yet with your mother's side of the family?
> *Peter:* No, and when I think about that, if you remember, we talked a couple of months ago, I have only two cousins left. One of them, Bill, is a doctor and living on Long Island. We talked about my getting in contact with him. And I haven't done it. At one point I decided I must. I must call him up, and I must . . . but I never did. And other than that, I decided to start off with my sister first and work my way up to him.

During the rest of this discussion we planned strategies for his forthcoming visit to his sister. In particular, he was puzzled about how to refer to his stepmother, since he could not even imagine using the term "mother" with her. We reviewed the issues he wanted to discuss with his sister and tried to predict her reactions and how he could handle them. I suggested that some of his sister's distancing from him would probably have to do with her hurt that he withdrew from her big-sisterly caretaking. He had never thought of it this way, but said that he had resented her attempts to "mother" him. When we looked at this from her perspective, he became curious to talk with her about her views of their respective positions in the family, and to check whether his distancing had hurt her.

Soon after this, Peter went to California and was amazed to find that he "really had a sister". The two of them talked for almost two days about their memories and their different perspectives on the family. Peter's only regret when he returned was that at the end of the visit he wanted very much to hug her and could not bring himself to do so.

Trigger family

Meanwhile, anxiety in the Arthur family was still high. Attempts to focus on the marital relationship of Mr and Mrs Arthur had not worked, as the marriage had been a difficult one and Mrs Arthur was feeling bitter, while her husband had become even more passive since her illness began. We decided that a session between Martha and her mother, to focus on the mother's feelings and enhance Martha's position as the oldest and most responsible of the children might help in the therapeutic process. It was hoped that emphasizing Martha's sensitivity to her mother might strengthen both Martha's position in the family and the mother's ability to let go. We arranged this time to do live supervision. The following segments from the transcript begin early in the session:

GM: I can't take any more snotty remarks.

(*Supervisor* (through earphone): But can she talk about the limited time?)

GM: I don't want to slap her. I don't want to get to the point where I beat up on her, but I'm afraid I might.

(*Supervisor:* Get their permission if you can, Peter.)

GM: I've never done anything like that in my life.

Therapist: Can you talk at all about, is it alright to talk about the fact that you have limited time?

GM: I don't want to talk about that. I want whatever time I have to be peaceful.

Therapist: Well, is it alright to bring in the fact that all this may have to happen soon?

(*Supervisor:* Very good.)

GM: But she shouldn't take an eight year old boy to a rock concert . . .

Martha: No. I didn't say that. . . . I don't know whether. . . .

(*Supervisor:* Peter, I really think you have to get down to the issue of death. You could have them talk a couple of minutes and then you come behind the mirror.)

GM: You just don't take an eight year old kid to a rock concert . . .

Martha: The majority of people that are going to be there. . . .

(*Supervisor:* That's not the issue. It's a ridiculous discussion.)

Therapist: Well. . . . You're talking about a rock concert here. . . You're both talking about a rock concert and not dealing with each other.

GM: . . . Where do you think they went?

Martha: I didn't know where they went.

GM: Well, anyone would know. . . .

(*Supervisor:* This discussion only makes sense in the context of her cancer and everyone's concern about her dying. Otherwise it would be a whole other discussion.)

GM: I'd stay away from her. . . .

Therapist: Let's get back. . . .

Martha: You didn't say that.

GM: I certainly did.

Therapist: Right now the situation is . . . You're not going to be around forever to check up on her.

GM: I'm gonna be around forever, because I'm gonna haunt her.

Martha: I want you and I to like each other.

(*Supervisor:* O.K. Let them talk about that. Give them the instruction to talk about how they can best relate to each other in this limited time and then come behind the one way mirror.)

(Peter and I then planned strategies for a few minutes and discussed the importance of interrupting and breaking through their fruitless arguing.)

Therapist: (back after consulting behind the mirror): The other kids, as well intentioned as they are, and as loving of you as they are, can't get near the issue.

They're so damned scared. Martha, you're making an attempt, but you're not getting too close either.

GM: She's pushing herself away without meaning to. She's trying to show her independence and that isn't necessary.

Therapist: Alright, so what we are left with is you alone. You facing what you are facing alone. That's the issue.

GM: That's right. But maybe I'm better off.

Therapist: You really think so? Because that's the issue we keep going around and around. And you keep saying you don't want to talk about it, but I don't think it's a good idea to run away from it. . . .

GM: Look, I know it's going to happen. I'll have plenty of time to think about it when it starts getting worse.

Therapist: I don't want to talk about your dying—that's for your medical doctor. . . .

(*Supervisor:* But her dying *is* the point.)

Therapist: I mean, I want to talk about the family's relationship with you, the way they care, and the way they treat you . . . that you are not alone.

GM: Oh, I'm not alone. All my children love me.

Therapist: They love you, but they can't share this with you right now.

GM: Joan and George are immature. Martha is trying to get herself established because she wants to be independent and for years Martha has, now this is just my opinion, I could be wrong. Martha has always wanted to show that she is independent of me, doesn't need me or anything like that, and I'm not saying she needs me, but I've always tried to show the kids they could be independent. We still could be close.

Therapist: Right now I think you very much need to share your feelings with somebody. Can you do it?

GM: I don't want to be a burden to my children. No. No. I can't do it.

Therapist: Is that a burden for them?

GM: Yes.

Therapist: Do you really think so?

Martha: No, I don't think it's a burden—I'd like to.

Therapist: No, no, don't talk to me. Tell her, tell her what you are feeling about that. Don't be afraid.

GM: I've been a loner all my life.

Therapist: Make her know.

Martha: I've tried. I've tried offering my shoulder, and I've tried just being there . . . I want to be there with you. I've wanted to be close to you, but no matter what I try. . . .

(*Supervisor:* Make it O.K. for the mother to talk to her now.)

Martha: You don't like the way I try. . . .

Therapist: Well . . .

Martha: . . . You always push me away.

(*Supervisor:* Make it all right now—in the present.)

Therapist: Martha, let her try. Tell her, for her as much as for you. Tell her how you feel. Help her.

Martha: But how can I? She won't talk.

(*Supervisor:* Get her to take her mother's hand.)

Therapist: Take her hand.

GM: Martha, there is gonna be a lot of time, I hope.

(*Supervisor:* Get Martha to tell her how she feels.)

GM: Martha, there's gonna be a lot of time, I hope. I'm not gonna go just like that.
Therapist: But you have to start telling her your feelings. You have to start.
GM: They all know.
(*Supervisor:* Get them to talk.)
   Therapist: Talk to her.
   GM: You know I love you. You know I care.
   Martha: I realize that. I realize you love me. You realize I love you.
   GM: I think, yes, I know you care.
   Martha: I don't want it to just be love without the caring.
   Therapist: Do you want to share what your mother feels about dying?
   Martha: I try to . . . Yes.
   GM: I don't know what I feel about it.
   Therapist: It's painful.
   Martha: It couldn't be more painful than not knowing . . . than not understanding, and getting mad at her for stupid things.
   GM: I don't even know what I feel about it. Would you believe that?
   Martha: Yes, I believe it.
   GM: I don't want to think about it.
(*Supervisor:* But are there times when she does think about it?)
   Therapist: Are there times when you think about it anyway?
   GM: When I'm by myself I think about it. I take a sleeping pill and go to sleep.
   Therapist: I think you really feel there's no one who could listen to you.
   GM: That's right.
(*Supervisor:* I think Martha wants to listen to her.)
   Therapist: I think Martha wants to listen. She very much wants to hear. And she's saying it.
   Martha: I could, Ma. Whatever it is, it couldn't be as bad as what I think and what I keep imagining you're going through.
   GM: I know what's going to happen. If I started telling Martha . . .
   Therapist: Do you hear what she says?
   GM: Yeah, I know what she's saying. I heard her.
   Therapist: What's she gonna do if you tell her? You think it'll be too much for her?
   GM: Yes.
   Therapist: You know what? I think you're going to be very surprised.
   GM: I don't want any of my children to have guilt feelings, because they've all been good kids.
   Therapist: And if you don't let Martha share this with you, I think you'll be giving her a bigger burden, that she'll carry around the rest of her life.
   GM: Look, I was 14 when my grandmother died. She died in my arms. I didn't expect her to die, but the day she said: "Mary, get up and do this, I'm gonna die tonight," I jumped out of bed and I knew she was gonna die. I took care of her and I watched her die. And I went out in the street and I broke down and cried. I sobbed. I woke up the whole neighbourhood. People opened their windows and said, "Mary what's the matter". I said my grandmother died. I couldn't say it. That was it. A week later I walked into a wall. I was going to put coal on the fire, because we lived in the country. I was 14.
   Therapist: Martha's not 14.
   GM: I never got over my grandmother's death. I wasn't prepared for it. I knew people died, but didn't really believe it till I lost my grandmother. That's like losing mother, father, everyone. She had brought me up.

(*Supervisor:* Can you get Martha to respond to her?)

    Therapist: Martha, where are you with this?

    Martha: Maybe because you never came out and said it, at certain times, or I don't come out and say it at certain times. I get the feeling that . . . Wait a sec . . . (Pause) . . . I know what I want to say. I get the feeling that it's always in the back of your mind.

    Therapist: I want to get to what may be in the back of your mind. You said before that knowing what your mother was feeling couldn't be worse than what you were thinking. But you didn't say what you were thinking.

    Martha: No. Just about her dying.

    Therapist: Yes, but you didn't say what you were thinking about that.

    Martha: I can't put it into words. I might get it wrong.

    Therapist: Try. Try as best as you can. There's no passing or failing here.

(*Supervisor:* That may help the mother talk about it.)

    Martha: I go to bed at night and I dream of her suffering.

    Therapist: Tell it to your mother.

    Martha: When I dream of it, I'm making her do it and physically that I . . . Could we change the subject?

    GM: No, we can't.

    Therapist: Don't hold back. Your mother's very strong.

    Martha: No, I haven't even slept a good full night in about 4 or 5 months. I go to bed, and the first thing I start doing is having nightmares about you.

    GM: Well, tell me what they are.

    Martha: Of you suffering and you being sick and me in my dreams going to mean well, and me ending up making you worse. That's basically it.

    Therapist: How do you feel when you think about this? How do you feel now?

    Martha: Right now? I feel more relaxed than I have in a while.

    Therapist: I don't believe you're telling me what you're feeling.

(*Supervisor:* But it's the first time she's talking to her mother about what's really going on with her.)

    Martha: I haven't thought about how I'm feeling right now. I'm feeling O.K. right now.

    Therapist: Isn't it a little scary too, Martha?

(*Supervisor:* I think the worst part is the feeling isolated and alone—she probably *is* relieved to tell her mother.)

    Therapist: Or is there a little part that is relaxing now that you're finally able to talk to her?

    Martha: I think it's more that, yeah.

    Therapist: Do you believe you caused your mother's cancer?

    GM: I never in my life said she caused my cancer.

    Therapist: Do you believe you caused your mother's cancer?

    Martha: I know it's a physical thing, but I also heard it comes from nerves, yes, it's possible.

    GM: Oh, for Christ's sake, I said you made an old woman of me 7 years ago.

(*Supervisor:* Is she afraid of that?)

    Therapist: Are you afraid you caused it?

    Martha: If I didn't cause that, I caused her a lot of other things.

(*Supervisor:* But is she afraid she caused the cancer.)

    Therapist: Are you afraid you caused the cancer.

    Martha: I don't know. It sounds unrealistic.

Therapist: Forget about what is unrealistic. Is that a feeling?
Martha: Yes, I think so.
Therapist: That must be quite a thing to carry around.
(*Supervisor:* Did her mother know that?)
   Therapist: Did you know that?
   GM: How did you do it?
   Martha: Just by being me.
   GM: Oh, Martha, where do you come up with these things?
   Therapist: You see, the fears that you have that Martha would be carrying a burden
if you talked to her could never be matched by the burden she is actually carrying.
Whatever you told her, no matter how horrible your feelings were, they could only
relieve the burden, because if Martha believes that you could share with her, some
of your feelings . . .
   Martha: Maybe I could help you instead of hurting.
   GM: What kind of feelings could I tell her?
   Therapist: I don't know.
(*Supervisor:* What does she think about dying?)
   Therapist: What do you think about dying? Not the fact, not the figures, but how
do you feel?
   GM: I am not afraid of dying. We all have to go sometime. You know at first, when
I got the cancer, the first time I was going on the plane to Hawaii, and I had the
cancer, I had the patch on my back. I had the surgery in the morning and I was
with Joan, and I was looking out over the mountain and everytime I'd look at Joan,
the tears would come and I'd say "Oh, My God, I won't see my grandchildren.
Billy is growing up. I won't be able to see this because I have cancer." And it hit
me. Then three quarters of the way to Hawaii, everytime I'd look at Joan, I'd be
remembered of all three of you. Billy would appear. Joan was married but didn't
have any children. I'd think that I'd never see her children or George's children. I'd
think of Billy growing up and of me not seeing him and it hurt me because all of my
life I prayed that I would raise my own children, because I never wanted you
kicked around like I was. All I ever asked God for was, let me live till I was 50.
That's all I want. But now that I'm over 50, I want to live. I heard something on
TV the other day. I was watching a show and some woman was saying, "I've only
got 6 months to live and I'm dying." And the interviewer said, "We are all dying.
Only you know when." And he was so right. I don't know when. But I am a hell of
a lot closer to it than a lot of other people.
   Therapist: How do you feel about that?
   GM: You know, in a way, I'm a lot luckier than a lot of people. I have time to really
appreciate things. I look at things. I appreciate my grandchildren a lot
more. I appreciate my kids a lot more. I appreciate the things that I do. I can
decide what I want done with my things, the few things I have, decide who
I want to give them to and so forth. A lot of people die and they don't settle all
these things.

This woman's articulation speaks for itself, and it seemed that once Peter was
able to help her open up with her daughter, her tension eased. The family
terminated by mutual agreement a short while later, although many issues had
not been resolved. On follow-up six months later, Billy's symptoms were no
longer prominent. He and his mother, Martha, were living together in a new

apartment, and Martha was taking virtually full responsibility for him. Mrs A. was able to talk quite openly and calmly about herself and while her health was failing, she seemed quite at peace. The relationship with her husband had not improved, but Martha, Joan and George had a much better relationship than during therapy. George, who had previously called off his engagement four times, had set a wedding date and seemed much more settled about this.

Trainee's family

At the same time as the family was moving towards termination, several very important shifts took place in Peter's family. By coincidence his uncle, Bill, whom he had finally decided to contact, invited him to his son's Bar Mitzvah the same week-end that Peter's sister was flying to New York on business. Peter decided to take the opportunity to visit his mother's grave which was nearby. He discussed this with his sister and they agreed to go together and to invite their father to go with them. On the day of the trip his sister called to say their father had decided not to go. Peter almost got caught up in this, feeling momentarily angry and frustrated with his father for this "typical manoeuvre of avoiding feelings". However, he was enough in control of his feelings that he decided against reacting, and instead replied matter-of-factly to his sister that that was O.K. and why didn't the two of them go alone together unless their father changed his mind. When he went to pick them up, his father said he had decided he wanted to go along to the grave and then to the family celebration. In the evening, on the way home they got into an argument about plans for the next day, and Peter said he suddenly burst out laughing in the discussion, realizing that for the first time they were connected together solidly enough to have a good argument and not be afraid they would lose each other again.

A word should be said about the timing of the shift from one level of supervision to the other. The process of work on the trainee's own family obviously can not be forced by the supervisor. However, by being open to the cues a supervisor can track the trainee's shifts and note when his or her anxiety is low enough to hear and deal with connections between clinical work and the family of origin. For example, during Peter's first year of training, he had been in the process of ending a five year relationship with a woman, which had greatly limited his ability to deal with family material. Obviously his own sensitivity to the issue of loss had compounded this life stress, which always seems to be a difficulty for family therapy trainees.[1] It seems highly unlikely that he could have responded to family of origin work during that year. Just as the therapist must be sensitive to the family's readiness to deal with certain problems, the supervisor needs to be sensitive to the trainee's timing. There are times when trainees are ready only for dealing with certain aspects of training, while at other times, as in this instance, the fortuitous situation of a certain case and a certain constellation of family circumstances leads to an opportunity for strong clinical growth in a condensed way.

The power of one's own system as it impinges on clinical work can thus be underlined. There may then be a merging of efforts on different systems which complement each other. As Peter put it, "I think there was a real period of merging, when I can't separate my progress in family therapy from the personal moves I was making. It was very interconnected. They were both sort of training grounds for me, and they both fed into each other".

Supervision and the Earphone

Since the earphone is a relatively new technique and not too widely used, a word should perhaps be said about its use (see Byng-Hall, Chapter 4). The earphone is an especially helpful tool in the supervision of beginners or of trainees who are very "stuck" and in need of a fair amount of immediate feedback to learn a new way of working. It is a very convenient and unobtrusive tool when you do not want the loud disruption of a telephone call, or when you want the trainee to stay with the process or intensify it. It can enable the supervisor to suggest much more subtle interventions, such as using small reframing statements to connote positively family members' behaviour in relation to each other. It can also help the trainees pull back immediately from a mistake, as in Peter's work, when he told the grandmother he did not want her to talk about dying, and was then quickly able to modify his statement.

The earphone can also be a useful way to help trainees stay "meta" to the content of the family's interaction. There are times when by talking to supervisees through the family's conversation, you enable them to keep a distance from family conflicts or attempts at collusion. At times, distracting trainees from the content is very important in teaching them to maintain a systems perspective and keep focussed on process.

There are also a number of disadvantages in using an earphone and a supervisor must beware of these. The biggest problem is that it can draw a supervisor into overfunctioning. Interventions are so easily made, that they can often be made too frequently or too soon, not leaving room for trainees to develop their work sufficiently on their own.

It is also important to recognize that having this immediate relationship with the family-therapist system, adds greatly to the complexity of the process of supervision. With so many system levels operating at once (family, therapist and his or her own family, supervisor and his or her own family etc.) it is easy to imagine situations where the complexity detracts from therapeutic effectiveness. Just by adding to the complexity of the interactions, supervisory remarks, unless made with considerable care, can overload a therapist, who may already be feeling an excess of inputs from the family.

Our general ground rules for this form of supervision are similar to those described by Montalvo (1973), in having a rather clear hierarchy of authority. The supervisor is in charge of the supervision, but the trainee has flexibility to move within those limits to do things in his or her own way. Before we begin, I usually tell trainees that if my suggestions are not helpful, or even worse, are adding to their confusion, they should just take the "bug" out of their ear as a clear signal to me that they have had enough. At that point my rule is to let them proceed on their own merits unless I become very concerned about the situation, at which point I say I will knock on the one-way mirror as a sign for them to come out for discussion. In fact this has never occurred. Setting up this structure ahead of time has generally helped to reduce trainee anxiety (and supervisor anxiety) about the possibility that things will not work out in the process.

As a rule of thumb for supervisory interventions, we work on the assumption that "less is better". As Haley has said, it is important to present no more than one supervisory idea at a time (Haley, 1976). This makes supervision a discipline requiring much rigour. It is extremely difficult to make instant decisions in relation to many levels of interaction and then frame them clearly and succinctly, but that is the objective. As the transcript presented clearly indicates, there were instances in the work with Peter and the Arthurs when the supervisory interventions came too soon, or were too frequent.

The tendency toward isomorphism, or repetitions of system problems at all levels of the system, is always a hazard. In this instance, the supervisor's urgency that the trainee resolve his issues mirrored the trainee's urgency with the family. Such trends can obviously become problematic with the availability of such immediate feedback as is available with the earphone.

On the other hand, the earphone offers unique possibilities for enabling trainees to integrate new skills by providing the immediate opportunity to experiment with new interventions modelled by the supervisor over the earphone.

Generally speaking, the use of the bug is optimal with beginners and with trainees having trouble making key transitions with families. Supervision of videotapes can be very frustrating when a trainee has become "stuck" early in the session, because one is then reviewing a series of mistaken efforts once the process has already become jammed. Telephone calls with live supervision can also be frustrating and demoralizing interruption for a trainee having trouble establishing authority and a solid alliance with a family. The use of an earphone is not as good for helping trainees develop their own style. Analysis of videotapes seems best suited to that part of the supervisory process, because of the degree of reflection it allows on each moment of the interaction (see Whiffen, Chapter 3).

Conclusions

While the material presented in this paper is only anecdotal, it suggests that by aiming supervisory attention more directly on those particular families with which trainees are having the hardest time, and then working backwards to the trainee's own family issues, the trainee's clinical competence may be greatly enhanced. In Peter's case, a number of factors were involved in his clinical development and in his helping the Arthur family move toward greater openness.

He felt that the earphone enabled him to push the issue of death far beyond what he would have done on the basis of discussion alone. The specificity of the therapeutic suggestions in that instance were particularly useful to him. He said that of his own accord he never would have asked many of the questions he did, especially about the grandmother's cancer and Billy's fears of her dying. However, once having said the lines, they became his. Later, in discussing the value of the earphone in his supervision Peter said:

> It meant a great deal to me. In a sense it was taking a risk. You do something you would never have done without someone suggesting it specifically. But now that you've done it, it's yours. Even though the words were suggested to me, I owned them—it was something I did. It's funny because you would think, theoretically, that I might negate the whole experience. I might say, I was just parroting her. But it had none of that at all. Somehow in the process of translating it, putting it into my own words, dealing with the family's reactions and mine, it gave me something very special. It gave me the ability to use it again, and relate that way.

The specificity of the supervision suggestions also made it clear to him how very toxic the issue of death was in his own family. Once he could see that asking a direct question about death did not greatly frighten the Arthur family, and, in fact, relieved them and enabled them to talk to each other about what was on their minds, he was stirred to work more on the emotional cut-offs in his own family. It helped clarify his need to learn more about his mother's death and its impact on him and the rest of the family. His confidence in dealing with the emotional issues involved in cancer seemed considerably strengthened by the time of the last transcript. His persistence in helping the grandmother to express her feelings paid off in her responsiveness which mirrored many of the feelings Peter himself had described to the family earlier. It is also interesting that his question to Martha about having caused her mother's cancer enabled her to describe her own painful fears of having brought on her mother's cancer, which paralleled Peter's own fears of having been the cause of his mother's cancer. It seems touchingly clear from Mrs Arthur's discussion about needing time to deal with feelings how much Peter's message about his own childhood experience had meant to her. All of these experiences, in conjunction with the profound shifts which occurred in Peter's own family, were part of his shift from a technique-bound and distant trainee to a highly competent and emotionally sensitive clinician.

Note

1. Over eight years of doing family therapy training, I have known only one trainee who was able to maintain his level of clinical competence while going through a separation or divorce. This clinical experience has led me to recommend routinely that those in the midst of a marital break up wait until the transition is over before beginning training.

References

Bowen, M. (1978). *Family Therapy in Clinical Practice*. Jason Aronson, New York.

Carter, E. and Orfanidis, M. (1976). Family therapy with one person and the family therapist's own family. *Family Therapy* (P. J. Guerin, ed.), pp.193-219. Gardner Press, New York.

Haley, J. (1976). *Problem-Solving Therapy*. Jossey-Bass, San Francisco.

Minuchin, S. (1974). *Families and Family Therapy*. Harvard University Press, Cambridge, Mass. and Tavistock Publications, London.

Montalvo, B. (1973). Aspects of live supervision. *Family Process* **12**, 343-359.

Palazzoli, M., Boscolo, L., Cecchin, G. and Prata, G. (1978). *Paradox and Counter Paradox*. Aronson, New York.

Weakland, J., Fisch, R., Watzlawick, P. and Bodin, A. M. (1974). Brief therapy: focused problem resolution. *Family Process* **13**, 141-168.

3. The Use of Videotape in Supervision

Rosemary Whiffen

Videotape provides three unique opportunities. First, it freezes time so that after the session a crucial sequence can be played and replayed enabling every aspect and angle of that behavioural sequence to be pieced together, something impossible to achieve during a session. Secondly, the therapist can see himself objectively as one of the contributors to the whole system, a very different perspective to the bewildering experience of receiving multiple and immediate family pressures during the interview. Thirdly, the effect of an intervention can be studied and its success evaluated.

It is indisputable that for any therapist it can be valuable to observe leisurely and in minute detail family interaction with all the inevitable reciprocities, circular behavioural sequences and redundancies. Videotape is an invaluable aid to the observation of non-verbal communications and of the families' use of space.

It is equally relevant for the therapist to study his own messages transmitted by a posture and tone of voice, as well as in his use of words. Thus videotape is a valuable self-teaching tool. Hirsch and Freed (1978, p.120) recall a statement about learning: "To read is not as effective as to be told. To be told is not as effective as to be shown. But to see for ourselves is perhaps the most insightful method of learning". It is also useful in supervision, either as a record when the supervisor cannot be present for live supervision or as an additional aid to the use of a one-way mirror.

The advantages of having a live supervisory session videotaped and viewing the tapes afterwards, is that it allows for a more leisurely consideration of what took place in the interview. This can be done either alone or within the supervisory group, in which case the supervisor and the group can share thoughts. Lurie (1978, pp.111-116) states that learning from videotapes helps to facilitate peer feedback and peer learning and to avoid over reliance on the "expert". It can also ensure that the family does not become "forgotten" in the emphasis on teaching-learning experience (Gruenberg *et al.*, 1978, pp.121-125). It is also useful if reviewed before the next session in planning strategies for the forthcoming interview. For these purposes, informed consent forms should, of course, be signed by the family members.

FAMILY THERAPY SUPERVISION
ISBN 0-12-794815-5
Copyright © 1982 by Academic Press.
All rights of reproduction in any form reserved.

Teaching Circular Function in Systems

One of the most critical but difficult tasks in teaching a systematic approach to family therapy is to help the trainee move from the causal-linear way of thinking to a cybernetic-circular approach. The opportunity of observing minute details of interchange between family members and the order in which this happens, allows the trainee to see that each event was in response to the previous one and that in time the sequence comes full circle, the same order being repeated over again. This enables the trainee to see that each part of the system contributes to the chain of events and that attributing cause to one incident in a cycle is inaccurate and often misleading. The trainee learns how to punctuate the system in new ways.

A useful exercise is to ask the trainee what caused the sequence, then to look at that sequence again but start a little earlier. A new version emerges; a new punctuation. This will help the trainee reframe interaction for the family, who often also sees one particular event as causal.

Example

In one family two adolescents seemed to be rebelling by a series of dramatic actions including running away from boarding school and taking an overdose of drugs. The family attributed their problem to this behaviour. It was noticed when reviewing the videotapes, however, how the parents' affect changed as soon as these events were introduced. From being morose, angry, pompous or uninvolved, they both became smiling and animated, and their intense interest in the details encouraged further discussion. They became like a family of four siblings having a gossip.

This was repeated in relation to the father's attitude to his wife's family — her husband's "outrageous behaviour" towards her difficult mother provoked the same sort of response from her. It was then noted that the adolescents' behaviour started after the last member of the older generation had died. There had been several members who had needed prolonged care or nursing and had taken up time and energy in the family for fifteen years.

These observations had been missed by the trainee during a typical session with rebellious adolescents, involving hectic swings from angry confrontation to sullen withdrawal. On viewing the videotape she was able to perceive the double messages being given between the generations. The insistence by the parents that they needed help with their uncooperative and impossible son and daughter and their covert enjoyment and encouragement of past and future escapades. It later transpired that they had been unable to indulge in such escapades themselves at their age.

The generosity displayed by the mother and father in the care of the older generation and of the children's service to their parents in replacing this lost function was positively connoted and therapy was under way.

Increasing Awareness of Therapist's Contribution to the System

As has already been stated, the therapist too has the opportunity of seeing himself in context as part of the family system. He can observe his own involvement and contribution to the functioning of that system in a way which is often difficult to do when with the family.

It is possible to observe the minutiae of family functioning and the way both digital and analogic messages are distorted or diverted, colluded with or provoked; words and movements so subtle and unobtrusive that they frequently go unnoticed in the ebb and flow of the family session.

Example

An experienced therapist, whose own father had left home when he was eleven, was working with a family consisting of a widow and two young sons. The father had been killed one night in a car accident two years before. The therapist's intention at this point in therapy was to help this family with their delayed grief reaction, but he was quite unaware of the number and variety of ways he colluded with the family in avoiding this. When viewing this session he noticed how at one moment he looked away, inviting a son to avoid answering, at another he got up to open a window at a crucial point, at another he changed the topic for reasons he could not understand himself even in retrospect. During the session he was aware of having difficulty in keeping the family to the task but was quite oblivious of the number of times he had led the family away by his own contributions or actions.

Use of Videotape in Supervisory Sessions

Supervision by viewing videotapes contains two elements. First, there is the management of the case including understanding the dynamics of the family, deciding on the focus for therapy and planning strategies of intervention. Secondly, it can be used to develop the skills of the therapist.

Management of case

There are several ways to avoid videotape viewing becoming time-consuming and tedious. The most important is to require the trainee to prepare for the supervisory session. He needs to review the tape he intends to present and decide on the issues he wants the supervisor to concentrate on. This may help to understand the dynamics of the family in the way the family system organizes around the symptomatic member. He may want to review the repetitive sequences he is aware of in the family but which he finds impossible to interrupt. He may need help with making a systemic hypothesis or in planning therapeutic strategies. The important thing is that he is clear about what it is he wants and, before the supervision, locates the parts on the tape which will give the supervisor the necessary evidence which will enable him to be of most help.

There can be few supervisors who have not experienced the tediousness of watching endless random extracts of a therapy session, and attempting to make constructive comments. The trainee may assert that he has already tried a particular suggestion made by the supervisor, later in the session and it had made no impact. He starts to run the tape forward, searching for this intervention, frequently unsuccessfully. He then resorts to a description of what he said and explains why he thinks it was ineffective. The supervisor is at a disadvantage without the evidence of the choice of words, the tone of voice, the posture and above all the timing and is less helpful than he might have been.

If it is possible, the trainee should make an annotation of the tape as he replays it and make a note of the revolution numbers in the margin; this enables quick identification of relevant pieces of tape and is well worth the time involved. It is also useful in recalling the session.

To begin with it is a common fault to choose sequences which are too long. If the camera is fixed and there is no cameraman, it has been suggested that the time span of attention for viewers is only four minutes. If there is a change of angle, close up showing facial expressions or some lively interactions in the family, the viewer's attention is held for longer.

It is not only the visual signals that are instructive but also the sound. Sometimes a therapist may imagine he has remained impartial, unruffled or non-judgemental at certain tense moments in the session. On listening to the tape he may find his voice gave him away and he may learn the reason for the subsequent defensive behaviour in the family. The tone, intonation and timbre of the therapist's voice is of the utmost importance in therapy and may be more influential than words, facial expression or body movements.

Video feedback to the family

When planning strategies of intervention it may be appropriate at a certain point to use video feedback to the family. This can be a powerful therapeutic tool and much has been written about it (Alger, 1973, pp.65-74; Alger and Hogan, 1971, pp.237-246). It is almost impossible to use this technique unless the therapist is used to studying therapist and family interactions from viewing videotapes. To have learnt something about oneself in this way enables one to have the necessary sensitivity and perspicacity in deciding on sequences to show the family.

It is so powerful a therapeutic tool that it is important to show the family a creative or amusing extract before confronting the family with more illuminating but often more painful sequences. The supervisor would also be well advised to bear this lesson in mind with their trainees (Lurie, 1978, pp.111-116). Confronting one's own image tends to be a traumatic experience even for the experienced therapist. Thus it is as important to study successful interventions and try to determine why the therapist was effective, as it is to study unsuccessful manoeuvres.

Skills development

Viewing video recordings can help the therapist improve his therapeutic skills and explore and develop his individual style. This issue is often part of a supervisory session which includes decisions on management issues, but it can also be centred specifically on skills development.

This involves the trainee in selecting a small sequence from an ongoing or new family session. The trainee need give little information about the family but should have a clear idea of what he was intending to achieve in the sequence he shows. He must isolate and present the problem to which he was addressing himself *at that moment*, stating his reasons for his choice of intervention, his intended goal and, in his opinion, whether or not it had been achieved.

The discussion with the supervisor and supervisory group then centres round whether they perceived the therapist as having achieved his stated goal. He may try out different ways of doing the same thing with a simulated family, using videotape which they then review. If he failed what could he have done differently? If he succeeded, what made the intervention succeed? In both circumstances the aim is to make him more aware of why he is effective, or not, and thereby make his skills more available to him on subsequent occasions.

It is important when using this method of teaching not to be diverted into a long discussion on dynamics, problems, choice of approach, management of the case and so on. As already mentioned, this means that this teaching exercise can be used when management is not discussed. It is also possible for the trainee to help the therapist achieve their goals using their own particular style, even if they are working within the broad framework of a particular approach, such as structural family therapy. There is a distinction to be made between choice of method and technique and personal style that teaching from videotapes can help clarify and develop.

Both these factors make it a suitable teaching technique for visiting trainers who do not intend to either manage cases or teach a particular method or for

trainers working with groups inside or outside their own agency for whom he or
she does not have responsibility for case management.

Example

The trainee in an interview with the parents and their thirteen-year-old
adopted son, about whose uncouth behaviour they were in despair, was
attempting to demonstrate to the parents how powerful their son had become in
the family. Each time the therapist demonstrated the boy's power in the session,
the father disqualified the therapist by laughing, shifting in his chair or making
some generalized comment on modern teenagers. The mother only smiled and
looked helplessly at the therapist, indicating her relief at seeing the therapist
rendered as impotent in the family as she was frequently made to feel. The boy
sat inert, with a large, satisfied grin on his face, seemingly well aware of what he
was doing.

This happened several times in a remarkably short space of time. The
supervisor further isolated one such repetitive sequence and the group examined
the movements of all the family members, who resembled well trained dancers.
Among other things it highlighted the way in which the therapist, by letting the
disqualification pass, invited the family to greater efforts to "get away with it"
on subsequent occasions.

The discussion included the trainee's admission that he found professional,
middle-class men difficult to confront. He role played with the group more
forceful and effective ways of standing up to the father's disqualification and of
mobilizing mother to support father, when the son came between them, rather
than disqualifying father in her turn in her own way. The trainee was
subsequently able to return to the family with greater confidence and effectiveness, and make his observations in a way that was heard by all the family
members.

Administrative Considerations

To use video for teaching purposes it is essential that the supervisor is convinced
of its value and is able to demonstrate its effectiveness to the trainees. Unless
there are technical staff available to work the equipment, finding an empty tape,
and setting up the camera and deck, can often be the "last straw" for the
therapist in an overcrowded day. There are numerous excuses to be found along
the way to avoid using it that day and inevitably the "crucial" session goes
unrecorded.

Unless the organization is as easy as possible, and this is often difficult to
achieve, the equipment will be left gathering dust in a cupboard. It is also

necessary for the therapist to have some understanding of how it works or the repeated frustration of ending up with sound but no picture or picture but no sound will soon discourage the most ardent enthusiast.

Time needs to be scheduled for viewing and editing, otherwise tape after tape remains unviewed and video becomes a tedious and pointless operation. Space and equipment for viewing is also important if there are several therapists using the same rooms and machines. Scheduling time in a busy timetable to study one's work and then finding no space or equipment, can lead to further frustration.

Camera Work

There are other aspects of video which are useful in a training programme. For instance, if there is a supervisory group observing behind a one-way mirror and there is available a camera which can film through the one-way mirror or through an aperture in the wall, it is excellent practice for members of the supervisory team to film each other. The cameraman's job is highly skilled and the trainees can be of the utmost assistance to each other by learning to follow with the camera the relevant sequence of events so as to catch the most useful information. At first it is easy to concentrate too much on the person who is talking. It may be more important to film the one to whom the person is talking, the bystander, or the small child on the edge of the action, or the dog. It is the significant interchanges, often non-verbal, that carry the loudest messages. The human face and sequences taken at close range can be more informative than a wordy interchange. To observe the functioning of a system requires distant shots, but close-ups show how the individual is *experiencing* being part of that system.

Another useful technical adjustment is to give the supervisor engaged in live supervision a microphone to add his comments (through a sound mixer) to the sound track of the videotape. This has several advantages. The supervisor's running commentary, valuable to the other trainee observers, is even more valuable to the therapist. It provides an extremely good way of supporting and validating the trainee's good moves. Critical comments are usually avoided, instead the supervisor says: "At this point I would. . . ." Quite frequently, however, the trainee carries out a similar manoeuvre later anyway, or if not it becomes clear what opportunities were missed. Not infrequently the supervisor will comment: "Look, he did well by going in that different direction". The disadvantage is that the sound track is complex and the tape is only understandable to those who observed the session. Thus it is essentially only for supervision purposes.

Sometimes it is necessary for family therapy programmes to decide between investing in videotape equipment or in a one-way screen. In my view there is no substitute for the immediacy and value of live supervision through a one-way screen with or without an earphone. However, it is possible to use videotape as closed circuit television. This enables the supervisor to view the trainee in another room while he is seeing the family and provides a facility similar to a one-way mirror. This amounts to direct supervision and the supervisory procedure is similar to that described in several other chapters in this book (Andolfi and Menghi, Chapter 15; Boscolo and Cecchin, Chapter 13; Cade and Seligman, Chapter 14; McGoldrick, Chapter 2). It is also suggested that the study of videotapes and constitute part of the training for all family therapy supervisors (Goin and Kline, 1978, pp.126-132).

Summary

In this chapter the use of videotapes in supervision has been discussed. The opportunities offered in teaching about family dynamics and circular functioning and the therapist's involvement in this, has been demonstrated. The use of videotapes in case management, and in developing the skills of the individual therapist has been looked at and some administrative difficulties and additional potentialities have been explored.

References

Alger, I. (1973). *Techniques of Family Psychotherapy: A Primer* (D. A. Bloch, ed.), pp.65-74. Grune and Stratton, New York and London.

Alger, I. and Hogan, P. (1971). *Changing Families* (J. Haley, Ed.), pp.237-246. Grune and Stratton, New York and London.

Goin, M. K. and Kline, F. (1978). *Videotape Techniques in Psychiatric Training and Treatment* (M. M. Berger, ed.). pp.126-132. Brunner/Mazel, New York.

Gruenberg, P. B., Liston, E. H. and Wayne, G. J. (1978). *Videotape Techniques in Psychiatric Training and Treatment* (M. M. Berger, ed.), pp.121-125. Brunner/Mazel, New York.

Hirsch, H. and Freed, H. (1978). *Videotape Techniques in Psychiatric Training and Treatment* (M. M. Berger, ed.), pp.117-120. Brunner/Mazel, New York.

Lurie, H. J. (1978). *Videotape Techniques in Psychiatric Training and Treatment* (M. M. Berger, ed.), pp.111-116, Brunner/Mazel, New York.

4. The Use of the Earphone in Supervision

John Byng-Hall

Introduction

What is the Earphone?

What is popularly known as the "bug in the ear" (Boylston and Tuma, 1972) consists of a small earphone inserted into one of the therapist's ears while the supervisor speaks into a microphone from behind the one-way screen. This means that the family does not hear the intervention, and unlike the telephone or supervision from inside the room, therapy is not interrupted. The earphone may either be a small radio receiver tuned to a radio transmitter, which has the advantage of leaving the therapist freedom of movement, or the earphone can be linked to the microphone by a cable which can, if necessary, be passed under the doors separating the therapy room from the observation room. Either system can be relatively inexpensive.[1] A one-way mirror is the only essential moderately expensive piece of equipment.

The control microphone handset, held by the supervisor can have either one or two (or more) earphones attached to it. This enables him to speak to co-therapists. He may then select both channels and specify to whom he is speaking, in which case the other co-therapist will know what instructions have been given, or he may choose to select only one channel in which case the other person does not hear what is said.

Its main uses, advantages and disadvantages

The earphone is the best tool for supervising process. Because the flow of interaction is not interrupted, the trainee's intervention resembles ordinary therapy. The family responds to the trainee's intervention as if it were entirely his, not someone else's. This provides immediate experience of the effect of various interventions; a much quicker way of learning techniques than by observing or reading about a technique and tentatively trying it at a later date; the earphone also allows the supervisor to add intensity to the intervention (see

47

FAMILY THERAPY SUPERVISION
ISBN 0-12-794815-5

McGoldrick, Chapter 2) by blocking the trainee's own homeostatic or diffusing techniques and by suggesting more potent interventions. The telephone, or "in the room" comment can diffuse the intensity by halting the proceedings for a few moments.

The disadvantages come from the fact that it is a powerful tool and deceptively easy to use. The supervisor, who is usually a therapeutic enthusiast, may get caught up in the therapeutic excitement because he can get very close to being the therapist himself. Almost every intervention can be parroted by the trainee. This is "echo" therapy. It is wise for the supervisor to keep in his imagination a huge loud speaker in one corner of the room. As soon as he feels like using that he knows that he is breaking the first golden rule which is that supervision is teaching the trainee, not treating the family. If he wants to do that he can walk into the room and take over. To move on to using the earphone as a teaching device requires practice and skill. The degree of concentration and attention to detail that is required is probably higher than in any other form of supervision. Once learned, however, it is a very rewarding technique.

The other major problem comes from the difficult experiential position the trainee has to cope with. The intervention is his but also is not his. This can sometimes lead to a feeling that, "I am my supervisor," or to feeling persecuted by an invasion of autonomy. It is vital that the trainees speak for themselves. Indeed this is the second golden rule. Because the trainee cannot reply to the message, or show openly how he feels about it at the time, plenty of space must be given for exploring the experience afterwards or during the break in the session.

Two trainees, experienced as therapists but relatively fresh to systems family therapy, wrote about their initial reactions after three months of starting live supervision. This response is published in Chapter 10, with additional impressions added by one of those authors six months later and another trainee after two years' experience. Much of what they have to say is about the earphone.

It must only be used in the setting of wider training

It is important to recognize that the use of the earphone can only provide one small aspect of training. Without understanding why and when a particular intervention is used the trainee will be lost when treating a family on his own. A conceptual formulation (see Byng-Hall and Campbell, 1981) should be taught as well. The wider therapeutic strategies of which each intervention is a part need to be understood and if possible planned before the session and reviewed in consultations with the supervisor during the session. Videotape (see Whiffen, Chapter 3) can be used to review the execution and effect of each intervention. A valuable addition is to add the sound of the discussion behind the one-way screen to the videotape recording. Although this makes for a complicated sound track it enables the trainee to understand some of the reasons behind each of the supervisor's communications.

Putting it into Practice

The supervisor has to learn: an experiential event

The author, once again learning from his students, invited them in a workshop to use the earphone on him. Smiling sweetly one of the trainees offered to do so saying, "As it is clear that we cannot improve John's therapy, I will give him experiences of various interventions". He could have been warned by the glint in her eye. He was given a continual flow of instructions, comments and formulations, one following upon the other so quickly that he could not apply his critical faculties at all. He felt confused, and somewhat panicky. There was a pause in the input and he was able to grasp that the role play family was doing a good job of presenting a psychosomatic family with a boy with stomach ache. The instructions then changed to a much more leisured format leaving sufficient time between each input. He had no trouble understanding them. Each sentence was short and to the point. He did not have to stop listening to the family while the instructions were given. By far the most useful supervisory intervention was, "Notice mother putting her hand on her stomach". He had not noticed this and the therapy from then on organized itself around that observation, and the author felt genuinely helped to do a better job.

Somewhat to the author's relief he learned that his supervision group had decided to pack all the difficulties they had experienced into the first half of the role play and the helpful aspects into the second half. They had proceeded to execute this plan with considerable gusto and enjoyment.

Much was learned from the ensuing discussion in which the supervision group rejoined the workshop. Perhaps one of the most significant discoveries was that no one observed that the author had been confused in the first half. It is as if he had gone onto automatic pilot, and by parroting some of the instructions, had put on a reasonable show. Practice also suggests that it is not always possible to know when the supervisee is confused. The supervisee must be given space to discuss this afterwards and also be given the right to remove the earphone if necessary. This right is rarely used but it enables the supervisee to screen out the earphone instructions if they are confusing. He may choose to come out of the session to find out what was intended. It must also be remembered that when unsettled, supervisees tend to blindly obey instruction. When there is no time gap between instruction and intervention and no transformation of the supervisor's input into the language style of the trainee — in short, parroting occurs — it is a warning that perhaps the supervisor should not give any instructions for a while or he should call him out for a discussion.

Differing styles of supervision for each training phase and each trainee

Different forms of intervention are more helpful for therapists of varying experience. For very experienced family therapists it is doubtful whether the earphone is suitable except for an occasional observation, as above, when the therapist can use this information in his own style. At the other end of the scale novice therapists can use precise instructions of what to do and say. Novice therapists lose fewer families with this help. As they become more skilled, and know what the supervisor wants, the instruction can be of a more generalized nature such as, "Now work structurally on that discipline issue". It is especially helpful if trainees can watch the supervisor's therapeutic work for a while. Then an instruction such as this is easier to follow because he has a model to use. Towards the end of the training period although the earphone is plugged in, it may be only used two or three times during the session, giving the trainee experience of largely conducting his own therapy.

The trainee who is an experienced therapist but in a different field, such as individual therapy, poses a particularly interesting problem. His personal authority has to be respected, as Loewenstein and Reder (see Chapter 10) point out so forcibly. On the other hand if enough good will and mutual respect can be built up, in the author's experience the earphone is the most effective way of breaking up a linear cause/effect approach and establishing a circular systems approach. It can be helpful to allow the first half hour or so of the first session to go by without any interventions. The supervisor should warn the trainee of this, saying that he needs to get a feel of the trainee's normal therapeutic style. After the trainee has demonstrated his therapeutic authority he may need specific instructions just as much as the novice. Repeated instructions to notice or include the whole family can be invaluable. In one single parent family the mother, recognizing a good listener, made an all out bid to capture the therapist for herself by pouring out her anguish. Repeated supervisory comments about what the children were doing, with instructions to ask the children what they did when Mummy was upset at home, made the psychoanalytically trained therapist aware of the interacting system, and of how it could be used. Prior to a later session he said, "Please help me if I get hooked by mother again".

Clinical example

The following excerpts from a session show something of the range of interventions of which the earphone is capable. Almost the entire supervisory input in a one-and-a-half hour session is given. The ratio of supervisory to therapeutic intervention is thus exaggerated.

A Greek family from Crete with a fourteen-year-old enuretic boy, Dinos were present. He was the eldest of four. Father's mother was living with the family and was invited to the first session. Neither father nor his mother spoke good English. Mother was fluent. Early in the first session the supervisor said, "Ask father when they came to England". This broke up mother's monologue and elicited the following information: father could speak English better than mother said he could: both parents had come to England nine years ago, leaving Dinos aged five and his sister aged two with their paternal grandmother. All three had joined the rest of the family in England three years later, by which time the two younger children had been born.

The supervisor (*S*) then said to the therapist (*T*): "Ask if there are any plans to return". Grandmother wanted to go home, father was not sure, whereas mother had a job and was in the process of buying a house.

> *S:* (through the earphone) Ask Dinos whether he is Greek or English.
> *T:* Do you think of yourself as Greek or English, Dinos?
> *Dinos:* I am . . . I feel both at different times. When I am with my friends I am English . . . .
> *S:* (through earphone) Note the youngest boy talking Greek to father.
> *Dinos:* (continuing) — at home we speak Greek.
> *T:* When people all speak Greek at home it helps everybody to feel you haven't really left Crete.
> *S:* (earphone) Good.

The session continued revealing that the children overtly tried to avoid an open alliance with one culture or another.

> *S:* Some time ask what language each of the children think in — Greek or English.

Five minutes later the therapist explored this, revealing, even to the family's surprise, that Dinos thought in Greek most of the time, except when with his friends. The rest of the children thought entirely in English.

> *S:* (earphone) Get Dinos to find out from grandmother when Cretan children are expected to be dry.
> *T:* Dinos, do you know when boys in Crete should be dry? Perhaps you can find out from your grandmother.
> *Mother:* (Interprets the question into Greek for her mother-in-law.)
> *T:* Dinos can do it.
> *Grandmother:* (in English) It does not matter in Crete, my daughter was not dry until 16.

The session continued, revealing a greater and greater difference between paternal and maternal sides of the family, and between Greek and English cultures.

Mother discussed furnishing the new house, and how it was difficult for father to help as his English was poor.

> *S:* (earphone) Say this must make them want to part sometimes.
> *T:* I think it means that sometimes you will want to be different, to do different things—perhaps go in different directions.
> *S:* (Discussion in observation room) He compromised it! He did not give it quite the punch that I wanted.
> *Observer A:* I wonder why.
> *Observer B:* Too painful?
> *S:* (To observation group) Perhaps that dilution is fine—we may not be experiencing in here how brittle it is in there.
> *S:* (earphone) When you're ready come out for a discussion.

In the break the therapist said that he had realized that he had pulled his punches. The supervisor discussed with him whether this reflected the family homeostasis or his own difficulties with separating parents. Having recognized that indeed it was a difficult topic for him, the therapist was free to think about the homeostatic mechanisms of the family, especially the role of the symptom. The trainee was told to return and explore as to who dealt with the wet bed clothes and pyjamas.

> *M:* We do it together, my mother-in-law washes when I am too busy, and me the rest of the time. We try . . .
> *S:* (earphone) Say that there is a message from the group.
> *M:* . . . to get it . . . .
> *T:* (interrupted and put his hand up to halt mother) Hold on a moment. I have a message from my colleagues.
> *S:* (earphone) Say that we are most impressed with how Dinos keeps his family together by giving enough work for both his mother and grandmother.
> *T:* (repeats message.)
> *S:* (earphone) Second part. He should wait before deciding to be dry until the adults have decided whether to stay in England or not. Only then will his job of keeping mother and grandmother together and so keeping mother and father together, be over.

Guide to Practice

Before starting supervision the ground rules of therapeutic responsibility should be reviewed with the trainee. It should be remembered that the balance of authority is even more on the supervisor's side than with other supervising techniques. If there is a dispute over which way to proceed Montalvo's (1973) suggestion that if the trainee comes out and persuades the supervisor that his own strategy is as likely to produce results as the supervisor's the trainee should continue with his own approach. As a general rule supervisors should pause before intervening, first, the trainee's strategy may work, secondly, the supervisor is often surprised by how frequently the trainee comes up with what was on the tip of the supervisor's tongue. Supervisors who never pause never discover the trainee's potential; neither does the trainee. This point was made for the author when his trainee followed his instructions well for about fifteen minutes but then seemed to be ignoring instructions more and more. The earphone had been switched off from the very beginning!

Montalvo (1973) suggests that the prefix "must" should be used when the supervisor takes authority for what happens in the session, otherwise the trainee can modify the suggestion. In the use of the earphone the prefix also guides the degree of authority of any particular supervisory comment. It should be assumed, however, that anything said is likely to be taken as "must", therefore if this is not intended then the prefix should countermand it, e.g. "Perhaps you might . . .," "Think about . . ."

Instructions

The tone of voice and prefix will convey the supervisor's intentions, e.g. "Say . . .", or "Change seats with . . .", "Go across to the girl . . .", "Take mother's side".

"Ask . . . ." is an important intervention and much of the supervision early in therapy is taken up with exploring issues which will enable a systems hypothesis to be formulated. This depends, however, on the type of therapy being taught. Structural family therapy gains systemic information more from observing and provoking interaction than from questioning.

Suggesting strategies

It is unwise to change direction without discussing this with the therapist first. Loewenstein and Reder describe how one trainee was completely floored by such a change. The supervisor in his own therapeutic practice may well be used to changing tack with the ebb and flow of a therapeutic session. Indeed an unexpected reversal can be used to break up a redundant feedback loop. Sudden unplanned changes in supervisory direction, however, merely break up the therapist's coherence.

If the strategy suggested is broadly along the lines planned, or in the direction that therapy is already going, and if the trainee will understand the shorthand, then interventions like the following can be used:

"Explore the parents' differences on that," "Decentre yourself," "Get father to negotiate with his daughter on that," "Keep the boy out," or more tentatively, "See if you can . . .", "Perhaps you might explore . . .", Sometime try . . .", "If you have a chance . . .", "How about changing the seating arrangement?" "In your own time . . ." "You don't have to use this idea but . . . ."

Drawing attention to something

"Notice how . . .", "See how they repeat . . .", or "Father is crying". Attention may be focused on something the therapist is doing, "You are leaving the children out". "Father is drawing you into a fight again." As has already been suggested, therapists have to be senior enough to use such observations. Beginners feel they have to do something immediately, and may just repeat the observation to the family, which may or may not be helpful.

Messages

Here the metaposition of the group's authority can be used to add impact to the intervention, and it represents a strategic move, akin to the written message from the group after a consultation (Papp, 1980; Palazzoli *et al.*, 1978).

Encouragement

Complimenting the therapist on a good move can be very valuable. It is as important for the trainee to know when he is doing well as it is to know when he should try something different. It is especially important with beginners. It can be a good way of keeping a trainee to a particularly difficult task, which he might drop without encouragement. Too many "Goods", "Well dones" or "Greats" can, however, become distracting, infantalizing and addictive. When the supervisor stops the trainee thinks the supervisor is disapproving. It is worth informing trainees that "live" encouragement will decrease with experience. Congratulations can, and often should, be given when the trainee consults behind the screen when compliments should be directed at particular aspects of his work.

Increasing intensity

This is discussed by McGoldrick (Chapter 2). Because the supervisor is partially outside the therapeutic system it is possible to engage issues too difficult to consider in the room. Skill is required in knowing when and how far to go. Families or trainees if taken too far too fast may take flight.

Decreasing intensity

If the intensity of interaction is escalating too rapidly the supervisor can say,

"Tell them to stop so that you can hear a message from your colleagues," or "Put your hand up and say hold it!" or, "Stand up and stop them!"

Rescuing trainees from the family system

Families which bombard each other and the therapists with talk can be helped by the therapist repeatedly telling them to stop so that he can hear what his colleagues are saying. This provides them with a model that listening is important. In families with very confusing intense forms of communication the supervisor may talk to the therapist for a while ensuring that he stops hearing the content and only notices the process. When cotherapists are used the supervisor can talk to only one therapist, making him observe while the other therapist not hearing this conversation will remain more within the system. Therapists can also be instructed to leave the room.

Adjusting style to fit the trainee

The interchange between supervisor and trainee is so intimate—the trainee hears the supervisor in his head—that careful mutual monitoring of personal communication styles is essential. This is best done with regular discussion. The author completes a genogram with each of his trainees. This serves a number of purposes, including fostering a sense of trust and intimacy. It is also possible to focus the genogram on communication patterns. One trainee revealed the fact that she felt that her father never told her the truth, and what is more only had useless rubbish to tell. It was predicted that she would find the earphone particularly difficult. Once this was out in the open she was able to share her doubts, anxieties and anger about invaded autonomy. The supervisor was able to follow her suggestions about pace and authority so that it was experienced as genuinely helpful.

Before starting

Role play is invaluable, both for supervisor and trainee. It must be remembered that role play families are often more difficult than normal families to treat, and even more difficult to supervise. If both can manage that, they can manage anything and the oft expressed initial fear of the "bug" is reduced.

Introduction of the setting to the family can be practised, e.g. "We work in teams in this Clinic, the rest of my team is behind that mirror. If they have any suggestions to help us they can give them to me through this (picking up and inserting) earphone. Now what is the problem? (or whatever is the usual introductory procedure)." Once the trainee is comfortable with the earphone the family will be as well, and discussion will be minimal. Sometimes children want to know more and then the earphone can be likened to those worn by announcers on television which enables them to be given up to date news.

Conclusion

The earphone is a highly versatile and powerful instrument which needs to be used with care. It must only be used in the context of a trusting relationship. Once mastered, it can add considerably to the effectiveness of training. Families also benefit.

Note

1. Specifications from Media Services, 49c Onslow Gardens, London N10 3JY, U.K.

References

Boylston, W. H. and Tuma, J. (1972). Training mental health professionals through the use of the "bug in the ear". *Am. J. Psychiat.* **129**, 92-95.

Byng-Hall, J. and Campbell, D. (1981). Resolving conflicts arising from distance-regulation: an integrative approach. *J. Marital Fam. Ther.* **7**, 321-330.

Montalvo, B. (1973). Aspects of live supervision. *Family Process* **2**, 343-359.

Palazzoli, S. M., Boscolo, L., Cecchin, G. and Prata, G. (1978). *Paradox and Counterparadox*. Aronson, New York.

Papp, P. (1980). The Greek chorus and other techniques of family therapy. *Family Process* **19**, 45-58.

5. In on the Act

Patricia F. Pegg and Anthony J. Manocchio

The model of live supervision developed and employed by the Centre for Therapeutic Communication differs from other documented models in the extent of the visibility of the supervisor and the openness of communication between supervisor and therapist. During a supervised family therapy session, the family, therapist, supervisor, learning team and video technician are all in the same room. The therapist and family form a unit, apart from which sits the supervisor, at a short distance which allows the supervisor to be able to hear the session, and to speak to the therapist in the course of the session. The learning team—comprised of course members of whom the therapist for that particular session is one—sit at a further distance from this unit. These course participants observe without interference in the session, without taking notes, talking, or smoking during the session.

The extent of team involvement and its implications for training and therapy are described in detail elsewhere (Olson and Pegg, 1979). The purpose of this article is to describe the method, rationale and consequences of this direct form of live supervision in which all interventions and instructions are made to the therapist in front of the client family.

The aims of the Centre for Therapeutic Communication (henceforth referred to as CTC) and general course structure are also detailed in the above-mentioned paper. However, it seems relevant to establish here that CTC run intensive short-term courses for professionals working in mental health, education and training, and welfare. Courses emphasize theoretical input, application, and skills of evaluation by which approaches and techniques can be valued for their relevance and efficacy according to the needs and goals of the professional, the agency and the client.

Course participants range in background from school counsellors to social workers, through specialized family workers and psychologists, and from psychiatric nurses to family doctors and psychiatrists. Supervision in the form described below is used in client work with families who have been referred from local authority social services, psychiatric and child guidance clinics and self referrals in times of crisis. The model has (and is) been applied to

57

FAMILY THERAPY SUPERVISION
ISBN 0-12-794815-5

training programmes in England, the Scandinavian countries and Germany.

It is frankly difficult for either therapist or family to picture what the first session will be like from a verbal description, for the model demands open communication of what have for so long been secret areas. The one-way mirror has traditionally served as protection for family *and* observers in the course of supervised interviews. And the even more delicately protected supervisor-therapist interactions have been, until very recently, almost exclusively individualized and private.

The goal of this mode of supervision is to focus on the applied knowledge and skills of the therapist—a fact which is stressed to the families before the session. The session is not only intended to help the family but is defined as for the edification of the therapist, and comments and instructions are made directly to the therapist in the course of the session. (This is not a rigid rule, however. When on occasion the family member responds directly to the supervisor's intervention, the supervisor does not ignore the family member, but directs the communication clearly and humanely back between the therapist and family.)

Before outlining the types of interventions made, a word on the model of family therapy taught. With the proliferation of institutes and agencies specializing in family work comes the development and modification of their specialized or stylized responses to the families they serve. So follows the theoretical issues "Should we teach an eclectic approach to family therapy?" or "Is it possible to teach an eclectic approach to family therapy?" We suggest that this would be better redefined as "Can we *avoid* an eclectic approach to family therapy?".

Born of the disciplines of psychiatry, sociology, psychology and anthropology, family therapy *is* an eclectic approach to working with people's problems, and like any applied behavioural science, an amalgam of theory, pragmatically-derived solutions, and feedback from practise. As pointed out in "The Book of Family Therapy", it is in the very nature of the profession to search "for conceptualizations from many different disciplines and many different frames of reference" (Mendelsohn and Ferber, 1973). In our opinion those family therapists who lit the horizon with their creative glow have been those who employed a wide range of techniques and methods in their practises.

The therapeutic goal which pervades CTC teaching is well expressed by Bandler and Grinder, who define the aim of creative therapy as expanding the clients' model of the world in ways "that make the clients' lives richer and more worth living" (Bandler and Grinder, 1975), and to alter the behaviour which diminishes the available responses of the individual to situations he encounters.

Drawing from the works of Haley, Minuchin, Satir, Bandler and Grinder and Watzlawick *et al.*, we aim to present a meta model which gives the professional both the perspective and the effective skills to afford them (him or her) broader scope in their professional goals and aspirations (sometimes referred to as imagination), and more options in their therapeutic responses.

Minuchin said very clearly in his workshop at the Institute of Family Therapy, in London, June 1979, that the reading makes access to family therapy theory rather easy. The problem for the professional is in applying these ideas in practice, in the face of the challenge most families present. CTC courses acknowledge this phenomenon, and their design reflects this concern. Courses aim to (1) teach theory of family dynamics and change (2) present methods and techniques of intervention (3) encourage integration and creative application of techniques.

While the therapist's use of self and own particular talents are held to be a part of professionalism, self-awareness and inner knowledge are nowhere proved to be inherent qualities of an effective therapist. Emphasis in training and supervision is on the dynamics and demands of the family system, the goals of the therapist, and the application of the method selected for employment. Therapists are encouraged to articulate their goals, the specific purpose of tactics they use, and to be able to evaluate its appropriateness and efficacy in the situation.

Courses are comprised largely of practising professionals. We stress the importance of acknowledging the skills and experiences course participants bring with them — to embellish rather than to scrape or analyse away. This attitude is concomitantly fostered in therapists, to recognize and to use the skills, interests and world view the clients bring, and to build on them as resources.

At the first meeting, the family is introduced to the supervisor as the therapist's teacher and supervisor, and one who may intervene in the course of the session. The supervisor's presence is perceived as an advantage (it was for this feature that most people join courses), and this belief is earnestly conveyed to the family. Families, in turn, tend to see the supervisor's presence as being for the benefit of their therapist, and, further, as an additional resource to their therapy. The therapist is responsible for sessions while being supervised — (that is, supervisors do not take control of such sessions) — and for subsequent sessions. The supervisor comments and instructs the therapist.

"What if they won't follow instructions?" is the question raised by supervisors new to this model — perhaps an issue of concern to all new to live supervision. It is the experience of the authors that no intervention has been rejected in the course of a session. Occasionally the clear or advanced therapist will beg a few moments to integrate an instruction later in a session, or may question the supervisor for further clarification. Since live supervision is a relatively new phenomenon, it may be that obedience to the supervisor's instructions has more to do with the Hawthorne Effect, than with any beneficial qualities of the mode itself (The Hawthorne Effect being the discovery that *any* new or special treatment, even abuse, can bring positive consequences to a work situation, because of the psychological and sociological needs of the individual at work, Mayo, 1945). Nevertheless, there is a responsibility on the supervisor to make resourceful interventions which are also clear and simple enough for the therapist to directly translate them into the session.

The forms of intervention fall roughly into five categories which are outlined briefly below:

(1) The *authoritarian* instruction: "I want you to do "X" or "Ask the mother . . . ."" The fairly obvious purpose of this intervention is to push the therapist to another level of involvement, to pursue more closely a certain line of information or to redirect a therapist who is moving in an unhelpful direction.

(2) *Supportive* interventions take two forms: (a) *Supplementary,* which encourages the line the therapist is pursuing by reinforcing the demands of the therapist—"Are you satisfied with the answer you got from the father?" or "What did you hear the father just reply?" (b) *Complementary* interventions, again, encourage the line of the therapist by suggesting a technique to take it further—"Have the teenage daughter move out of the family circle while you discuss this point".

(3) *Explorative* interventions demand that the therapist halt the progression of the session momentarily, consider, and articulate how she perceives the system, how she defines her goals, and in which ways she might best work with the family at this point. In this intervention the supervisor might ask the therapist—"What do you see as the resources of this family? And how could you use them?" or "What would be the next best thing you might do in the session?" Sometimes the therapist is encouraged to ask this question of the family members: "What do you think is the most useful step for us to take next?" This intervention is particularly useful for therapists who continue talking when they have stopped saying anything useful in a session. It demands conceptualization of goal and method, and clear communication thereof in words as well as action.

(4) *Collaborative* interventions utilize a tacit agreement between therapist and supervisor to create a therapeutic double bind in the course of the session. "Slow down—don't go too fast with this family. They are probably working harder than they ought to on this problem. Be careful with them." Here the therapist and supervisor take therapeutic advantage of the fact that the family cannot question the supervisor directly, to employ Haley's strategy of resisting change (Haley, 1976).

(5) The supervisor employs an *educational* intervention to highlight an aspect of the session for the training of the therapist and the learning team—and, inevitably, the family. Here the supervisor interrupts the session to comment on a pertinent dynamic, an issue of content, or a particular method.

Most sessions are videoed, and the supervisor may here use an instant playback of the session to illustrate what has just happened within the family system, or between family and therapist. Video analysis is a powerful, immediate feedback technique in therapy or supervision, and here the supervisor uses the video to teach from what has just happened, and to suggest or elicit alternatives from the therapist, family or learning team (Olson and Pegg, 1979).

During such an intervention, the session shifts to another level — use of video or a blackboard for a quick linguistic analysis — to look at the events of the session in terms of the Meta Model (Bandler and Grinder, 1975). Educational interventions are brief (5-10 min.) cognitive learning experiences for therapists and families, who in fact respond very positively to these kinds of interventions. We will see below where Scandinavian CTC colleagues make educational interventions the focus of the post session, demanding that the clients remain to partake, and if they will, to contribute to post-session analyses and strategy building.

The most obvious feature of this model of live supervision is that the family see and hear all the interventions and interaction between their therapist and the supervisor. This means that interventions are functioning on two levels: the operational level, that of instructing the therapist what to do next; and, secondly, in that all comments, queries, changes of direction, theory, etc. are heard and become part of the cognition of the family.

The supervisor's visibility demands clear, simple and constructive framing of interventions during the session, for, whether instructing or inquiring, the supervisor is modelling clear communication. Perhaps most significantly, what is being demonstrated is that it *is* possible to speak of what is not usually openly discussed — at least in the presence of clients: namely, the therapist's perception of the session, and the therapist's actual performance in the session. We assume that it is beneficial for the family to be exposed to the same input as the therapist whose ideas and options of behaviour are being expanded by the teaching and supervision.

From the forms which interventions can take, as described above, it is clear that they can be employed to focus the therapist on issues of either process or content in the family. Case examples might better indicate how this actually operates in a session:

A course participant social worker brought to supervision a family which had come to her agency with an insistent, if rather unspecific request for financial assistance. The family cited difficulties in running the household and "family needs" as reasons for their request, and hence had agreed to appearing for a family interview. Early in the session, the mother referred to an illness. The therapist did not seek further information on this point. After the mother mentioned her illness for the third time, the supervisor instructed the therapist "Find out what the mother means by her 'illness'". The therapist asked, received a brief reply about a sore throat, then returned to the generalized issues of family and financial difficulties. Ten minutes later, the supervisor intervened again. "Get more information about what the mother means when she says she is not well." The therapist proceeded slowly and generally in that direction for some minutes, still without putting a direct question about the mother's health. "It is still unclear about the mother's health," the supervisor intervened. "Ask her how she knows about her illness and how much she knows about it." So directed, the therapist discovered that the mother had been diagnosed as having cancer of the throat—and that no one else in the family was aware of the diagnosis. The focus of the session was redefined in relation to the information about the mother's health—present and future implications for the family, plans to be made, and how the family would deal with what was to come. By putting the problem into a fuller context, the therapist/social worker was able to offer more appropriate treatment.

Of course not all problems transform into family therapy issues, nor should the therapist try to redefine them in those terms. But the importance of obtaining as much information as possible about the problem, its context and how the family see it is a basic principle of a number of approaches to family therapy (Bandler and Grinder, 1975; Haley, 1976; Watzlawick et al., 1974). This rather dramatic example indicates the difficulty of even professional workers in obtaining full, appropriate information.

In a similar case, a single parent family was brought in by a worker who was helping the mother prepare to leave the psychiatric rehabilitation programme in which she was a participant. The therapist, who was analytically orientated, concentrated on the mother's separation anxiety and fears about the future. The supervisor interrupted the session and instructed the therapist to brainstorm with the young mother her interests, skills and dreams about possibilities for the future, and to record these on the blackboard in the therapy room. The scope of the young woman's resources and experiences became visibly clear through this exercise, and the session, quickly moved to developing real plans for the woman's future and that of her small children.

In this instance, the family remained for the post-session, during which her brainstorm list was used by the supervisor to teach about focussing a session, and about identifying client strengths. The client responded spontaneously in the post-session to comment upon previous counselling efforts, and to contribute with feedback about the evening's session. It seems significant to note here that early in the therapy session, the young woman had spoken in a whisper. Part of the supervisor's intention in suggesting that the therapist write up the client's responses on the board was to make her replies accessible to the rest of the people in the room. As the brainstorm progressed, however, the woman's voice grew, and as she spoke in the post-session, she directed her statements clearly to all present. She was identified as a contributor to the group.

The example of a process-focussed intervention comes from a family session which took place in the family's home. The family had been referred by a psychiatric institution where the wife was involved in a day programme. The problem, as clearly defined by the husband, was, aside from her chronic depression, that she was unable to listen to him, that they could not talk together. This he could document with numerous examples, which included her behaviour during the session. The couple had two active, talkative children around the ages of four and six years. Each time the wife was questioned by one of the co-therapists, the husband leaned over and spoke with his children.

This took place with predictable regularity until the supervisor stopped the session, and instructed the videoman to locate on tape an example of the co-therapists talking with the mother. Off the screen, the mother could be heard mumbling some response to the co-therapist's earnest questions. On screen the videoman had picked up the father speaking with the two children. The supervisor used the opportunity to teach the supervision group about behaviour which maintains problems and strategies appropriate in such instances. The father responded with the amazement people do in seeing unexpected behaviour on the video screen. It is important in these cases not to blame or interpret the behaviour: the supervisor must frame the intervention so that its content opens new possibilities for the therapists, and perhaps for the family.

A criticism of this model is that strategies so openly developed cannot have the power of those slipped into a session, and that, therefore, therapy so practiced will not be as effective as where the family is not aware of the therapist's perceptions or plans, or where the family is levered with the statement that "My colleagues behind the screen don't believe you can fulfil the task I have in mind for you".

In the first place this model does not exclude strategies developed without the presence of the family. Family therapy sessions and post-sessions are parts of an overall course of theory, video analysis and discussion of sessions. Nor is the model based in the tenet that everything must be discussed before the client all the time. Strategies and approaches are planned and evaluated without the presence of the family. But this way of training and practising therapy does question the assumption that the power of a therapist lies in what is *not* seen, rather than what is seen by the client.

This issue proceeds to one of the main theoretical bases on this mode of live supervision. The therapist, learning team, and supervisor must speak out in front of the family in terms which they can *use* in front of the family. This may seem a self-evident point, but it is a key point of application which is generally not part of training. Professionals are trained to discern dynamics, pin-point problems, to devise attacks — but often this is done in language which is difficult to translate into in-session dialogue and (harder still, as Minuchin stated) into action.

Dark, rich symbolic interpretations are creative in literature, but, it is fairly well accepted, not necessarily useful with a working class alcoholic, or the mother of a schizophrenic. This tradition of not speaking openly about the client in front of the client leads to a vacuum: a practical absence of skills for face-to-face interaction through which the therapist can communicate his intentions and behavioural goals to the family in a constructive and active way.

This issue proceeds to one of the main theoretical bases of this mode of live supervision: the demystification of therapy. It is our explicit opinion that the therapist, while by training and experience an expert, is not a mystical personage, nor is the field one of mystical powers. This demystification of role and function is a consistent theme throughout training and supervision.

The model itself is one which simply cannot be utilized in a situation where the therapists' work is held to be unquestionable, or the secrets of the trade of danger in the hands of the "eavesdropping" family. Everything happens in the open. The therapist is instructed, sometimes halted, questioned about the session or its progression all in front of the family. By having to respond in this open arena, the therapist must sharpen her skill of reframing, and of responding in a clear and constructive fashion to the demands of the supervisor or of the family.

Demystification is also achieved as the clear communication between therapist and supervisor is modelled in their interaction. Verbal skills appear as integral features of Satir's (1964) and Bandler and Grinder's (1975) basic approach to family therapy as a communication issue, in the emphasis of the Palo Alto group on reframing and the verbal depiction of problems (Watzlawick *et al.*, 1974), and in the verbal acrobatics of skilled therapists like Haley (1976), Minuchin (1974) and Palazzoli *et al.* (1978).

Furthermore, the family see that the therapist, too, is capable and willing to learn. Contrary to the expectation and frequent concern that the family will be exposed in all its emotional vulnerability, it is the therapist who is defined as the learner, as the vulnerable one under the guidance of the supervisor. But the family, as well as the therapist, are exposed to the learning and evaluation which takes place at a meta-level—that is, above the level of the session's actual content. Psycho-analytical interpretations of the therapist's behaviour or motives are *never* considered or made, either in the course of a session, or in post-session analysis.

A consequence of this approach is that training sessions are redefined as situations where therapist and family are working together toward common, though distinct, goals of enrichment and change, rather than one individual doing something to a small group of others. This, of course reflects an approach to therapy as a co-operative effort at problem solving, with the onus of responsibility and consequences resting with those with the problem.

This assumption of responsibility is reflected, too, in the intensive, short-term format of CTC courses. It is a model applied in management training and language contexts where the client (student) is served with information, skills and feedback—and expected to practise, develop and apply the learning on their own. It was probably those at the Palo Alto Brief Therapy Centre who most clearly described the period of contact and affect as a product of the assumptions and expectations of the treater (teacher) (Weakland *et al.*, 1974). Certainly

America's National Training Laboratories, and the internationally-known Berlitz Language courses have experienced sufficient positive feedback from their short-term approaches to continue with that format. Both therapists and families on CTC courses have reported positive reactions to intensive, short-term contact.

Families are often invited in this model, to attend post-sessions which follow the therapy session. These generally consist of feedback to the therapist from the observing colleagues, video analysis of the session, and discussion of strategy for future work with the family. CTC colleagues in their supervision and training practice in Scandinavia are in fact demanding that clients remain for the post sessions. "People are the best experts at their own problems," says Wirtberg. Clients are asked to take part in evaluative discussion of their impoverished life maps: the ways in which they cause or maintain problems, and to contribute to the development of a therapeutic strategy for further treatment. Wirtberg and Pettit believe that more therapeutic affect occurs in these post-sessions than during the therapy sessions, as clients are exposed to clear discussion of their techniques of problem maintenance and take part in the discovery of options to enlarge their world picture (Wirtberg and Pettit, 1979).

What has for so long been hidden — a veritable taboo between practicer of and practiced on — is here dealt with openly. But this model of supervision is not as radical as might seem, it has been used for many years in the fields of physio-therapy, dentistry, surgery, without fear of danger to the patient.

As the family is invited to attend all or part of the post-session, their involvement underlines other aspects of the demystification process. First is the importance of learning from clients. Therapy, although it has its meaning in application, is theoretical. It does not seem unusual for students of therapy to get hooked on learning the theory, and forgetting what is to be learned from the mouths of the clients. This model creates the circumstance where they are expected to learn from the client, as part of the post-session learning group.

The second aspect is detailed in the work of Truax and Carkhuff (1967). Their extensive research in training and practise of psychotherapy and counselling lead them to conclude that it was openness to feedback from the client that modified and reinforced the skill and sensitivity of the therapist. Openness to client feedback, they said "is probably an essential quality of any effective therapist; through it he comes to trust his own experience" (Truax and Carkhuff, 1967).

Perhaps the greatest drawback of this model is the initial response when it is described, for both family and therapist (especially therapist, from our experience) react with disbelief, sometimes bordering on alarm, at the thought of talking before a group of people. This is really overcome only after it has been experienced. It has proven to be the cause of withdrawal from therapy in a small percentage of cases.

The model makes a heavy demand on the supervisor. It is obviously not possible for the supervisor to fall asleep or pace around, as is the case with the protection of one-way mirrors. Given the feedback of others who have tried to supervise in this manner, the ability to give useful interventions before the family is one which takes considerable concentration and skill.

Other drawbacks must be similar to those of other modes of live supervision: implementation of instruction, for example, can be difficult whether the instruction is served by a warm body or through an "ear bug".

We have not yet been able to measure the effect of having an audience on the family or therapist. An informal survey suggests that the larger percentage of families forget about the observers during the session. There are undoubted cases of both family members and therapists who freeze under these circumstances and are unable to register their discomfort. On the other hand there is the "player-syndrome" where some therapists report being stimulated to better performance by the presence of an audience.

Of course this audience effect can work against a therapist, as the skilled family can play the audience against their helper. Sometimes the family members, whether to disqualify the therapist, or to relate honestly to the supervisor, communicate verbally or non-verbally to the supervisor during the session. Here the therapist must exercise authority in regaining the family's attention in full.

Another issue, which probably occurs with other methods of live supervision, has to do with differing value systems. The therapist who has severe reservations about openness before clients is caught in a genuine bind in this form of supervision. Course membership would suggest that these professionals self-select themselves out of attendance. Verbal skills and openness are difficult for some participants, but those who attend courses are usually eager to develop those aspects.

Direct Open Supervision is a model of live supervision born of necessity — the unavailability of one-way mirror facilities for CTC's first family therapy course in the early 1970's. We believe it has evolved into a model with therapeutic and educational benefits unimagined at its inception.

The model is useful in its mobility: it does not require equipment or props. Family work has been supervised in homes, course locations, and referring agencies. Of course, there is room and need for research on the effects of this approach. Response from trainees and clients has been positive, in survey and evaluation. Therapists raised and supervised by an individualized, interpretive approach have expressed relief and pleasure at the openness both amongst colleagues and clients.

References

Bandler, R. and Grinder, J. (1975). *The Structure of Magic*. Vol. 1, p.18. Science and Behaviour Books, Palo Alto, California.

Haley, J. (1976). *Problem Solving Therapy: New Strategies for Effective Family Therapy.* Jossey-Bass, San Francisco.

Mayo, E. (1945). *The Human Problems of an Industrial Civilization.* Harvard Business School, Boston, Mass.

Mendelsohn, H. and Ferber, A. (1973). Is everybody watching? *The Book of Family Therapy* (A. Ferber, H. Mendelsohn and A. Napier, eds.), pp.331-444. Houghton Mifflin, Boston, Mass.

Minuchin, S. (1974). *Families and Family Therapy.* Tavistock Publications, London.

Olson, U. J. and Pegg, P. F. (1979). Direct open supervision: a team approach. *Family Process* 18, 463-469.

Palazzoli, M. S., Boscolo, L., Cecchin, G. and Prata, G. (1978). *Paradox and Counterparadox.* Aronson, London and New York.

Satir, V. (1964). *Conjoint Family Therapy.* Palo Alto Calif. Science and Behaviour Books.

Truax, C. B. and Carkhuff, R. P. (1967). *Toward Effective Counselling and Psychotherapy: Training and Practice.* Aldine, Chicago.

Watzlawick, P., Weakland, J. and Fisch, R. (1974). *Change: Principles of Problem Formation and Problem Resolution.* Norton, New York.

Weakland, J., Fisch, R., Watzlawick, P. and Bodin, A. (1974). Brief therapy: focused problem resolution. *Family Process* 13, 141-168.

Wirtberg, I. and Pettit, W. (1979). The use of the meta model in supervising family therapy. Unpublished manuscript.

6. Supervisory Discussion in the Presence of the Family

Elizabeth A. Carter

Methods of family therapy supervision, like techniques of family treatment, have proliferated in recent years without particular regard for whether or how they might or might not fit into an overall theoretical framework. Passed along by word of mouth, or observed at workshop demonstrations, supervisory techniques applied without notice of the principle of isomorphism may serve to confuse the therapist in training and/or deliver double messages to the treatment family. Isomorphism, the tendency for patterns to repeat at all levels of the system, strongly suggests that as the supervisor deals with the trainee, so will the trainee deal with the family, and the family members with each other.

Applying this principle to the issue of boundaries, it is important to clarify at the outset of supervision who is in charge of what. In the model described below, it is established that the supervisor is in charge of the procedures and the quality of the supervision, the trainee is responsible for the procedures and quality of the therapy (and remains so even when bringing the family in for live supervision), and the family is responsible for decisions and actions related to change. I have found that this clarification reduces the tendency of supervisors to anxiously take over treatment responsibility, which leads inevitably to the therapist's anxiously over-functioning for the family, while the family does nothing (except perhaps, complain about the therapist's failure to change them). In one way or another, I think that every method of supervision must deal with the potential triangling of supervisor, trainee and family or pay a price in impaired training, treatment, or, most likely, both.

With the knowledge that his or her method of supervision will have strong impact on every level of the training and treatment system, it behooves the supervisor to use a method of supervision that is consistent with the family therapy theory being taught to the trainees, and which respects the boundaries between the sub-systems involved.

FAMILY THERAPY SUPERVISION
ISBN 0-12-794815-5

The Setting

The method of supervision described in this paper is one of many used at the Family Institute of Westchester (New York), where the author directs the family therapy training programme. The Family Institute of Westchester is a small private institution chartered by the State of New York for post-graduate training of mental health professionals in family therapy. A part-time, multi-disciplinary faculty of eight family therapists, most of whom also teach at the major universities and hospitals in the New York area, are responsible for teaching a student-body of 40 to 60 trainees (the majority of whom are social workers) over a two to four year period. The basic curriculum is geared for three years: In the first year, basic family systems concepts are taught, the clinical emphasis is on family evaluation and engagement, and the goal is to shift trainee thinking from individual toward systems thinking. In the second year, the workings of triangles are taught, with the clinical emphasis on identifying and tracking the emotional flow through nuclear and extended family triangles, and developing techniques for assisting the family to interrupt those patterns which are dysfunctional. At the end of the second year, the trainee is expected to be a relatively consistent "systems thinker". In the third year, focus is on more of the same, with particular attention to the special knowledge and techniques helpful with different types of family problems. The methods of teaching include didactic lectures, reading and discussion, faculty demonstration, viewing of edited videotapes, and the small supervisory group. In addition to direct clinical supervision, the small groups take up related systems problems such as trainee difficulties in a work setting suspicious or inimical to family systems therapy; how to start a private practice (i.e. dealing with the mental health system in the private sector); and study and work on the trainees' personal families.

The heart of the clinical training is the supervisory group, where four or five trainees meet for half a day with their supervisor every other week from autumn to spring. Supervision is both live and by viewing videotaped sessions. Treatment families come from both the trainee's work setting and from our own small clinic, thus cutting across all economic and class lines, with the majority probably falling into the middle class.

The Complexities of Multi-Method Training

The theoretical orientation of the faculty is family systems theory. The majority follow the framework of Bowen (1978); some teach Minuchin's (1975) structural method, and there is current interest among the faculty in the possibilities of adding strategic therapy. It is our belief that all of the above theoretical frameworks "see" family process in a very similar way. A family problem involving a distant father and over-involved mother and child is Bowen's "triangle", Minuchin's "coalition across generational boundaries", and the strategic therapists' "dysfunctional cycle of interaction". However, the above frameworks differ sharply in their views of where and how to intervene in the system, their differences being related to divergent answers to questions about change. What kind of change? How much change? How does change come about?

We thought when we started multi-method training that the advantages for the trainees in learning several of the major systems approaches to family therapy were obvious. We did not fully anticipate the problems of such an undertaking, which raises many difficult questions for faculty and trainees alike. In what order should these methods be taught? What are the criteria for differential use of the methods? What methods of supervision fit and do not fit the various theories, and most important of all—if we do not teach a single method (a "true religion"), how can we avoid the murky, so-called "eclecticism" which can produce a therapist who strings together unrelated concepts from both individual and systems theory and applies them with techniques unrelated to either a particular theory or a coherent view of change?

So far, we have many questions and few answers to these problems. Operationally, we have tried to make some gross distinctions to reduce confusion: most trainees seem to grasp Minuchin's structural method in a usable form in about a year, whereas Bowen's more fully elaborated theory of family process and more complex, long-term method of therapy requires at least two years of training for comparable proficiency. Adding strategic family therapy will certainly compound our problems. Our ideas at the moment are that appropriate paradoxical or other strategic interventions, although appearing deceptively simple, are based on a very sophisticated understanding of the family emotional system and should be taught to advanced trainees. Finally, we will face programme problems since it is not at all reasonable to think that a given trainee can or would want to learn three or four different methods in as many years and end up master of none. (I feel that I owe the reader, and myself, another chapter in a few years to see how all of this comes out.)

As for the differential use of the two major methods now taught, in general, most of us recommend the use of the brief structural method with chaotic, multi-problem families, with rigid child-focussed families with symptomatic children, and in settings requiring brief therapy (e.g. inpatient wards). Bowen's method would then be recommended for all other problems, and might also be used for a "phase II" course of treatment after a child's symptom has been relieved, if the parents are motivated to continue, and if the setting permits long-term work.

It is probably clear that the above schema is rudimentary in the extreme and relates to the teacher's experience and preference rather than to any hard evidence that one method is superior to another, either in general or with particular problems. I think this is not different from the basis on which given single methods are taught in most training programmes. The conviction of the teacher that his method is useful, and his own clinical confirmation of that through sufficient satisfactory outcome (whatever that is), seems to me still the basis from which most teachers operate, in spite of the "softness" of this basis as opposed to a "hard data" research basis for development, choice and evaluation of method. Bowen, Minuchin and Palazzoli all speak and write of research as the basis for their theories and as evidence of its good outcome, but it is my impression that, aside from their own training programmes, the majority of therapists teaching and learning their methods probably disregard this and focus instead on their concepts and techniques. Although it is understandable that clinicians tend to develop a narrow focus on the "practical" aspects of the work, it would seem important in our teaching institutes to promote a focus on the research and evaluation that can keep us open rather than partisan. This is a goal toward which we hope to move, however slowly, at the Family Institute of Westchester. While we work towards the day in which research-theory-practice-evaluation-and-teaching are all part of an integrated process, it is at least possible, we believe, to avoid blatant incongruity among the components that we do have in place: theory, clinical practice, and the teaching of these.

Supervisory Discussion in the Presence of the Family

This method of supervision, in brief, consists of a live family session conducted by a trainee with the supervisor and other trainees from the supervisory group present in the room during the interview. There is usually a large chalk board in the room containing the family's three or four generation genogram, drawn there by the trainee before the family arrives. When the trainee has concluded the interview, or reaches a place where he or she feels "stuck" and uncertain how to proceed, the trainee tells the family he wishes to consult with his colleagues and invites them to remain for the discussion. (I have never seen a family turn this invitation down.) The trainee, supervisor and other training group members then proceed to discuss the family, and the treatment interview they have just witnessed, while the treatment family listens. No comments or questions are directed to family members, nor are they permitted to participate in the discussion. When the family has been dismissed by the trainee, who remains in charge of time, the group discusses in greater detail the therapist's conduct of the interview and explores, if relevant, the connection between the therapist's difficulties with the treatment family and his difficulties in his own personal family system.

Before the family arrives, the trainee is given a few minutes to present the family situation and his perception of his own difficulties with the family to the group. This is expected to be brief and highly focussed. I give trainees four or five points of information needed to orient us to be helpful, ending with a statement from the trainee on what help he wants from us today. This part of the format forces the trainee to actively prepare for his presentation and reduces the trainee tendency to do unto the supervisor what the family does unto him: overwhelm with circumstantial detail. If the trainee chooses to do so, this presentation to the group may be made in the presence of the family, before the interview.

A specific contract is made between supervisor and trainee before each session as to whether the supervisor will interrupt during the session to address the trainee or will wait until the trainee ends or interrupts the session himself. Most trainees choose the latter course at first but then come to appreciate the advantages of being helped to shift course during the interview.

Trainees vary in how they present the invitation to their families. Some are open about their status as trainees; others refer to it as a consultation group. They usually describe it as an "opportunity" for the family and themselves. Initially, when the trainees are ambivalent and anxious about the process, many families "refuse". As the trainees become willing and then eager, almost all families accept the invitation, whatever hour of day or evening the group meets.

Congruence with Theory

It should be clear that such a method of supervision would make sense only with a theory of change which considers education and intellectual understanding by family members as useful, and which values openness between therapist and family in the course of treatment. The post-session exploration of the therapist's personal family could only be appropriate if the theory finds this area relevant to proficient conduct of family treatment by the trainee.

This method would not be used by structural or strategic supervisors, who consider understanding absolutely or relatively useless in the face of emotional resistance, and who seek power and leverage by use of authoritative prescriptions, tasks, and strategies rather than through direct explication. The use of a three-generation genogram, which may open the door on a multitude of problems, would not be appropriate in brief therapies which focus on the presenting problem. Finally, having the supervision group present to reveal themselves directly would not be at all feasible in strategic therapy where the group plays a part (enhanced by their mysteriousness) in the treatment itself. Similarly, the exploration of the role of the therapist's personal family situation would not appear relevant to any therapy model where brief, highly focussed, observed, technique-oriented treatment all protect the therapist from remaining caught in the family system. However, exploration of the therapist's personal family, is in my opinion, an essential element in any long-term, single-therapist form of treatment in which a multitude of intense emotional issues arise and need to be explored and dealt with in detail in treatment.

Advantages of this Method of Supervision

For the family

(1) The anxious, uptight family usually benefits from being "off the spot", and is frequently able to calm down enough to think about their situation and hear indications of possible new directions to pursue.

A trainee brought in a young woman, Joan, whom she had been seeing individually for depression and trying (unsuccessfully) to motivate to undertake work on reconnecting with her family of origin, from whom she had been almost totally cut off. Since Joan's family was chaotic and violence-prone, she resisted any attempt by the therapist to discuss renewing contact with them, and Nancy, the therapist, had been trapped into arguing with Joan about this.

In the supervisory discussion, the group members acknowledged the extreme difficulty of this work, while reviewing the benefits for Joan if she could find a way to reconnect at least with some of the family. One member of the group told of his work on his own family, which was similar to Joan's, emphasizing the particular strategies he had begun with and how slowly and carefully he had planned and proceeded. He spoke briefly of the beneficial results in his own life. The supervisor then asked the trainee, Nancy, if her own experience in a very close personal family network had trapped her into pushing Joan toward this "ideal". Nancy agreed that this was probable.

In the post-session, after Joan's departure, Nancy explored her central position in an enmeshed family and planned specific moves to try to define herself more clearly within her family. She reported within several weeks that Joan was working on a plan to contact her father ("inspired by the story of the man in the consulting group") and that she, Nancy, was working on not pushing her. Her personal family work, gaining more "space" for herself within her family, was proving to be helpful in this regard.

(2) The family which denies involvement in problems and tries to pin everything on an "identified patient", benefits from hearing a preponderance of non-blaming opinion on the operation of the system as a whole, especially in the absence of any opportunity to use characteristic defensive manoeuvres to obscure or wipe out the therapist's point.

A trainee, Carl, brought in a child-focussed family in which all problems were perceived to reside in the 16-year-old daughter. Marital and extended family problems were alluded to and then brushed aside as irrelevant. The family was at the point of considering individual therapy for the girl.

Carl conducted what he later said was a "typical" session with the family: the older daughter sulked, the younger ("good" daughter) smirked, while father criticized the older girl, alternately silencing mother's feeble attempts to mitigate his criticism and the therapist's attempts to focus elsewhere. After a particularly vehement harangue by father, Carl stopped the interview, turned to the group and said, "Here's where we're stuck". Father said, "You're damned right, for once," and sat back triumphantly while the family, the trainee and the group laughed.

The subsequent discussion of the family was conducted with reference to a three-generation genogram on the chalk board. "Here are the areas father won't let me discuss," said Carl, and engaged the group in a discussion of bitter extended family feuding on father's side of the family. During the discussion, father's attempts to interrupt became a running joke, accepted good naturedly by father. When his criticism of his daughter was labelled by the supervisor as evidence of his "great concern that she not turn out like his black-sheep sister", his posture became less defensive and more interested. The group expressed concern for father's over-responsible position in the family and suggested ways that both the family and the therapist could acknowledge his concern and thus reduce his anxious criticizing. The daughter's role in provoking father's criticism was outlined, as was mother's peacemaker role in the middle. Strong emphasis was placed on the role of the extended family feud and the avoided marital difficulties, as fuel for the family anxiety level which triggered the same old dance in the nuclear family triangle.

As the family was leaving, father asked, "Am I just allowed to say that all of this finally makes some sense?". Carl jokingly replied, "No, you're not," and then as the door closed behind them, whispered: "That's because this is the first time you ever shut up long enough to hear it". The post-session, in addition to discussing Carl's relationship with his own father, focussed on ways to calm down over-anxious talkers who obstruct work in family sessions without becoming engaged in a prolonged power struggle with them.

(3) The hopefully calm, thoughtful, and non-judgemental tone of the discussion can model a different climate in which to view and work on the family problems.

(4) The supervisory session can provide an overview, or roadmap, which becomes a shared reference point in treatment, identifying relevant issues and pointing to directions for the future work and goals of therapy.

Trainees report that the family members refer back to the supervisory session throughout the rest of treatment with comments such as: "So that's what the group meant!" — "I think I'm falling into that trap that the group talked about." — "Well, I guess the group was right when they said that sooner or later I'd have to deal with my mother, so let's go." etc.

For the trainee therapist

(1) Previously "obscure" events such as earlier deaths, events in extended family, etc. gain new prominence and relevance in the group discussions and give added clout to the therapist's efforts to focus on these in treatment (as in the previous example), or may reveal therapist resistance to the pursuit of certain themes.

John and Susan, a couple in their forties, were invited to a supervisory session because the trainee, Carol, felt they were "stuck" in their marital disputes and in the therapy. Susan had been married before, her first husband having died when their girls were very young. Most of their five years of marriage had been marked by endless battles over the raising of the girls and the therapy had focussed on these disputes, with and without the children present, with no results.

Following the interview, which simply "re-hashed" the latest argument over the children, one of the group asked the trainee, Carol, if the couple and the children were able comfortably to talk about Susan's dead husband, Charles. Carol, somewhat surprised, said she did not really know. The subject of Charles "had not come up" except during routine taking of the genogram at the initial evaluation. The group members then raised many questions about Charles' death and whether it had been dealt with sufficiently by the family to permit the new marriage and family to proceed without his "ghost". During the discussion, Susan sat quietly crying in the background.

In the post-session, the trainee appeared very shaken by the impact of this "overlooked" issue and immediately related it to her own failure to come to terms with her father's death several years ago. What really shook her up, Carol stated, was not just underestimating the importance of this issue to the family, which could happen to anyone, but rather the fact that she had not even noticed it at all, nor asked the most routine questions related to the first husband, something she would surely have done, for instance, if there had been a divorce.

(2) Toxic issues, which the therapist and family may have been tiptoeing around, can surface matter-of-factly in the group discussion and will then be available for future reference and work. The openness of this session is a model for future sessions for the therapist and the family.

Two middle-aged women, involved in a long-term lesbian relationship, had consulted a trainee about problems related to the behaviour of the teenage daughter of one of them. The women shared a household and the raising of four children, two girls and two boys, from a marriage that had ended in divorce and cut-off from the children's father.

The beginning of the interview, which was attended by all six members of the household, consisted chiefly of criticisms of the oldest girl's behaviour and arguments between the women as to how best to handle it. The trainee, Sharon, conducted the interview skillfully, and gave not the slightest indication that there was anything at all out of the ordinary about the family.

As the atmosphere became "sticky" with the tension of an obvious but avoided issue, the supervisor interrupted (as had been agreed) to ask Sharon matter-of-factly whether they had ever explored in family sessions how the children felt about having two women as "parents", rather than the usual family with a mother and father. The trainee winced slightly but answered calmly enough that they had not. Before Sharon could direct this question back to the family, the children's mother said she had been worrying about it for some time, but she hadn't quite known how to bring it up. Slowly, the topic was addressed by the children, with the teenage girl finally asking her mother if she were a lesbian. The mother answered evasively, but one of the younger children pressed the issue by asking, "What's a lesbian?" This led to explanations by both women and a chance for the children to talk about both their positive and negative reactions to their mother's partner as well as their mixed feelings about belonging to such an unusual kind of family. The supervisor interrupted again later in the interview to say to the trainee that this might be a good point at which to ask everyone how they felt about the complete cut-off from the children's father.

In subsequent meetings, Sharon reported that the older girl's problem behaviour had subsided as therapy focussed on defining a clearer role in their lives for mother's partner, and re-establishing visitation between the children and their father.

(3) Significant factors missed or underestimated in evaluating a family will be picked up in the group discussion.

(4) There is little likelihood that the therapy will remain stuck in the same place following this type of session since so many others besides the therapist are privy to the thinking of the group.

(5) There is a relief for most trainees in openly resigning from the position of "omniscience" into which they tend to get locked.

For the members of the training group

(1) The major benefit for the trainees is learning to find the words and phrases with which to ask, directly but non-judgementally, about the anxiety provoking issues in the family. Trainees report that they learn how to phrase questions about death, homosexuality, incest, alcoholism, child abuse and other difficult issues in a way that does not blame anyone, does not ask "why", and which elicits information about the systems patterns in which symptoms are embedded.

(2) This format provides an exercise in putting systems characteristics into focus to avoid siding with particular family members. If a trainee comments about father's "explosive temper with the children", without mentioning mother's interventions, the supervisor can insert the missing piece. Trainees pick up on this quickly and learn to describe problems in triangular rather than

individual or dyadic terms. Trainees are further prevented by the format from escape into emotionally reactive invective ("that controlling bitch"), a form of "individual diagnosis" which militates against maintaining a systems perspective on the family problems.

(3) The openness of this method is as instructive a model for the rest of the group as it is for the family and the therapist.

(4) The observation of the interview in the room is more interesting and "alive" for the group since even one-way glass filters affect and permits observers to "drop out" or "act out" by getting bored, distant, distracted or judgemental. The impact of direct exposure to the family emotional field heightens respect in the group for family and therapist alike.

(5) The ground rule of speaking to the therapist rather than to family members protects the family from several disjointed interviews and forces group members either to make comments or be silent. The common trainee method of reducing their own anxiety through extraneous questioning of the family is eliminated. This rule also counteracts the tendency of the supervisor to take over the interview, a process that would be subtly abetted by the family's orienting themselves towards the "expert", and the trainee's willingly slipping into the background. Hopefully, the supervisor's comments to the trainee will be phrased in such a tone that the latter's authority with the family is not undermined.

Group Preparation

Very few trainees need to be warned about being hostile toward the family or the therapist during the discussion. On the contrary, the major pitfall is a tendency of group members to make overly-protective, indirect comments, thus repeating what the therapist is probably already doing with the family. The supervisor is well advised to prepare the group on this score and then model it in his or her comments during the discussion. The less advanced the group, the earlier in the discussion the supervisor should speak up to set the tone.

Another common tendency in the group is to avoid disagreement or differences on the grounds that this would confuse the family. The supervisor, while agreeing that a hostile, competitive atmosphere in the group is not helpful to the family, will have to put some effort regularly into encouraging the open expression of differences where they exist.

The most difficult task for the group is finding brief, matter-of-fact ways of commenting to their fellow trainee about his handling of the interview in the presence of the family. The supervisor should be alert for covert "protection pacts" between family and therapist and between therapist and group. Again, supervisor modelling will be most influential in demonstrating this facet of the process.

The Post Session

After the family has left, the group discussion is separated into two parts: (a) expanded feedback to the therapist on his/her conduct of the interview, including the role of his personal family situation if relevant, and (b) family or other families with similar problems. It is usually necessary to encourage the group to offer critical feedback to their fellow trainee, and, again, it is the supervisor who can help distinguish constructive criticism from competitive put-downs. The connections to a trainee's personal family are never explored in the presence of the family on the grounds that (a) a therapist loses authority with the family if turned into a "patient", (b) the treatment session and the group discussion belongs to the family—it is their time, money and problems that count, and (c) therapist self-disclosure is helpful to a family only *after* the therapist has dealt with his own problem, not during or before when his own anxiety around the issue is bound to be high.

Summary

At the Family Institute of Westchester, faculty teaching long-term family treatment, chiefly Bowen's method, find that the above format for supervision permits both family and trainee to unhook from power struggles and from emotionally reactive traps by providing a calm, open, reflective, non-blaming forum in which to think about problems at hand and become interested in finding out new ways to deal with them. The method has the further advantage of not requiring any special equipment or technology.

References

Bowen, M. (1978). *Family Therapy in Clinical Practice*. Aronson, New York.

Carter, E. and Orfanidis, M. (1967). Family therapy with one person and the family therapist's own family. *Family Therapy* (P. J. Guerin, ed.), pp.193-219. Gardner Press, New York.

Minuchin, S. (1975). *Families and Family Therapy*. Harvard University Press, Cambridge, Mass.

Palazzoli, M., Boscolo, L., Cecchin, G. and Prata, G. (1978). *Paradox and Counter Paradox*. Aronson, New York.

7. The Use of the Family's Relationship to the Supervision Group as a Therapeutic Tool

Caroline Lindsey and Jane Lloyd

Introduction

In this chapter, the authors examine some important characteristics of the relationship which develops between the family and the supervision group during the course of therapy, including the family's responses to the different supervision methods used. Ways in which we have used our understanding of this relationship both to further the formulation of the family and as an important therapeutic tool will be discussed. The application of these ideas in the engagement and treatment of a "holocaust" family will be described.

Background

The main reasons for the development of techniques of live and videotape supervision are to assist the trainee to become more quickly and accurately effective; and, through the strength of the supervisory group, to combat the powerful homeostatic forces in the family and oppose the tendency of the therapist to become a part of the family system. These techniques have inevitably brought the process of supervision and therapy much closer together so that in some situations it becomes difficult to distinguish the therapy from the supervision.

Thus, the use of supervision techniques to meet training needs should not be seen in isolation from the therapy of the family—the techniques themselves constitute interventions and are a part of the therapeutic process. This view may surprise those unfamiliar with the use of live supervision or videotape techniques, who commonly express anxieties that such techniques interfere with the private and intimate nature of the therapist-family relationship and breach

81

FAMILY THERAPY SUPERVISION
ISBN 0-12-794815-5

principles of confidentiality. Further, they suggest, that these methods will engender paranoid feelings in the family and will undermine the therapist. These concerns are understandable, and are also commonly expressed by informed clients in anticipation of therapy. However, our experience is that the supervision group and the techniques it uses facilitate and enhance the therapeutic process rather than oppose it.

For most family therapists, the way in which the physical arrangements are made for a therapy session are just as important as they are for individually-orientated therapists, and they would support the traditional view that the therapeutic situation depends on three main components — the therapist, the patient and the physical setting in which the therapy takes place (Winnicott, 1958). When the mirror and the video-recording equipment is introduced in a sensitive and self-assured manner it is accepted by the family as one of the ways in which the therapist is going to pay attention to their needs. In our experience it does not militate against successful engagement but rather constitutes an important part of the therapeutic process, particularly in providing valuable diagnostic information. In this paper we will focus on the use of live supervision rather than video-recording, which has been discussed in detail elsewhere (see Whiffen, Chapter 3).

Live Supervision as a Therapeutic Intervention

The potential to use the supervision group for therapeutic purposes rather than for supervision alone will vary depending on the experience of the group. It is optimal when a group of therapists share a common theoretical background and know and trust each other; but even in less experienced groups the supervisor can draw the trainee's attention to the diagnostic information which the family's relationship to the group provides.

In our setting the choice of a live supervision technique usually depends on the particular needs of the trainee. In our experience this choice will usually also be acceptable to the family. However, as will be shown in our example there are advantages in being flexible about which particular technique to use, in order that the therapist's needs and the family's needs can be fitted together as creatively as possible. Examples of the techniques of live supervision used are:

(1) Observation through a one-way screen with a mid-session consultation with the supervision group to formulate a hypothesis and make an intervention by sending a message to the family.

(2) Brief instructions or comments sent to the therapist through a telephone or earphone.

Information about the family is gained in many ways but here we would stress the relationship of the supervision group to the family and vice versa. For instance, it is a familiar experience that each member of the supervision group behind the screen will sometimes respond to a family in the same way. For example, the group may become excited and giggly, angry and rejecting, depressed or paralysed, and this has been found to be indicative of a significant dynamic process in the family. Equally, however, we feel that the way the family relates to the group behind the screen is significant and provides information useful for diagnosis and therapy. We have noticed that families may use the supervision group in one or more of the following ways.

Containment

Examples of this role (commonly seen with deprived and depressed families) are:

(1) Where the group is perceived as providing additional support and care to the family and therapist. This may result in diminution of anxiety, with a subsequent reduction of chaotic behaviour in the children or a relaxation of tension in the parents sufficient to enable work to continue. We further enhance this role by mentioning the names of the members of the group behind the screen. In our main clinical example we suggest that the presence of the group greatly enhanced the family's ability to talk freely about the concentration camps. In another family the children brought Christmas cards, which they had made themselves, for their therapist, and also for the supervisor (C.L.) behind the screen. This seemed to be an open acknowledgement by the family of their positive experience of the therapeutic team.

(2) Where the group is used as a recipient of unacceptable, angry, rejecting and destructive feelings, often related to the family's view of the outside world.

If therapy has already been established, such a response to the group can be used to understand the current and historical processes in the family which have given rise to this response. This happened in one family where the parents were questioning how to use their authority with the children constructively. Their own childhood experiences had been of a negative and punitive kind, and in adulthood they had committed themselves to a democratic family life-style, which made it difficult for them to justify any form of limit setting. In a session in the middle phase of therapy the therapist was attempting a detailed piece of work to establish the parents' expectations of behaviour from their four children. During the session two of the children started throwing plasticine at the screen. This we understood to be an expression of the family's hostility to the group, which represented a world which did expect limits to be set and hierarchies to be valued.

If the group is used for the projection of such negative emotions at the outset of therapy, it may prevent the successful engagement of the family in therapy. An example of this was with a family consisting of a divorced father and his adolescent daughter who had recently taken a serious overdose. During the first interview, the girl made various comments that the supervision group should be in the room rather than behind the screen. The therapist explained that we found that this method worked best with families but they could meet the team at the end of the session. The girl was incensed by the message sent by the group after the mid-session break. She refused to attend the next session, to which her mother and father came alone. Her mother was furious at her daughter's treatment by us, saying, "I've just come to tell you how stupid you all are, I'm not surprised she won't come again . . . I was paranoid when I was her age". Sometimes it is possible to predict such a response and take appropriate steps. Our main clinical example illustrates this.

Reality testing

The life experience of the family may have led to significant distortion of perception both within the family group and in their relationship to the outside world. The family can then use the group to explore its fantasies. If the group is sensitive to this, it can respond with a technique such as relabelling or positive connotation, which may be much more powerful when coming from the group than when offered by the therapist on his own. In our main example we shall show how the group was used to counter the family's extreme fear of the unknown. In another example an adolescent girl who had committed a minor misdemeanour at school, said in a first session that she feared that there were police inquisitors behind the screen, who would accuse her of doing wrong. She was a member of a heavily enmeshed family from whom it was extremely difficult to achieve independence especially as they regarded the world as offering no additional advantages to their comfortable family life. In another example (personal communication from Mrs Gillian Parker) where videotape and camera were used, a girl who had consistently had her experiences denied by her mother in a schizophrenogenic manner, found it enormously relieving and helpful to speak her thoughts into the camera and have them replayed accurately later.

Most families involve themselves predominantly with the therapist and only show limited curiosity in what the group has to say. In these cases the relationship between the family and the supervision group will have less therapeutic significance.

Clinical Example

As mentioned earlier, some flexibility in the choice of supervision technique can greatly enhance the therapy. In this example the trainee was experienced and did not require detailed supervision of technique. This enabled the group to modify the way it worked as the needs of the family emerged. In this case live supervision contributed greatly to the successful outcome because we took account of the relationship of the family to the group and used it therapeutically, in addition to offering supervision to the therapist.

Mr and Mrs L referred themselves and their two children, Anna (nine) and Kate (seven) to the clinic by telephone. Following this contact, Mrs L made several more calls in which she expressed worries about keeping records and confidentiality. The therapist picked up considerable anxiety about the referral and yet also a strong motivation to come. The group discussed ways in which both supervision and support for the therapist could be ensured in what seemed likely to be a difficult initial session. It was decided that anxiety could be reduced by not using the one-way screen and video-recording initially, but that the supervisor (C.L.) should be present in the room with the therapist (J.L.) so that live supervision would be provided. Consultations outside the room during a break or when requested by the therapist were also arranged (this decision was taken out of consideration of trainee needs).

Engagement phase

The first ten minutes of the session were spent explaining the methods being used with an emphasis on the issues of confidentiality. The members of the team were referred to by name to diminish the sense of unknown, potentially hostile observers. The outcome of this introduction was that the family then agreed to the presence of observers behind the screen and to the use of the video-recording. Nevertheless, both the therapist and supervisor continued to experience an atmosphere of great fear, far in excess of the usual anxieties of a family at a first session. Characteristically this was not nearly so apparent to those behind the screen. It also did not obviously link with the reason given for seeking help — their worry that they were neglecting their children. The key observations of the supervisor, sitting silently in the room, were first, the fear, and second, the behaviour of the children, who spent the session climbing over their mother, drawing attention to themselves in various ways, looking disgruntled and truculent. Mr L sat a little apart from his wife and children.

During the consultation behind the screen (J.L. and C.L. with the group) it was recognized that, in terms of what had been observed, the parents' complaint that they neglected their children contrasted with the overly close physical contact of the children with their mother. The observation of both the process and content of the session led to a view of the children as being in a strong, even controlling position in relation to their parents. In attempting both to validate the parents' obviously profound sense of their need for help without confirming their negative view of their parenting abilities, we hypothesized that the "neglect" they were describing was related to a problem of intimacy and separateness in the family, which led, at times, to the father's exclusion. This was put to the family after the break.

> *Th:* You talk, Mr and Mrs L, about neglecting your children, by not giving them enough of your attention . . . . (Father grunts acknowledgement).
>
> *Th:* And time. And we had a feeling it might be difficult for you to be a group of four . . . . In the room, Mrs L, you and Anna and Kate seemed very close together . . . in fact, you really were on top of your mother, Anna and Kate. I could hardly see you at times, in the first part of the session.
>
> *Th:* (turning to Mr L) And you seemed a little out on a limb.
>
> *Th:* (turning to whole family) I don't know whether that is how you are at home — but maybe you were taking this opportunity to get very close together.
>
> *Th:* (pauses and then goes on) Perhaps one of the difficulties is how you are either terribly close together or very separate. And that doesn't seem quite right to you as a family.
>
> *Mrs L:* . . . there's not a tremendous amount we do as a four, it is three and one.

In the second session it was felt that the family was sufficiently engaged for the supervision to take its usual form with C.L. behind the screen with the group. The family's behaviour was observed to be very different with the parents much more in charge of the children. After consultation, a message to this effect was given to the family and the validity of the observed change was confirmed by Mr L who said that it was as a result of the group's intervention following the break in the first session: "When you felt we were on top of each other".

Later in this session there was a discussion about a family choice of activity. The family presented as a problem Anna's insistence on going out with her grandmother instead of going to the cinema with her parents and sister; an outing agreed by the family. A telephone message from the group confirmed both the need for parents to make decisions but also the need for some separateness for the children. "They are very impressed how you have worked together to come to agreements but also that you, Anna, could stick to your decision and do something separate now that you are ten."

This initial exploration of the problems of intimacy and separation which had been experienced as helpful then led into the revelation of the source of the family's fear and their difficulties with relationships. Mr L revealed that the first five years of his life had been spent in Auschwitz, where he had survived together with his mother. More than fifty percent of the L family were in concentration camps and most of them did not survive. Until the family came to the Clinic, Mr L had only shared his concentration camp experience with his wife. His father died before the end of the war, but Mrs L senior is still alive and in close contact with the family. She came to a session later on in the therapy and filled in details about concentration camp life for Anna and Kate. It seems likely that mother and son survived partly as a result of Mrs L's need to fight for food for her child. In the same camp were Mrs L's sister and her two children, only one of whom survived. Since the war the two sisters had lived close to each other. Mr L is afraid of what will happen to his mother when his sister follows her nephew to America and she no longer has daily contact with someone who shared her suffering. This raises an important therapeutic point for the supervision group. At the point of revelation of Mr L's holocaust experience, both J.L. with the family and C.L. and the group behind the mirror, experienced a paralysing sense of horror, such that J.L. reported that the next ten minutes of the session passed as if in a dream. We used this emotional response to say to the family (in a message) that we realized that we would never be able to understand fully the nature of the experience that Mr L had lived through. The importance of the capacity of therapists to be able to make this acknowledgement is reiterated throughout the literature on working with holocaust survivors (Herman, 1980).

Mr L admitted to few memories of camp life beyond playing in the mud in the yards. His facial expression was usually masklike; he experienced all laughter as attack. He had to be persuaded of the importance of exploring the past for the sake of Anna and Kate. But his willingness to do so was a mark of great strength in him since the problem of communicating with the children about the holocaust experience has usually been found to be enormously difficult for parents (Davidson, 1980). Family therapy techniques of drawing up family trees with children were useful here (Dare and Lindsey, 1979; Byng-Hall and Whiffen, 1980).

The camp experience led to an extremely close relationship between Mr L and his mother which she attempted to dilute by remarriage when he was 18. Mr L recalled his intense fear of English schools and his difficulty in integrating into an essentially beneficent institution. He feared the teaching staff and became the target of bullies because of his foreign accent and inhibited behaviour. Thus to the holocaust experience and its sequelae were added the problems of immigration. He now works at home with his wife selling life insurance. He has made a few close friends but depends to a great extent on his wife and family to whom he clings for the fulfilment of his needs.

Mrs L had spent the first five years of her childhood alone with her mother and grandparents while her father was in the army. She felt that the peace of her early years was disrupted by her father's return, the arrival of three siblings and serious marital conflict between her parents. She felt an outsider in her family and left home as soon as possible to become a nurse.

Mrs L brought to the marriage needs complementary to those of her husband, that is to be emotionally essential to another person.

Both children had been named after family members who had died in the camps. But they were unaware of the significance of the names they bore. Characteristically for children of survivor parents, they showed fears and anxieties which could not be related to current family events.

The therapeutic goals

In addition to the impossibility of fully understanding the holocaust experience, it is important for the therapist to recognize the inevitability of the "mourning without end" of the victims which the holocaust requires of its survivors. Within this context, the essential goals to be achieved with the children were *communication* and *clarification* of mystifying information about the family history and experience (Krell, 1979). There were three further important issues related to the holocaust experience and complemented by Mrs L's family history which required work and which had been reflected in the process of the first session. (1) The family's relationship with the outside world. (2) Family relationships. (3) The marital relationship.

Relationship with the outside world

The whole family was suspicious and frightened of the outside world. Mr L had obvious reasons for this; he and his mother had been at the mercy of the camp guards. This experience had been reinforced by the bullying during his English school days. Mrs L saw herself as standing on her own without family support to face the outside world. Their story was sufficient to account for the family's fear as well as their eager search for help.

The first few sessions were carried out in the presence of the group behind the screen. In each of these the group was used to help the family work through some of the fear of the outside world by the fostering of a relationship with an interested, concerned, helpful and available outside group of people. This was done by: (1) the nature of the positive messages sent by the group, with which the therapist allied herself; (2) the way in which the therapist referred to the group and talked about them—even in subsequent sessions when the group was no longer present and supervision was by videotape; (3) the therapist's fostering of the relationship with group members by encouraging the children to telephone and to meet them at the end of a session; (4) the choice of the telephone rather than earphone, so that messages were openly received.

Session 1: examples of messages from the group

(1) *Th:* My colleagues, like myself, are really very impressed by how you have learnt to govern in your family. You have made a major step forward in learning to take charge.
Mr L: That was obviously what was missing.
(2) *Th:* (to the children) Do you know your drawings are very much to do with what we have been talking about? You are both drawing pictures which show us how frightening it is when you don't know things.
Anna: (firmly) Yes.

Session 2

Anna asked many questions about the group and camera. Explanations were given and she was encouraged to greet the group and to meet them later.

Th: I think you will have to meet them afterwards so you know these mysterious figures in the background.
(On this occasion the family did not feel ready to meet the group after the session.)

Session 3

Kate made faces at the screen in the early part of the session.

Th: Kate still seems to be worried about the people on the other side . . . do you want to meet them?
Kate: We were discussing that in the car. . . .
Th. It might be quite sensible to find out if they are friendly.
Anna: Are they?
Th: I think you ought to meet them.
Kate: Could we meet them?

They agreed they would like to meet the group at the end of the session, which they did. Later in this session the therapist used the group to give her support for working on the horrors of Auschwitz and to indicate to the family that she had a group to support her and them.

Session 6

Maternal grandmother was present. Therapist used the material from the supervision group to further the task of recognition of the holocaust in the family by openly acknowledging the number of deaths of family members in the camps.

Th: I showed the genogram to my colleagues and what they said, and I think that was right, was that we ought to make a special mark for the people who died in the concentration camps because they were a special group of people and they would then stand out on the family tree.

From the therapist's point of view, the supervisory group was essential to contain her feelings of horror and grief. This enabled her to work on the problems with the family without being blocked by their fear and sense of persecution which arose from discussion of the experience.

Family relationships

Mr and Mrs L were unable to take charge of their children. For Mr L parental control had links with the inhumanity of the camp guards (Davidson, 1980). He also had no father on whom to model himself. Mrs L experienced any expression of aggression as destructive and related this to her parents' violent and unresolved rows. It seemed that they had needed external permission from the group to allow them to change. Mr L said: "That was obviously what was missing".

Marital relationship

Following session six, therapy continued without the group, or reference to the group, once marital issues arose. They worked on the issues of intimacy and dependency. In order to emphasize the properly private nature of marital issues, the therapist chose to use video and discussion for supervision rather than the observing group.

Discussion

(1) We have tried to show that an experienced supervisory group has the advantage of having a dual purpose (a) of supervision, (b) of the use of itself as a therapeutic and diagnostic tool.

(2) Experienced trainees can participate in making a choice of supervision technique appropriate to the needs of the family at a particular time, having previously experienced the range of techniques available and their usefulness.

(3) To use the group in this way necessitates a group in which the members share a theoretical framework (to some extent), and also know and trust each other.

(4) The diagnostic aspect of the relationship of the family to the group can also be used by a supervisor in a less experienced group.

References

Byng-Hall, J. and Whiffen, R. (1982). Family and marital therapy. *Handbook of Affective Disorders* (E. S. Paykel, ed.). Churchill Livingston, Edinburgh.
Dare, C. and Lindsey, C. (1979). Children in family therapy. *J. Family Ther.* **1**, 253-269.
Davidson, S. (1980). The survivor syndrome today: an overview. *Group Analysis* **13**.
Herman, S. (1980). The meaning of death: experiences with survivors in Holland. *Group Analysis* **13**.
Krell, R. (1979). Holocaust families: the survivors and their children. *Comprehen. Psychiat.* **20**, 560-568.
Winnicott, D. W. (1958). Metapsychological and Clinical Aspects of Regression Within the Psychoanalytic Set Up. Collected Papers (1958). Tavistock Publications, Belsize Park.

Part III
The Learning Process

8. How to Translate Different Dynamic Perspectives into an Illustrative and Experiential Learning Process: Role Play, Genogram and Live Supervision

Helm Stierlin, Michael Wirsching and Gunthard Weber

It is essential to examine the supervision of family therapy in the context in which it takes place. Before all questions of content and other aspects we must ask: which therapist, from which professional area, within which conceptual framework is treating which family?

The Contextual Framework

In the Federal Republic of Germany the systemic perspective is not widely used. Understandably, proponents of established psychotherapeutic orientations and primarily somatic-orientated psychiatrists remain sceptically noncommittal or openly reject this new approach. The degree of rejection often seems to correlate with the position in the professional hierarchy. This reserve on the part of the establishment contrasts with the interest, rapidly increasing in the last few years, in systems-orientated work among the actively engaged members of the psychosocial services. Unfortunately, however, the number of those able and available to give training and supervision in family therapy is small. With these conditions in mind we have looked at possibilities for training and supervision and at the same time paid careful attention to the situation of the trainer and the context in which the students work.

The programme which thus emerged consists of four main elements: basic groups, live observation groups, a first interview seminar and seminars and workshops for limited periods.

FAMILY THERAPY SUPERVISION
ISBN 0-12-794815-5

Copyright © 1982 by Academic Press.
All rights of reproduction in any form reserved.

The basic group

The basic group consists of registered participants grouped according to interests, place of work, the part of the country they come from, etc.: they meet every fourteen days and work on their own initiative on theoretical and practical issues of family therapy. Every third or fourth session is supervised. These basic groups have the following advantages: a relatively high number of participants (up to 80) could thus be taken into the programme; such a mutually supportive basic group by its solidarity underpins the work of the individual members and the joint endeavour acts as a counterbalance to institutional resistance. In our experience, it is extremely hard for a single person alone to introduce and sustain systems-orientated work in an institution on a lasting basis. The position of isolated trained workers in many institutions is comparable to that of the client in individual-centred therapy: in both instances an individual has the (almost impossible) job of changing a system. For this reason we have recently been supervising increasing numbers of whole teams from counselling centres. The self-regulatory nature of the basic groups promotes the involvement, creativity and self-reliance of its members and discourages a passive noncommittal stance. The basic group also makes it possible for the family therapeutic supervision to be keyed to the needs of the group and the context within which its members work. In this way one group might work on basic theoretical concepts, another begin with their own families of origin, for a third it might be more important to discuss the conflicts its members face when they have to provide individual-centred diagnoses in their psychiatric clinic or to conduct "supportive" individual therapy, while others might be concerned with the specific problems of families of cancer patients, addicts or psychotics, etc. Each group decides independently on the main theme of its work.

Live observation groups

These groups are open to advanced participants who are continually involved in the conduct of family therapy and who are able to bring families for supervision to our observation room equipped with a one-way mirror. It has proved valuable to have regular sessions of the live observation group in which we do not observe a family. Rather, we discuss in detail the theoretical implications of the previously observed therapeutic sessions and possible therapeutic strategies and steps.

First interview seminar

Trainee participants are allowed to take part in the continous weekly first interview seminar for a period of six to nine months and to conduct first interviews under supervision.

Seminars and workshops of limited duration

Every year we hold ten to 20 seminars and workshops of limited duration. These usually centre on a particular subject. About half the leaders come from our own group and half from outside.

At the present time we see the extension and integration of the system perspective into psychosocial and medical fields as our most important and urgent task. For this reason we accept for our programmes only participants with complete qualifications and work experience. To increase the spread of our work we have instituted a training group for supervisors.

The Conceptual Framework

Our group has developed a series of family dynamic perspectives that encompass various dimensions of systemic interaction and provide the rationale for therapeutic interventions. These also shape our training concept.

At present we are working with five central concepts, primarily developed by Stierlin. Like the lens of a telescope each brings an aspect of the complete situation into sharp focus, while the other aspects remain invisible or blur on the edge of the field of vision. Each concept is open, integrative, and constantly developing.

Each concept must:

(1) Indicate the direction of therapeutic treatment according to the context and systemic constellation, describe the individual contributions, subsystems, and the family as a whole, and be applicable to other social systems.

(2) Allow the analysis of circular, cybernetic processes instead of linear cause and effect chains of reactions.

(3) Above all encompass patterns of relationships acting over long periods of time.

(4) Assimilate observable behavioural aspects of which the participants are aware as well as complementary processes of which the participants are unaware and which are revealed only through the observer's interpretation.

Three of the five concepts focus on the currently active processes, the "here-and-now" of the horizontal systemic level; two concentrate more on the vertical, historical aspects.

We report below on the way this theoretical model is expressed in our training programme. At present our foremost training goals are:

(1) To give the student a dynamic framework or model through which she or he can observe and assess the *various dimensions* of systemic interaction. This involves making the concept "fluid" and helping the student to grasp it through his own experience.

(2) According to system constellation and phase of the therapeutic process, to provide the student with guidelines for therapeutic intervention.

Brief description of the five perspectives and examples of the exercises used to illustrate them during the training programme[1]

Related individuation

Our first observation concerns differentiation: how do the parts of the system delimit themselves (e.g. the subsystems parents — children)? How far is a member of the system able to distinguish between "self" and "non-self"; to recognize those are *my* thoughts, feelings, perceptions, and those his or hers? Individuation is incomplete if the parts are unable to re-establish a relationship with one another. We go on to observe the quality of relational integration: is a coherent whole, a closed form recognizable? We differentiate the disorders of the individuation process, fusion and isolation. Fusion implies extreme under-differentiation: all is one, we are one unit, all have the same thoughts, feelings and perceptions; what you think, I think, we see the world through the same eyes. In contrast, isolation means the failure to relate to one another. Empathy with the mental processes of others is lacking, boundaries are rigid and impervious, exchanges between the individual members and subsystems are minimal. This often also is true of the relationship of the family to the outer world. Nothing enters and nothing leaves. An impression of the quality of related individuation is conveyed by the quality of the dialogue: how far are the individual members able to express different positions, while reacting to what the others say, to the fact that they disagree, adjust, or delimit their own ideas?

This perspective is made comprehensible by means of role play: with the same spontaneously grouped "family" the two extremes of fusion and isolation are enacted. The family has in each instance the same task of planning the next holiday; the rules the group leader gives are, however, different. In the first enactment (fusion) the rule is, "All have the same ideas, perceptions, needs; we are a family, a unit, there is no conflict or difference of opinion, no one may say 'I', only 'we'. Every projection and attribution must be agreed on and accepted as one's own thoughts". The therapist has the task of discovering what the members of the family really think, want, perceive.

The same "family" then performs the same task, but with the contrasting rule: "The parents do not speak to one another, they gave that up 15 years ago. They never refer to what the other says, there is no conflict, the other just simply doesn't exist. The children have no guidance, they just have to cope as best they can". The therapist has the task of trying to make the parents talk to one another.

Both tasks are impossible for the therapist. He experiences in this failure the specific resistance of a fused or isolated system and the feeling of menace and danger that he evokes by trying to change the system: a mounting confusion in the fused family (the expression of fear of separation) and massive destructive conflict in the isolated family (the expression of fear and of closeness and intimacy).

Interactional modes of binding and expelling

Here we are concerned with the direction and intensity of the central relational tendencies in the system. We distinguish between centripetal (binding) and centrifugal (expelling) interactions on the various psychological levels. On the ego-level thoughts, feelings and perceptions are attributed to others in a mystification process. One person intrudes into the feelings and thoughts of the other. In situations of expelling or neglect there is only disinterest for the interactional partner. On the id-level binding takes the form of manipulative satisfaction of various needs such as regressive gratification or sexual over-stimulation, expelling or neglect amount to the reverse. Finally, on the superego-level loyalty bindings and moralistic demands become overriding. In contrast, anomie represents the complete neglect of all moral rules and laws.

It is precisely in the interactional modes that the dialectical nature of the chosen concepts is revealed: every binding at the same time implies neglect. Every instance of neglect or expulsion carries with it a strong binding effect in that the expelled individual becomes involved in a life-long effort to engage the attention, interest and emotional investment of the neglecting parent (or substitute).

To demonstrate these modes, we again use role play with the spontaneously formed "family" and present as a problem: "The family is referred to the therapist by a third party because one of the children is failing in school". The first attempt unfolds in a binding family. In this family the rule is "We are a closed family, we let nothing in and nothing out; we never give any clues away. We're a completely normal family, we've no problems. On no account can anyone leave the family group". The therapist has the impossible task of making therapeutic contact with the family.

The second time we let the group play an expelling family. Here the rule is: "No member of the family is interested in any of the others. No-one is prepared to do anything for anyone else. There is a total lack of loyalty and moral precepts". The therapist has the task of bringing the family to a therapeutic discussion. As before, he or she fails, but gains a valuable learning experience.

Delegation and delegational conflict

Here we describe missions which are often handed down over generations.

They are expressed in the meaning of the Latin verb "delegare": "to send out and to entrust with a mission". We distinguish two aspects: *What* is demanded of the delegate, and the *relational aspect*—the strength of the loyalty bond between the delegating person and the delegate, on how long a leash is the delegate held? Missions are relevant on various psychological levels: ego missions involve exploration, the gathering of experience or the performance of specific intellectual tasks: id missions involve the proxy fulfilment of parental libidinal or aggressive needs; and finally, to carry out missions on the superego level the delegate takes over superego functions for the delegating person such as tasks of self-observation, functions of conscience, or realization of certain ego ideals.

Depending on the kind of mission characteristic overdemands and/or conflicts can arise:

(1) Overdemands—the missions overtax the capabilities of the delegate;

(2) Contradictory missions—for example, the delegate must achieve dazzling success on the ego level while remaining a spoiled bound child on the id level;

(3) Loyalty conflict resulting from different delegating persons—the delegate must, for example, be ally to both parties in a parental conflict. The demonstration of this perspective during training had the best chance of success when it is integrated with experiences undergone within the trainee's family of origin: the group members discuss in small units the meaning of their first names: for example, who chose the name, who has the same name in the family, what does the name mean, with what expectations is it associated, who has ever changed their name? etc. Furthermore, the analysis of cases and the use of videotapes in which missions and mission conflicts are worked over are aids in demonstrating the delegational dynamic.

Multigenerational perspectives of debts and merits

This dimension introduced by Boszormenyi-Nagy is closely related to the delegational concept. It concerns the disclosure and negotiation of accounts of debts and merits in the family: who has justified claims to make? Who is indebted to whom? Where are there unsettled accounts? Who has done something positive or negative to whom? Have particular achievements on the family's behalf been acknowledged and recompensed? Injustice, derelictions of fairness and family loyalty are often inherited over generations, and underlie recurring patterns of conflict. In the context of this perspective we frequently stress the significance of unconsummated mourning and derailed grief.

To demonstrate this perspective we again go back to the experiences of the student within his or her own family. Small groups discuss the following two main questions: what topics have I so far avoided within my own family and what feelings do I experience when I think about discussing them? The reconstruction of the family of origin in a genogram and in a family sculpture is helpful here. In addition, videotapes of multigenerational sessions can be shown in which a dialogue of reconciliation over several generations is introduced.

The state of mutuality

Though all the perspectives so far presented describe characteristics of systems, they neglect, however, one central systems parameter. The last in our series of perspectives, the state of mutuality, attempts to fill this gap. It comprises both "positive and negative mutuality" as complementary or symmetrical relational patterns and also reveals the character and intensity of the "malign clinch" in which the family has become entrapped. This enables us to gauge the homeostatic tendency of the system: how fixed and narrowed are the behavioural patterns and rules within the family? To demonstrate these patterns we give the members of the "family" the rule that in their roles they must entirely disqualify, disparage, discount or ignore whatever the others say but at the same time make sure the others stay in the field. The theme of their discussion is lack of money in the family. After a short time a symmetrically escalating power struggle develops. From the recurring behavioural sequences it then becomes clear that this system's dynamics do not derive from the individuals, but rather from its rules. If the members of the "family" are then asked to behave differently it becomes clear how they all, even in this short time, have been drawn into a rigid behavioural and relational pattern from which they can only release themselves with a considerable effort.

Relating Teaching Style to Therapeutic Style

This style of teaching—in which each main point is illustrated by various techniques—is at the same time a model of the therapeutic process, since according to a given perspective, the therapist can apply a variety of strategies and techniques. In the different phases of the therapeutic process we focus on its specific aspects and our procedure varies accordingly. In the "Live Supervision" we try to synthesize the described approaches. At the same time the question remains crucial which strategies lead to which practical consequences in which situation and at which developmental stage of the therapy. To be able to answer we must keep two basic family therapeutic models in mind.

Encounter work versus systemic work[2]

We refer to the two basic models "healing through encounter" and "healing through systemic change", which we designate briefly as family therapeutic encounter work versus systemic work. The models show similarities as well as differences as to the goals of the therapeutic procedure and this entails different methods in the supervision.

Encounter work

The goal of the encounter model is as rapidly as possible to initiate a liberating, individualizing dialogue in the family. The therapist helps the family members to talk about previously taboo, massively fear- and shame-loaded themes—family secrets, disappointed expectations, injustices, deep hurts, unacknowledged grief. He often communicates less through his words, than his attitude: we can talk about everything, we can survive all fears. Many important aspects of this work resemble psychoanalytic procedure. The scene and impetus of these changes are the relatively frequent therapeutic sessions. Encounter work is most indicated when it meets with sufficiently individuated systems with potential for change and communication in which a reflective and constructive dialogue is still possible.

Case studies, genograms, and family sculptures are suitable teaching tools for encounter work. Technical questions are discussed around videotapes and tape recordings. Live supervision can take the form of a consultation. New insights into the dynamics of a given case are not simply a matter of explanation, but are allowed to emerge gradually in the course of therapy. The teacher therefore intervenes very little in the session.

Systemic work

Here we mean system work as practised by our Heidelberg group along the lines of the Milan team (Boscolo, Cecchin, Prata and Palazzoli, 1978).

The goal is the most rapid possible survey of the important relational and systemic forces in the family and their restructuring by maximal use of the resources of a team of experienced therapists and observers. The teamwork and interventions designed to produce systemic changes often take the form of a paradoxical prescription. Systemic work in this sense appears most appropriate where there is a massive malign clinch, a chronic rigidified homeostatic situation as, for example, in families with psychotic or chronic psycho-somatically sick members, ongoing attempted suicide problems, etc.

The goals of the current session—the rapid study of the relational dynamics, the work on, and initiation of, systems changing interventions—require that the therapists refrain from all intrepretation right up to the final prescribing phase. Wherever they sense resistance, they must retreat and reset their course. They try to obtain information about the way in which the members define their relationships to one another and how, for example, they form their coalitions, be those overt or covert.

In contrast to "healing through encounter" the model "healing through systemic change" requires longer intervals between sessions (four to six weeks).

Live observation is in most cases the best means of instruction for systemic therapy. At best all sessions with the family take place in front of a one-way mirror. There must be a competent group of therapists who *together* bear responsibility for the treatment. This is necessary to ensure an interchange free of anxiety and competitiveness between the groups on both sides of the mirror as well as the success of most difficult interventions which may provoke acute systemic reactions and even frighten all participants—for example, the prescription to continue or escalate arguments and fights within a family or that the anorexic member of a family should continue fasting. The supervisor is at first a member of the observational group and changes later to a "meta-position", namely she or he now relates herself or himself to the work of the family, the therapists, or the observer supersystem. Through such live observation the students learn to do systemic work autonomously and to apply the basic concepts of this procedure to other therapeutic situations where they must cope without the support of a group.

An Illustrative Case

The A's are a young married couple, who came to us by a somewhat unusual route: indeed at the time they did so they had as yet no real problems, but feared that their marriage could run into difficulties in the future. They came as it were prophylactically.

In the background lay the cancer of the 31-year-old husband, who two years before had had to undergo a major operation, one of the results of which was that he became impotent. He is still uncertain whether he will survive the illness. His 28-year-old wife had herself while still young undertaken terminal care of a cancer-stricken parent. She had first met her husband only weeks before his illness and married him soon after the operation.

The first sessions were mainly characterized by the clients concerted defence and attempts by the therapists to undermine that defence. In the course of eight months this resistance nevertheless increased and the therapy came practically to a standstill. In this phase, after protracted discussions, we decided on a change in therapeutic strategy. The approach used so far "Healing through Encounter" had already ended in a blind alley. All attempts to get the couple to talk about their feelings in this extremely difficult situation only exacerbated their fears and strengthened their resistance, as did all efforts to introduce fear- or conflict-loaded themes. The already restricted relational and communicational pattern shrank further, and the sessions became more difficult, painful and boring. Hence, after eight months' therapy, at the end of the fifth session we made the following intervention:

Because of our limited experience with cancer patients we have made a serious error: we have treated you as a couple who came to us as a result of marital conflict or sexual problems. In this way we failed to understand with what great strength you master a situation which is more difficult than most we have seen until now. Today it has become clear to us that you require all your strength for this hard test and cannot afford to indulge in such trivial problems as marital and sexual conflict. Instead your strength is shown precisely in the way in which you have up till now resisted all our efforts though otherwise we are experts in changing families. It is easy for us to end the therapy today. We know that you will go on living as you have until now, whatever happens. We would ask you, however, to come to us again in 6 weeks so that we can make a general assessment of the situation.

This intervention had the following aims:

(1) In admitting their mistake the therapists withdrew from the symmetrical escalation and could no longer be confronted as "advocates of change". In this way they paradoxically achieved a new power.

(2) The couple's "symptoms"—suppression of feelings and avoidance of conflict—were accorded a new meaning as a particular strength and ability adapted to survival in a difficult situation.

(3) Change was thereby admitted to be impossible and nonsensical, and the homeostatic tendency of the system was confirmed. Accordingly, the therapy was declared at an end and an appointment made only for a check-up.

At the next appointment (six weeks later) Mrs A made a much more insecure impression. She spoke of multiple fears. The following is an excerpt (about 15 to 30 min) from this session. Mr and Mrs A sit opposite two therapists (Th. 1 and Th. 2):

Mrs A: Well I'm someone who can't just forget about important things, like politics and so on and that's why it's so important for me that Hans is there and I can talk to him. When I've got it out and he's said what he thinks too, then we're bearing it together. But I get so mixed. On one hand I've got myself and I make myself frightened. On the other I just can't forget about what I see on the telly or hear on the news. Hans says, you know you get all upset about things like that so leave it alone. But they still don't give me any peace.

Th. 2: Just what is it that frightens you?

Mrs A: It's hard to say.

Mr A: (interrupts) As I see . . .

Th. 1: (stops Mr A) Just a moment.

Mr A: I just thought, because I'm here too.

Th. 1: Ah, yes, but she is just swallowing her feelings again.

Mrs A: Swallowing.

Th. 1: Just, it's gone now.

Mrs A: (Laughs)

Th. 1: (to Th. 2) Hm, that's why she's laughing.

Th. 2: Hm.

Mrs A: It frightens me. Like a liquid or something. Sometimes I think it's going right through me. I feel it all over, I can't say what, like death or destruction of the world, it's not that easy, it's something like . . . it's loneliness, too.

Th. 1: Hm. Where do you feel it physically?
Mrs A: In my stomach.
Th. 1: What does it do there?
Mrs A: Well, it's like as if I, then . . . it's a feeling, as if the nerves stretch and I've less appetite and so on.
Th. 1: Tension?
Mrs A: Yes.
Th. 1: What else, it goes tight or. . . .?
Mrs A: It hurts somehow. If I press on it so, it goes away. (Appropriate gesture.) It's the same in other situations, if I'm afraid of something, it comes again.
Th. 1: Hm. Mrs A could you imagine that you yourself are this feeling in the stomach. Imagine you are this feeling and say "Cramp yourself together". Be the feeling yourself and tell us everything the feeling does to Mrs A.

From this short passage it is already clear that the therapists have abandoned the prescription based on the paradoxical strategy introduced at the end of the previous session. That final intervention had clearly made Mrs A insecure. The therapists are making a mistake in entering into the patients' fears even more in that by their questions they encourage their expression. The effect of the prescription is diluted, the resistance increases again and the therapists again are in the position of advocates of change (i.e. of the ability to admit burdensome feelings) in an escalating struggle, in which the couple defends the homeostasis ("No change"). Expression and result of this power struggle is also that Therapist 1 now reaches for stronger weapons and tries to introduce techniques of Gestalt therapy.

Th. 1: Go on.
Mrs A: Now, I've got to talk like a feeling?
Th. 1: Yes, everything that the feeling does: I . . . .
Mrs A: Oh that's difficult. It'd be easier for me to say why I've got the feeling. What that feeling does? It hurts me.
Th. 1: I hurt you. What else?
Mrs A: I take you away from other things which you might be doing in this time. I make you sad and more depressed. (*Th. 1:* Hm.) And more hopeless, I make you afraid of what's going to happen. (*Th. 1:* Hm.) I'm always on your mind (short pause). I make you unsettled and less patient and sometimes so bewildered, unconcentrated.
Th. 1: Hm. And what does this feeling do to you physically?
Th. 2: I make you, your body . . .
Mrs A: I make it cramped. I cramp the body.
Th. 1: I cramp your body.
Mrs A: I cramp your body. I cause it pain.
Th. 1: How does the feeling do this?
Mrs A: I concentrate everything on me, me the feeling.
Th. 1: O.k. Now be Mrs A and answer the feeling. The feeling has just been speaking to you and you answer the feeling.
Mrs A: It's so hard for me to resist the feeling.
Th. 1: It's so hard for me to resist you.

Mrs A: Resist you, yes. It's so hard for me to resist you. I try to distract myself and think about something else, something positive and do something sensible.

Th. 1: But you are stronger.

Mrs A: Yes.

Th. 1: Do you, Mrs A, have a chance against this feeling?

Mrs A: The feeling is less when Hans is there. Well, then I can get away from the feeling more. With other people it's not so. This special form of feeling is . . . it's to do with loneliness, with negative loneliness.

Th. 1: Has the feeling recently got stronger, has it got stronger in comparison with Mrs A?

Mrs A: I think so, yes.

Th. 1: Tell the feeling that, "You are always getting stronger".

Mrs A: (Laughs)

Th. 1: Now what is that laugh for?

Mrs A: Laughed. To talk to the feeling like that, I find it difficult. It's difficult for me.

Th. 1: Perhaps it is also hard to say, "You are always getting stronger".

Mrs A: It's such a foreign body then, though what is a foreign body? You are for me an opponent, but then I say that to myself. That's what's hard: I'd rather talk about the feeling that gets stronger all the time, because it's part of me (short pause).

Th. 1: Have you, Mrs A, a chance against this feeling?

(Short pause)

Mrs A: I don't know.

Th. 1: Hm, have you a greater chance, with your husband together against that feeling? (Mrs A: Hm) Do you want to say that to him?

(Longer pause)

Th. 1: He's sitting there.

Mrs A: I think, that he knows (laughs).

Th. 1: I would like you to say that to him.

Mrs A: (Laughs)

Mr A: Says it at home so often.

Mrs A: (Laughs)

Th. 1: What might happen, if you say it to him now?

Mrs A: I don't know, why I should say it to him now. Something's shut up in me now, because . . . just because you say, that I should say it, that I should then really say it, because I mean, that's nothing new, that's so important for you to know (in Mr A's direction), that's something that I've said in so many ways already. Or is it different with you (to Mr A)?

Mr A: Now, I've also got the feeling. . . .

Mrs A: Yes, well that wasn't quite true, just because I'm supposed to say it.

Th. 1: Yes, I can see that too, that . . .

Th. 2: I've also got the feeling, the feeling that we're getting a bit bogged down at the moment.

Th. 1: Yes, perhaps I've pushed you too far in the direction of feelings and it's better. . . .

The resistance has reached its peak. The couple are now openly allied primarily against the active Therapist 1. The therapists realize their mistake and react with uncertainty.

A member of the supervising team now offers Therapist 1 a short consultation outside the room.

At this point it is clear to all participants that the chosen method to reach Mrs A's fears through an intervention based on Gestalt therapy or to bring the couple to talk to one another by direct approach, has led to a blind alley. The supervisory group recommends a continuation of the paradoxical strategy aimed at systemic change linked to the prescription of the previous session.

> *Th. 1:* (After returning from consultation with the supervisory group). Yes, the observation group have reminded me of our general session in January and told me I'm on the wrong track again. I've been called back. They said we already knew then that it's too much to excite so many emotions and I should pay more attention to your strong points. You, each of you, manage to cope very well on your own and it's better not to excite too many feelings. . . . Perhaps you've been doing the right thing in not having too much contact with one another, so that these feelings couldn't get too strong.
>
> *Mr A:* Oh, well then. Some of it is because of something we really can't do anything about, that we're really not together that much. And it could also be the consequence of our experience when Liesel still lived in O., where I've often thought, if it's only for half an hour. But then we found that we don't get anything out of it, because we can't make contact with each other quickly enough. I'm there and then I suddenly notice that nothing's happening. Basically I don't really want to.
>
> *Th. 2:* When it comes down to it, you do what's the right thing for you, don't you?
>
> *Mr A:* And that's because I'm in the situation, if there's lots going on and if I know I'm going to be in the office until 5 o'clock and Liesel has to leave at 6.30, and then sometimes it varies a bit, I know. If I go home now, we've only got one and a half hours, but then it's even less, and I say to myself, it's better not at all.
>
> *Th. 1:* Than it being all stiff and cramped. In fact one could say that you two have become more independent recently.
>
> *Mrs A:* Oh yes, I do think I've become more independent. There are points when being together is important for me, for example, meal times and bed times together. Those are important points. But otherwise, in comparison with at the beginning, I have my priorities, the job comes first. The experiences I have there and the contacts I make and the acknowledgement I get, are to me very important for our relationship, because I can see, if I didn't have that, I could get really fixated on Hans.

Both partners react with obvious astonishment to the change in strategy and begin to become more open again. Mr A too, the cancer-sick index patient, takes more part. The more the therapists maintain a reserved and positively reassuring approach, the more the interview turns to relevant themes such as emotions in the couple's relationship.

> *Mr A:* Truth to say, I was afraid of that.
>
> *Mrs A:* . . . that he would disappoint me, I believe that.
>
> *Th. 1:* So you're very happy if she has something of her own. You would be afraid,

if she put everything on you and was totally fixated on you and said "only you", that'd be no good.

Mr A: Yes, if I imagine that I'd come home and. . . .

Th. 1: All needs and demands were directed at you.

Mr A: Yes, if I think of our last vacation, the woman of the house where we were staying, gets all dolled up when her husband comes home, and so on. Then I thought, if I were coming home and Liesel got herself all especially nice just for me, I really wouldn't be pleased, instead I'd think, here comes another day's work.

Th. 2: Yes, I think Liesel's grasped that perfectly and found the right balance of distance and closeness.

Mr A: I've said, I could never marry a woman who only wanted to stay at home. I can't really say exactly when we made this decision, when I understood it. Anyhow, our relationship has shown that it's true, that I really suffer if I have to disappoint Liesel, and it's anyhow a problem, just strengthwise, if I come home and I see, oh yes, Liesel's all lit up, physically too, and me, I just stand there and feel helpless (gestures with both hands hanging down). Just that, if she says: I've been sitting here all day and waiting for you.

Mrs A: But I just don't do that. I can't imagine that . . .

Mr A: For me it'd be . . .

Th. 2: Liesel's really doing the right thing there.

Mr A: Yes, by and large I think so. Now we've come to the point that Liesel has said, she wants to make her own room more comfortable, and I think that fits in well here. Yes, that's really interesting, we've got three rooms, Liesel's room and my room are on either side and the living room is in the middle.

Mrs A: But the work room up till now has just been a store room for our things.

Mr A: We meet in the living room, we two . . .

Th. 1: Is it just your wife, or do you too think that you'd like your own room, your own area . . .

Mr A: Yes, yes, she's already further than I am . . . we're just starting out in that direction.

Th. 1: I'm not quite clear, is that the bedroom too?

Mrs A: No, no, we have a proper bedroom, we weren't talking about that.

Mr A: Yes, I hope that she feels also happy in that.

Mrs A: For your sake I shall try hard . . .

Mr A: This would be a real problem for me, something would have to happen, this I could not stand in the long run. But I hold this important, since it connects with the illness when the thought hits me: wait, just a moment, if I get perhaps more seriously ill again and would have to cope with that fact and I would then have the feeling, we have lived two years together and this amounts to nothing else that Liesel says, when I was by myself, all was different, and now everything is so bad, well, this would cause me great discomfort. Yes, sometimes this thought hits me. For example, right now, when I come home and Liesel tells me, "The week was terrible," the news on the telly was bad, and so one bad thing after the other and I would have to think, heavens, if I would no longer be here, if I would die, what would then be left? . . . And when I think of all that I am happy that Liesel can work by herself, that she has her own interest, that she knows other people.

Mrs A: It has been this way for some time. I think it positive that I am not totally tied down in a marriage, as I have imagined it could be. Tomorrow, for example, I have to talk in F. to participate in a conference and I shall go there by myself, not thinking of myself as the wife of Hans. In this, I feel a sense of independence.

Otherwise, I would be anxious, I would have to give up too much. That would mean a lot to me.

Mr A: Yes.

Th. 2: I would like to ask you something, Mr A. You've said there could come a time when you would have to talk about these things: illness and death. I would like to ask you now. Has she really enough of a life of her own, your wife, can she openly talk about this, or would she still need more reassurance?

Mr A broaches himself the theme of his uncertain life expectancy which so far has been tabooed. This give Therapist 2 the chance to address the important question as to how Mrs A could live on in the case of her husband's death.

After the therapists aligned themselves with the position implicit in the couple's resistance, a surprising change occurred. Above all, Mr A, the cancer patient, talks about his fear, that he could die of his illness. In the therapy both show that they need to maintain a relatively large, geographical as well as emotional distance from each other, in order to be able to live with the emotional burden. This is expressed, for example, in their living arrangement: each has their own room at either end of the apartment.

The supervisory team made it possible to abandon the strategy which though aimed at expression and communication of feelings, nevertheless produced the opposite — the suppression of emotion. The intervention originated by the supervisory team had a paradoxical effect — the partners were able to speak about themes which they had previously avoided. The important theme of sexuality, however, remained untouched and was only referred to indirectly (bedroom).

This example shows, also for other situations, that progress achieved through a paradoxical intervention (here above all the opening of communication) was not exploited, because the therapists again reverted too quickly to an "encounter strategy" (here more precisely a strategy geared to mobilization of feelings). In the case presented, the therapists' room for manoeuvre seems to have been limited by one of the myths about cancer, "With cancer patients above all no tricky method employed that might possibly be burdensome". But in other situations also, therapists working with systemic approaches, are prejudiced towards "Encounter work" as the best and most truthful therapy, while paradoxical prescriptions are only admitted for exceptional emergency solutions. Live supervision seems particularly suited as a means to correct this impression.

Summary

This chapter shows how the various perspectives of our Heidelberg model shape our training programme. Within this programme trainees form so-called basic groups (Basisgruppen) which facilitate training outside the formal programme and encourage individual initiative. Also, they make it possible for a small number of trainers to reach a large number of trainees.

The different perspectives of our model require different methods for making it illustrative and experiential. Foremostly we emphasize role play, work with one's family of origin and live supervision. Jointly these methods help the trainees to cope with different families and different problems during different phases of the therapeutic process.

Notes

1. For a fuller account of the Heidelberg Dynamic Concept see Stierlin (1979), *Delegation und Familie*, Suhrkamp, Frankfurt.
2. The term "encounter", translation of the German "Begegnung", is being widely used and possibly abused. We employ it nonetheless because it seems best suited to grasp two seemingly contrasting meanings of Begegnung — confrontation and reconciliation.

References

Palazzoli, M. S., Boscolo, L., Cecchin, G. and Prata, G. (1978). *Paradox and Counter Paradox*. Aronson, New York.
Stierlin, H. (1977). *Psychoanalysis and Family Therapy*. Aronson, New York.
Stierlin, H. (1979). *Delegation und Familie*. Suhrkamp, Frankfurt.
Stierlin, H., Rücker-Embden, I., Wetzel, N. and Wirsching, M. (1980). *The First Interview with the Family*. Brunner/Mazel, New York.

9. The Use of Analogic and Digital Communication in Training in Systems Perception and Intervention

Phoebe Prosky

This paper describes an approach to the training and supervision of therapists which teaches them to identify dysfunction in families and to intervene through the use of a concept of congruence and incongruence in family members' digital and analogic modes of information exchange.

In this approach, identification of elements of dysfunction in families is made by the recognition of points at which a discrepancy occurs between the digital and analogic elements in their communication processes.[1]

The human communication process can be described as taking place primarily in two major modes or coding systems—the analogic and the digital, which combine to produce in our experience a communication package known as the overall meaning effect. When these two modes carry the same message, the overall meaning effect is congruent. Frequently, however, they carry discrepant messages resulting in an incongruity in the overall meaning effect.[2] A common example is the frequently noted variance between verbal and non-verbal communication.

Bateson (1972) has clearly delineated the digital and analogic modes of communication in "Steps to an Ecology of Mind". The digital mode encompasses all rational operations. It is the capacity to infer and deduce according to the rules of logic. It is linear in temporal orientation. It is an operation of the left hemisphere of the brain. Its medium is the written and spoken language and its symbols are words and numbers. That which best distinguishes the domains of the digital—language and mathematics—from the analogic is the arbitrary nature of their symbols: they bear no substantive relationship to the entity portrayed. For example the word "big" has no corresponding characteristics to that which it describes and is smaller than the word "little". The word "table" bears no resemblance to a table. The number seven has no implicit relationship to the actual magnitude referred to, and it is

109

FAMILY THERAPY SUPERVISION
ISBN 0-12-794815-5

only coincidental that the cross-bar makes it larger than the number one, which refers to a smaller magnitude, since the cross-bar in no way represents an increment of six.

The analogic, because of our tendency toward intellectualization, often appears to be the "everything else" of communication after the words have been considered. Among its processes are sensation, intuition, creativity, extra-sensory perception.[3] It is synchronistic in its temporal orientation. It is an operation of the right hemisphere of the brain. It easily incorporates polar opposites in ways which appear paradoxical in digital terms. In place of words and numbers, the analogic code in kinesics (body movements) and paralinguistics (attributes of speech which accompany words, such as tone of voice, rhythm, etc.). Its coding is distinguished from the symbols used in digital coding by its correspondence to the real magnitude or quality in the subject of discourse: the loudness of a person's voice *is* the loudness — it is not represented by an assigned symbol but is coded in its own medium.

Bateson says that the logician's dream of words replacing the analogic in evolution is not occurring. Analogic

> communication serves functions totally different from those of language and, indeed, performs functions which verbal language is unsuited to perform. When boy says to girl, "I love you," he is using words to convey that which is more convincingly conveyed by his tone of voice and his movements; and the girl, if she has any sense, will pay more attention to those accompanying signs than to the words. . . . It seems that the discourse of non-verbal communication is precisely concerned with matters of relationship — love, hate, respect, fear, dependency. . . .[4]

The analogic is generally processed outside of awareness. Bateson suggests that the subconscious processing of the analogic field is a necessary aspect of its being the major modality in communicating about matters of relationship. He suggests that the fact that it is processed subconsciously takes it out of our direct control and therefore gives it the trustworthiness needed in conducting relationships.

From this it follows that in a therapeutic endeavour, attentiveness to analogic communication is of vital importance. The processing of interpersonal transactions for their digital-analogic congruence is also extremely useful, both as a way of identifying problem areas and making interventions. Therapeutic interventions are more effective when they are made in digital-analogic congruence on the part of the therapist. When incongruent, the statement is eroded, produces a bind for the client system and generates a state of mistrust. To teach trainees to use both of these modes at once, both in perceiving and in packaging their interventions, gives them a means of identifying the problem areas and a way of maximizing their therapeutic impact.[5]

Trainees come to us highly conscious in the digital mode. The major challenge then posed to us in training therapists to monitor digital-analogic congruence lies in finding ways of raising a process ordinarily outside of awareness to full consciousness.

The use of the digital mode to teach awareness of the analogic is highly limited. To again quote Bateson,

> . . . it must follow that to translate kinesics or paralinguistic messages into words is likely to introduce gross falsification, due not merely to the human propensity for trying to falsify statements about "feelings" and relationship, and to the distortions which arise whenever the products of one system of coding are dissected onto the premises of another, but especially to the fact that all such translations must give to the more or less unconscious and involuntary (analogic) message the appearance of conscious intent.[6]

We must therefore indicate the analogic through training methods which do not first translate these events into the digital mode. This forces us to innovation, since, as Bateson further states, "There is, in fact, almost no formal theory dealing with analogue communication . . . no equivalent of information theory or logical type theory".[7] We are impelled to identify the analogical field experientially, in its own terms (i.e. analogically).

To do this the supervisor may create and/or highlight elements of analogic exchange between supervisor and trainee or among trainees in the supervisory group by amplifying his own analogic communications so that they are more readily perceptible or by repeatedly identifying analogic events.

The supervisor may call awareness to the analogic through prolific use of analogic verbal forms — a special case of the verbal — such as metaphor, imagery, and all poetic language, in which words are used primarily to create a pattern or shape rather than for their linear, descriptive value. The most striking example of analogic verbal form is onomatopoeia, in which the sound of the word imitates that which it represents.

Another way to increase trainees' facility with the analogic is to have them work with family sculpting. This modality describes the network of emotional relationships among family members by the physical positioning of the members to represent visually the shape of their system. It is a modality without words whose product can be perceived completely in analogic terms. Trainees working with sculpting learn to utilize their analogic capacities to perceive, communicate about and intervene in systems.

Another access to analogic awareness is through the implementation of techniques which diminish or block digital functioning. Work with images and guided fantasy calls predominantly on analogic processing and utilizes the digital in an ancillary capacity as a vehicle for the communication of the analogic events. Other techniques are capable of producing a complete cessation of digital processing, giving access to experience which is purely analogic. Among these are rhythmically repetitive activity such as walking, jogging and mantra repetition, and meditations which collect digital functioning to a concentration on one point and then drop that point and with it the whole digital operation. An experience of the purely analogic state is worth a thousand words of description.

The East has long sought after the development of analogic capacities, as the West has digital. Immersion of the trainee in Eastern philosophy is a further access to analogic awareness. (A few books of particular usefulness are listed with asterisks in the bibliography.)

A continual focus on analogic communication in the process of training results in an increasingly conscious familiarity with the analogic mode. As trainees increase their analogic awareness, they begin to hear and use the digital and analogic concomitantly. They are then in a position to identify incongruences between the two and to determine and utilize the digital-analogic congruence of their interventions.

To work toward personal congruence is required of trainees if they are to be able to recognize congruence and intervene congruently. A state of digital and analogic congruence is not easy to achieve. Most people are replete with incongruences between the two modes of communication. Yet if therapists attempt bimodal intervention in areas in which they themselves are incongruent, they introduce further incongruences into the transactional field, thereby mystifying rather than creating a therapeutic impact. Training of this nature must include therapeutic elements.

Training in this way sets in motion a process which only will have begun when the initial course of formal training has been completed. Like a Chinese scroll or a Contac capsule, it discloses its substance across time. It anticipates the emergence of a mature therapist.

An important implication of this approach for trainers is that it requires of them substantial and developing congruence. If, as Ram Das (1976) says, "Therapy is as high as the therapist," so training is as high as the trainer. To be a good trainer means not only to be in possession of a body of knowledge but also to develop consciousness toward continually greater congruence. This presents the trainer with an on-going challenge no less rigorous than that presented the trainee.

In summary, the trainee who develops a concurrent awareness of digital and analogic processes has an excellent tool with which to identify problematic areas and intervene effectively in family systems.

Analogically derived methods exist for the training into balanced awareness of the analogic with the digital.

Training in digital and analogic congruence requires substantial congruence on the part of the trainer.

Notes

1. This is not to imply that the communication discrepancy is the cause of dysfunction, but rather that it is a reliable indicator of areas of difficulty intrapsychically and interpersonally.
2. The origin of such incongruity may be repression or suppression, conflict, or dissimulation respectively in the order of awareness of the discrepancy.

   The incongruity has elements of the double bind phenomenon, but is a much broader concept in that it stops short of the requirement that the transactional field in which the discrepancy occurs cannot be commented on or escaped. As a concept it therefore fits over many more transactions than does the double bind.
3. Including such receptors as are referred to by "the sixth sense", "the third eye" in Eastern thought and "the third ear" in social work terminology.
4. Op. cit., p.412
5. The trainee needs to learn to notice that a parent has told a child to speak up in such a frightening tone that the child is immobilized. The parent's words and tone are incongruent. Point of intervention. The trainee needs to learn to make his own words and tone congruent in intervening.
6. Ibid., p.413.
7. Ibid., p.291

References

Bateson, G. (1972). *Steps to an Ecology of Mind*. Chandler, San Francisco.
*Castaneda, C. (1968). *The Teachings of Don Juan*. Balantine, New York.
*Castaneda, C. (1971). *A Separate Reality*. Simon and Schuster, New York.
*Castaneda, C. (1972). *Journey to Ixtlan*. Simon and Schuster, New York.
*Castaneda, C. (1974). *Tales of Power*. Simon and Schuster, New York.
*Castaneda, C. (1977). *The Second Ring of Power*. Simon and Schuster, New York.
*Herrigel, E. (1953). *Zen in the Art of Archery*. Random House, New York.
*Rajneesh, B. S. (1975). *The Way of the White Cloud*. Radneesh Foundation, Poona, India.
*Ram Das (1976). *The Only Dance There Is*. Aronson, New York.
*Ram Das (1977). *Grist for the Mill*. Unity Press, Santa Cruz.
Shands, H. (1970). *The War with Words*. Mouton, Paris.
*Suzuki, S. (1970). *Zen Mind, Beginner's Mind*. Weatherhill, New York.

10. The Consumers' Response: Trainees' Discussion of the Experience of Live Supervision

Editors' Introduction

Part I of this chapter (Loewenstein and Reder) was unsolicited. It was written after the first three months' experience of live supervision and was intended originally to be a journal article about initial reactions to live supervision. The editors persuaded the authors to allow it to be published in this book, and apart from a request to shorten the article somewhat, no specific editorial suggestions were made. It is, then, an unsupervised piece of writing. Both authors were senior trainees, experienced in other forms of therapy but relatively fresh to family therapy. They attended the same supervision group in the Advanced Family Therapy Training Course, Department for Children and Parents, Tavistock Clinic.

Dr Peter Reder was asked to write a postscript (Part II) at the end of his first academic year, Professor Loewenstein having returned to the U.S. in the meantime.

To give the chapter a sense of continuity Alec Clark, who was completing his two year training, was asked to give his responses to these contributions and also to add some of his own thoughts in Part III.

PART I: TRAINEES' INITIAL REACTIONS TO LIVE FAMILY THERAPY SUPERVISION

Sophie F. Loewenstein and Peter Reder

Summary

Performing therapy in front of a one-way mirror, and linked to the supervisory team by one of a number of communication devices, creates many conflicts and

115

difficulties. Problems about self-exposure and self-esteem, autonomy and loss of ego boundary, and compliance and authority are discussed. Different communication devices have varying effects on the trainee, whose reaction will vary according to his personality and level of experience. This medium of supervision can be enormously valuable to trainees provided that trust is established within the supervisory team.

Introduction

Exposure, shared responsibility, shared emotions and common problem solving will be experienced by families entering therapy. Since congruence between practice and education for practice is an acknowledged educational principle (Walrond-Skinner, 1979) these are also the experiences facing students entering family therapy training. In this chapter we shall report some of our own and our fellow trainees' first reactions to the innovative and exciting training model introduced by the first generation of family therapists—live supervision. We realize that the issues to be raised are common to all training programmes, and even to all learning. However, we shall describe how the drama and immediacy of live supervision highlights these universal training difficulties.

The structure and rationale of family therapy training programmes have been extensively discussed and reviewed (Montalvo, 1973; Liddle and Halpin, 1978; Rickert and Turner, 1978) but we could only find two articles by trainees (O'Hare *et al.*, 1975; Gershenson and Cohen, 1978). Only Gershenson and Cohen detail trainees' experience of live supervision. They emphasize the stages of learning from anxiety to independence and discuss the changing relationship of trainees to their supervisor. We feel that the trainees' viewpoint and feelings about the process of change deserves further discussion; it might prepare trainees for the intensity of the live supervision experience, as well as sensitive supervisors to the impact of this method on students.

The Structure of Live Supervision

The essence of live supervision involves performing family therapy in front of a one-way mirror. The supervisor[1] and other team members watch and listen from behind the screen and are able to give direct feedback to the trainee-therapist (TT) in the consulting room through a variety of communication devices. Although these devices have been described (e.g. Boylston and Tuma, 1972; Birchler, 1975) the literature does not provide comparisons between them, nor does it adequately reflect how subtle variation in their use can have quite a different impact on the trainee.

The trainee's situation in the interviewing room can be conceptualized as the TT standing on the interface between two intersecting systems. The therapy system is divided into two sub-systems—the TT and the supervisory team—by the one-way mirror. The screening mirror is more, or less, permeable depending on the device used by the supervisor to communicate with the TT, and it thus forms a semi-permeable boundary between the supervising team and the TT. The family is the second system, and when the TT joins the family in the interviewing room, he enters a position on the interface between the two systems. In such an ambiguous boundary position, the TT, interacting with both systems, feels himself pulled toward one system or the other, with important psychological consequences.

We shall comment on these consequences, as well as consider the impact of the intrusiveness and obtrusiveness of different devices and their varying usage.

The Experience of Live Supervision

Live supervision can be an immensely valuable teaching method and a most profound training experience. However, for the trainee encountering this setting for a first time it potentially arouses intense emotions, touching upon the following major intrapersonal and interpersonal conflicts, all of them superimposed on the basic anxiety of being a therapist, in a session, with a family.

The shame of self-exposure and problems of self-esteem

On the simplest level, the anxiety of "being watched" and "being talked about" may arouse dormant paranoid fantasies, in which the TT becomes more preoccupied with the people behind the screen than involved with the family. The experience of being observed performing an activity that, admittedly, one has not mastered, can even precipitate an extreme sense of helplessness and incompetence accompanied by a fantasised omnipotence of the supervisory team. For at stake is the core of one's professional self-definition, that of a competent therapist. It is not just a particular skill that is being observed, but the very capacity to use the self in the therapeutic encounter. Supervision by video-playback raises similar issues (see Whiffen, Chapter 3).

Importantly, the team behind the mirror represents the TT's professional reference group and their respect determines his sense of professional self-esteem and identity, not to mention such mundane consideration as career advancement. The TT is essentially in danger of making a fool of himself in front of the very people he values the most!

Exposure of one's work is all the more threatening because it occurs also in front of the other group that regulates one's self-esteem, one's clients. When the supervisor actually enters the therapy room, the TT's worst fears can be confirmed; loss of dignity, even disgrace, in front of his clients. Messages via the telephone and especially the earphone, being more private from the family, may feel less humiliating, although being rigged to an earphone can feel embarrassing.

While all adult learning is painful, learning under live scrutiny tends to dramatize such pain. It is therefore no wonder that one of our colleagues, an experienced social worker, talked of her imminent first live supervision session as being a matter of survival, while another trainee characterized live supervision as a life crisis.

However, we have all found that the anticipatory fantasy of live supervision is far more frightening than the actual experience. Moreover, we can confirm Gershenson and Cohen's (1978) observation that trainees' reactions change over time as they acquire greater confidence in themselves and the setting. Some of us, as suggested by Olson and Pegg (1979), may even come to enjoy an audience and be energized by their support. It will be a source of relief, reassurance and pride for a TT when he finds that his fearful fantasies about his "inadequate" work are not confirmed; instead his supervisor and colleagues express respect and confidence in his competence.

Trainees for family therapy are often professionals who bring years of experience to their training. This may result in greater vulnerability to exposure since their prior knowledge and acquired identity as a therapist is apt to feel endangered. Trainees with even greater experience and self-confidence may worry less about exposure, but feel more conflicted about potential loss of autonomy and the expectation of obedience.

Autonomy and loss of ego boundaries

Second to the shock of self-exposure is the interference with a basic sense of ego boundary and autonomy. The presence of other team members continuously reminds the TT that he is only *part* of a total thinking and feeling system. He is no longer independent in his work, and there are times when his own judgement will have to be suspended. Whenever the TT receives a message, his thoughts, otherwise totally directed to the therapeutic process, become diverted. He must evaluate each incoming suggestion and find ways of integrating it with his own thinking. The TT may experience "The Voice" coming from the earphone as invading his mind with ideas that may or may not be congruent with his own, without allowing him any time to reflect upon them. Messages may be alien because the TT does not understand their meaning or theoretical implications; because the TT disagrees with the suggestion; or because they are on some level incompatible with his therapeutic orientation.

A trainee followed his supervisor's directions and, against his better judgement, began the session discouraging a family from placing their delinquent boy in an adolescent unit. The TT attempted to explore why the family wanted to expel this child. When the supervisor advised to switch tactics and side with the family's resistance instead of working against it, the TT became confused and felt out of control. Within a few minutes he felt compelled to leave the room for consultation in order to escape his sense of paralysis.

Messages may also be disturbing if they are on a different (or meta-) level of communication (Bateson, 1972) from that in which the family and the TT are currently engaged, and they may appear incongruent with the current interaction. However, it is those very messages which unbalance the system and facilitate change.

The earphone is the most intrusive device of all, both cognitively and emotionally. On the emotional level, we would suggest that live supervision, particularly through the earphone, recreates the primitive mother-infant symbiotic union (Mahler *et al.*, 1975) in which the supervisor/mother functions as an auxiliary ego. Such intimate fusion is a regressive pull toward boundary confusion and loss of identity and it is bound to initiate feelings of helplessness and dependency. Just as differentiation in a child is interfered with by an overly intrusive mother, the TT's sense of autonomy may be disrupted by the over use of any communication device. For example, if the supervisor suggests a course of action that the TT was about to take, she robs him of the opportunity to demonstrate his own competence. Or, the TT may have a strategy in mind and his supervisor, unknowingly, suggests some other plan, preventing the TT from taking initiative. As with an infant, rage is one possible reaction. Another response may be the trainee relinquishing his own sense of responsibility and investing all authority in the supervisor. A danger of dependency in one's supervisory team was demonstrated by a "graduating" colleague: he commented on his anticipated isolation in his future work setting and uncertainty about his work when ongoing feedback was absent.

We feel that, as with an exploring child, the TT must at times be allowed to make mistakes in order to learn from them. Over use of supervisory feedback can deny the student this crucial aspect of all learning.

The TT's decision to initiate consultation with his colleagues behind the screen is one form of supervision in which autonomy, dignity and therapeutic authority is preserved. Seeking consultation is recognized as an honourable professional activity and valued even by senior family therapists. Indeed the Milan School of Family Therapy (Palazzoli *et al.*, 1978) include periodic consultation as an integral therapeutic strategy. Consultations with the supervisory team have a number of advantages. They allow the therapeutic rationale to be clarified and conflicts to be negotiated. Such consultations are also a form of emotional refuelling (Mahler *et al.*, 1975) and a confrontation with the person behind the *"ghost in the machine"* (Koestler, 1968).

We would emphasize that a trainee's sense of regression and ego boundary disturbance is most extreme during his introduction to the live supervisory experience. As with conflicts about self-exposure, most of our colleagues have found a growing sense of autonomy as they progressed through their training, while continuing to be supervised live.

Although live supervision may feel a threat to autonomy, it must be recognized that it puts into practice the intersystemic connectedness in which mental health professionals actually function. After all, no clients can be viewed apart from their social context, and any therapeutic efforts must take into account all the social systems to which clients and professionals relate. Supervisory messages are inevitably in a trainee's mind, even without an earphone! Thus the apparently isolated encounter between an individual client or a family and an individual worker always involves the interaction of numerous social systems. Perhaps it is high time to dispel the illusion of total independence and therapeutic autonomy of the individual mental health worker.

Compliance and authority

Montalvo's suggestion that the novice trainee "may feel as if he is under remote control" (1973, p.345) points not only to autonomy conflicts but also raises the closely related issues of control, authority and compliance. Some of the literature (Haley, 1976; Montalvo, 1973; Rickert and Turner, 1978) stresses the importance of obedience in a vertical relationship between supervisor and trainee, and Rickert and Turner even suggest that "ability to work in a hierarchical model" (1978, p.133) should be a criterion for student selection.

Decisions regarding obedience assume great immediacy when an instruction is received through an earphone or the telephone in the middle of a session. For supervisees who have not fully "worked through" childhood obedience issues, the expectation of carrying out sometimes verbatim instructions will feel infantilizing. Indeed, most adults would find it embarrassing to echo automatically someone else's ideas. We have observed that some TTs make a conscious effort to rephrase the message and therefore own it. Others may repeat the message verbatim, but delay its delivery, because they want to insist on their own timing. Sometimes the TT tries to repeat a message verbatim, but unwittingly alters its essence by changing an important emphasis or a critical word.

A TT was instructed to ask the mother of unco-operative boys, "Do you always accept such rudeness from your children?" Uncomfortable with the provocative nature of the question, he hesitantly enquired, "Do you always accept such behaviour from your children?" thus failing to raise the affective tone of the session.

We have the impression that in the midst of a family therapy session, a drama of clashes of will may be enacted!

There are, however, individual differences voiced by our colleagues. Novice trainees may actually prefer detailed instructions on how to proceed during the session, while more advanced trainees prefer to receive general observations. Likewise, we have found in our group discussions that novice trainees are particularly eager for, and energized by, active encouragement when on the right track. The more experienced trainee, however, may find such praise superfluous.

Students in general tend to complain about infantilization and traditionally resent authority. They use subterfuge, evasion and avoidance to redress the balance of power, such as failing to report, in supervision, errors or other activities that might displease the teacher. It is the peculiar nature of live supervision that such time-honoured student survival techniques have become impossible. Compliance to the teacher's wishes is built into the teaching method and it is this aspect of live supervision that might appear most coercive to some trainees, tending to inhibit development of an individual style. On the other hand, it is only reasonable to expect that creativity will be developed *after* fundamental techniques are mastered.

Running parallel with the issues of resistance and resentment of authority is the supervisee's recognition that the supervisor knows more and is in a position to be more objective. There is a feeling of gratitude for the "powerful voice" which offers generous help in moments of stagnation, perplexity or chaos.

A TT found himself in confrontation with an apparently united family who insisted that the school-refusing son should be sent to boarding school. The supervisor directed her TT through the earphone to initiate a dialogue between father and son about the boy's own wishes. When the boy just shrugged his shoulders and other family members started diversionary tactics, the supervisor repeatedly sent the message, "Make father get an answer!" Eventually the boy answered, revealing his fear about going to boarding school and the conflict became relocated in the family.

The mirror as barrier

We have so far discussed the semi-permeability of the screen in terms of its linking functions. It must also be remembered that the screen is a barrier, with the potential of creating dissonance between the TT and his supervisory team. Every session has its own momentum and emotional climate which the screen inevitably distorts. There will be times when the TT, having successfully joined the family will be more in tune with their pace and their feelings than the supervisory team. Live supervision provides a natural temptation to accelerate the pace of therapy through overactive instructions. This is frequently beneficial, but at times rapid pacing may be unrealistic to both TT and the family (see case example of Montalvo, 1973, p.254). The TT may intuitively become alert to the importance of following the family's lead, using cues that do not permeate the mirror.

A TT began to hear that the family he was treating had a long history of physical illness in different members. Just before he could follow his own plan to construct a genogram, his supervisor telephoned through a strategic instruction. The TT followed the new course into a fruitful, but limited, area. Two sessions later he was able to return to his plan of a genogram and through it learned a major family secret about illness, the sharing of which was crucial to initiating change in the family.

Ever-ready feedback may also interfere with the natural point-counterpoint rhythm in which understanding and resistance succeed each other for both family and therapist. A TT's resistance to supervisory guidance may seem surprising unless it is realized that his identification alternates between the supervising system and the family system, as mentioned earlier. When in identification with the family system, he may experience their resistance and act upon it. He may fail to understand the meaning of the message, or feel that it is unfair. The TT may feel defensive, protective of the family, indignant or hurt. Conversely, when identified with the supervisory team, there is danger that the TT loses empathic understanding with the family's predicament. We have found that when there is a good enough relationship between supervisor and trainee, the dissonance between them, once explored in consultation, can be a most valuable diagnostic aid. It will point to areas of counter-transference in the TT, or defences in the family that may have to be worked with, or respected.

Trust and transference

It is clear from the above discussion that we consider live supervision a humanly risky procedure, particularly in its early stages. The element which will help the TT weather regressive pulls, paranoid feelings and threats to self-esteem and autonomy, is a safe, "good-enough" holding environment, in which mutual trust among team-members prevails. Such trust must transcend the inevitable sentiments of sibling competitiveness, rivalry for parental approval, pairings and hostilities that are bound to arise in any working team/family, as Palazzoli et al. (1978, p.16) have observed.

As in all groups, we think that the supervisor's style of leadership sets the tone of mutual goodwill and professional integrity. The nature of her ongoing comments to the observing team members, as well as her willingness to include other team members' ideas into the supervisory messages, will be an important demonstration of respect.

In general, supervisees find it reassuring if symmetry is occasionally introduced into the team relationship.

An important incident in building a trusting climate of learning in one of our training teams was when the supervisor agreed to simulate a session in which roles were reversed, and she was supervised "live" by her trainees. The trainees playfully took the opportunity to alert the supervisor to the experience of excessive communication through the "bug in the ear", and she gracefully accepted the message.

In addition, the opportunity to role-play the live supervisory process can alert the team to its vicissitudes as well as further the trial and error process through which a team develops its preferred style of cooperation.

Reports in the literature stress the importance of mutual confidence (Boylston and Tuma, 1972) or rapport (Rickert and Turner, 1978) in the live supervisory relationship. We are convinced that the intimacy of contact between supervisor and TT, and its regressive pull when an earphone is used, introduces a stronger transference than might be expected in an ordinary supervisory relationship. The nature of the transference will vary according to personalities, age and gender of the participants, but its intensity should be recognized. Many trainees report with surprise the occasional arousal of excessive feelings of love and hate toward their supervisor. Trainees who have problems with narcissism and counter-dependency might actually find it difficult to participate in live supervision without the transcending effects of a positive relationship.

Evaluation of Communication Devices

In general, one-way communication is intrinsically frustrating. Some trainees have been heard mumbling to the earphone. Others have tried to invent a sign language to send back messages such as: "I agree," "Say that again," "I don't want to say that yet," "Why?" "Please help me".

The supervisor's entrance into the therapy session may be experienced by the TT as a welcome rescue manoeuvre, or as a transgression into his therapeutic domain. Moreover, this style of intervention runs the risk of presenting the family with a model of failure and incompetence, the very problems with which they themselves might be struggling.

On the other hand, a supervisor's respectful joining a "colleague" during a therapeutic impasse can provide a powerful ally without any demeaning aspects. Such an intervention can even be a critical therapeutic strategy. Although both are possible training methods, a clear distinction needs to be made within the team, between supervising a trainee on *his* own work, versus the *supervisor* treating a family through the medium of her student.

Telephone calls tend to be disruptive of the session's ebb and flow because the call itself creates a shift in the session and time required to complete a telephone transaction may even render the message redundant. However, a short break in the session can be useful. Telephone calls may also be appropriate when the team wants to send its own message to the family, via the TT, who can then choose to join the family in considering the usefulness of the message.

Our evaluation of the "bug in the ear" closely parallels that of other trainees. Boylston and Tuma (1972) review the advantages and disadvantages of the earphone for training individual child psychotherapists. They briefly mention trainees' reactions as focusing on: potential over-heavy reliance on supervisory guidance; the danger of feeling limited responsibility for a case; supervisors being out of tune with the process in the room; supervisors being exhibitionistic and correcting the trainees too quickly; preference for general interpretations, rather than specific messages (p.95). In addition we worry lest the earphone foster the illusion that only one specific message is the *right* one at a particular time, coupled with the belief of supervisory omniscience. In spite of these reservations, we feel that the earphone can be a challenging learning tool, given mutual trust, respect and sensitivity. It is quite possible that it accelerates learning to a degree that justifies its discomforts. Reactions to the earphone certainly vary widely. One colleague commented that its impact was quite minor, for him, compared to the impact of the whole unfamiliar context of live supervision.

Finally we consider the opportunities for mid-interview consultations so valuable, that we shall miss them in our future professional lives.

Conclusions

Live supervision is an enormously valuable learning tool, offering opportunities for immediate feedback on one's work, ongoing therapeutic guidance, and acquisition of the system perspective of family interaction during one's actual practice. All team members have the opportunity to see the supervisor apply theoretical ideas to live material with unparalleled immediacy.

The teamwork concomitant of live supervision has many advantages: the team provides each member with support; it affords stimulating intellectual discussions about common experience and common cases; it offers protection from isolation; it multiplies learning opportunities because each member is involved with all cases; and it recreates a setting equivalent to the therapeutic one.

However, live supervision introduces a number of important variables into the therapy session. Trainees will re-experience conflicts associated with basic childhood developmental crises, such as trust, autonomy, initiative, self-esteem and obedience. They will need to confront issues of narcissism, regression and control. These subsidiary processes all co-exit, sometimes compete and certainly influence the ongoing major process of family therapy. We wish to stress that only an atmosphere of safety and trust will securely contain these subsidiary processes. Most of us come to appreciate the enormous value of receiving honest feedback on our actual work, sometimes for the first time in our professional lives.

PART II. MID-TRAINING PERSPECTIVE
Peter Reder

As we anticipated, the supervisory relationship takes time to develop, during which both supervisor and supervisees change. Therefore, as with all developmental processes, some perceptions will alter while others remain. The trainee grows in competence and confidence, his self-esteem increases and anxiety lessens. Concurrently, his ability to use the supervisory group as peers develops. For example, instead of being preoccupied with demonstrating his competence to his supervisor he is increasingly prepared to be "sucked in" to the family system, even "go mad" with them, trusting that he will be rescued by other members of his team. The TT also develops sufficient trust in his supervisor to allow her to disregard the censorship of his observing ego and to follow instructions which he might otherwise question.

Contrary to his customary style of practice, a TT followed supervisory instruction to escalate a piece of family interaction to absurdity. The father was encouraged to lecture to his wife, standing up and wagging his finger like an omniscient professor. To the TT's delight (and relief) this helped all family members see an aspect of the couple's relationship *in extremis*: mother's ability to agree with father's advice, yet never follow it through, which rendered him helpless and ridiculous as he escalated his unheeded advice.

Therefore, it seems that the initially alarming experience of live supervision, especially via the earphone, does modify over time. Nevertheless, many of the conflicts remain and need to be appreciated and worked through. For example, the TT will still experience a dilemma of feeling dependent on, or independent of, his colleagues and hence dependent/independent in his work. In particular, the conflict remains about owning and being responsible for ideas utilized during the session. Even experienced trainees tend to prefix their reporting of a supervisory message to the family with: "My colleagues suggest, and I was also thinking myself, . . ." or, "My group is sending a message that I was about to say myself, . . .". So that even after many months of working together the TT still wishes to demonstrate his competence to his supervisor and own his ideas.

The development of a trusting and sharing supervisor/supervisee relationship can be one of the most gratifying aspects of live supervision. It is clear on reflection that every such relationship is special and each trainee has individual characteristics which must be recognized and respected by his supervisor. These characteristics include personality, transference phenomena, previous experience, beliefs and pace of change. Hence, both supervisor and supervisee must accommodate each other, and this takes time. A creative relationship can develop when the supervisor learns to modify her input according to the individual characteristics of her trainees. Again, it is the immediacy of the live supervisory setting that highlights this universal aspect of teaching and learning. For example, the supervisor needs to continually monitor whether her messages are acceptable to her trainee in length, in frequency, in timing, in content and in clarity. Experience has shown that as members of the therapy team become increasingly used to each other's style and the TT learns from his supervisor and gains in ability, the frequency of supervisory messages decreases. Consultation behind the one-way screen can then become the principal method of communication.

It seems worth re-emphasizing in conclusion the importance of individual differences in the live supervisory experience and reaffirming the value of a trusting group atmosphere.

PART III. A GRADUATE'S PERSPECTIVE
Alec Clark

As a graduating trainee I am largely in agreement with the sentiments expressed in Part I of this chapter, given that the greatest discomfort is experienced initially, and that it is quickly replaced by a feeling that one's competence is being enhanced by encouraging support. The extent to which this support can be offered and received depends upon the concurrent development of the team relationship. Once the trainee feels himself to be an accepted member of the supervisory "family", almost anything goes. Different communicating devices may vary in their impact, but the impact of the vehicle of communication is secondary to the impact of what is being communicated in the general life of the team. If this—the context and container of the trainee's therapy—is sound, then almost any device can serve to carry quite a wide range of advice, instruction and expletive!

A major training issue in the use of live supervision needs, however, to be explored further. As trust between the trainee and the team matures, that relationship can be used increasingly as a way of countering the family system with the therapist's system. Disagreements between the therapist in the room and the team behind the screen can become strategic ploys. The very dialectic of the disparity of view between team members in and out of the therapy room can be used to probe, test and unbalance the family system. Mysterious messages can be directed to the family by the ghosts behind the screen. In all these ways, the live session becomes a means for the team to intervene quite dramatically in the therapy. "Live Supervision" has then become something more than a training method; it has become a therapy technique in its own right, which is different in kind from that in which a lone therapist works with a family, and seeks his supervision elsewhere and at another time (see Lindsey, Chapter 7).

To quote Rabkin (1978):

> Having a motley group behind a one-way mirror to which one returns every now and then . . . is very helpful. From this perspective, what is actually happening is a collision between two different programmes, the therapist in the room being merely the advance guard of one system. The therapist draws the fire but is not actually the main attraction. Two invisible systems collide, and it is at the interface that all sorts of interesting things happen.

When the use of the one-way screen can be described thus, we have left the training mode behind, and we are in a distinctive therapeutic mode. The authors recognize this when they cite the routine use of the one-way screen by the experienced Milan group of therapists.

The issue for training can be spelled out thus. All trainees are exposed to the one-way screen in training; some will eventually work in a context without this resource; some will find a context with such a resource, where the team will continue to be a part of the therapeutic "weaponry". Should not these alternative outcomes be reflected in alternative training techniques? An analogous question could be raised about how one learns to fly in aircraft. Presumably, if one is going to fly in bombers, one must learn how to fly with "the team in the air"; if one is to fly fighters, one must learn how to fly with the backing of "the team on the ground". Both kinds of training are to do with flying and with teamwork, but training techniques have to take as much account of the differences as they do of the similarities. What will happen to the trainee therapist who has grown accustomed to delivering messages to the family "from my colleagues behind the screen", when he is eventually on his own? Does the future fighter pretend he is still a member of a bomber crew, and create a fantasy group whose messages he composes himself, pretending they are not his own? (I confess I have already done this on one occasion, with some effect!)

There is, indeed, one communicating device amongst those listed by the authors which may lend itself quite readily to a live-supervision technique which is geared specifically to train for eventual autonomy; that is the earphone.

Like the authors, I also admit to the peculiar potency of this device, which I found particularly heady. It gave opportunity for grandiose introjective identification. With his words literally in my head, and directly available for my lips to mouth, I could believe, "I am my supervisor"! (Who was it said, "I and my Father are one"?) But it is precisely this feature—the facility of the earphone to foster dependency—which renders it especially useful as a tool for training for eventual autonomy. To return to my aeronautical analogy, pilots who are later to fly solo are first trained in a two-seater, dual-control craft, where the trainee must mirror what his instructor does in order to learn to fly at all. Because of the direct mechanical links between the two control systems, it will not always be obvious, even to the trainee, who is actually flying the machine. But one day he learns with horror (but not without a little pride) that his instructor never had his hands anywhere near the controls—and his "graduation" has begun.

In summary, there is no doubt that live supervision facilities are essential for adequate training in family therapy, but more careful attention needs to be paid to their use as a component of that therapy, and the implications which follow. It may be that the earphone could be used more explicitly as a device for enhancing individual skills in therapists who will not expect to have a team behind the screen as a regular support to their work.

Note

1. As a shorthand, we shall arbitrarily refer to the supervisor as female and to the trainee as male.

References

Bateson, G. (1972). The logical categories of learning and communication. *Steps to an Ecology of Mind*, pp.279-308. Ballantine, New York.

Birchler, G. R. (1975). Live supervision and instant feedback in marriage and family therapy. *J. Marriage Fam. Counsel.*, **1**, 331-342.

Boylston, W. H. and Tuma, J. (1972). Training mental health professionals through the use of the "bug in the ear". *Am. J. Psychiat.* **129**, 92-95.

Gershenson, J. and Cohen, M. S. (1978). Through the looking glass: the experience of two family therapy trainees with live supervision. *Family Process* **17**, 225-230.

Haley, J. (1976). Problems in training therapists. *Problem Solving Therapy*, pp.169-194. Jossey-Bass, San Francisco.

Koestler, A. (1968). *The Ghost in the Machine*. MacMillan, New York.

Liddle, H. A. and Halpin, R. J. (1978). Family therapy training and supervision literature: a comparative review. *J. Marriage Fam. Counsel.* **4**, 77-98.

Mahler, M. S., Pine, F. and Bergman, A. (1975). *The Psychological Birth of the Human Infant: Symbiosis and Individuation*. Basic Books, New York.

Montalvo, B. (1973). Aspects of live supervision. *Family Process* **2**, 343-359.

O'Hare, C., Heinrich, A. G., Kirschner, N. N., Oberstone, A. V. and Ritz, M. G. (1975). Group training in family therapy—the student's perspective. *J. Marriage Fam. Counsel.* **1**, 157-162.

Olson, U. J. and Pegg, P. F. (1979). Direct open supervision: a team approach. *Family Process* **18**, 463-469.

Palazzoli, M. S., Boscolo, L., Cecchin, G. and Prata, G. (1978). *Paradox and Counter-paradox*. Aronson, New York.

Rabkin, R. (1978). Who plays the pipes? *Family Process* **17**, 485-488.

Rickert, V. C. and Turner, J. E. (1978). Through the looking glass: supervision in family therapy. *Social Casework* **59**, 131-137.

Walrond-Skinner, S. (1979). Education or training for family therapy? A reconstruction. *Family and Marital Psychotherapy: A Critical Approach* (S. Walrond-Skinner, ed.), pp.200-224. Routledge and Kegan Paul, London.

11. From Trainee to Trainer

Rosalind Draper

Introduction

From trainee to supervisor: the transition is described in six stages by the author who graduated from trainee to staff within The Advanced Training Programme in Family Therapy in the Department for Children and Parents at the Tavistock Clinic. Focusing on the relationship between supervisor and trainee the author identifies crucial aspects of this transition which the would-be supervisor needs to be able to recognize and practise. In conclusion the author identifies some supervisory skills that have to do with finding the right pace for supervision.

Over a period of two academic years the Advanced Training Programme in Family Therapy seeks to provide a sophisticated kind of apprenticeship. Trainers train trainees who are themselves experienced postgraduates, often teaching or training others in their own agencies. Thus simultaneously they are trainees for two days a week and trainers back home for three days a week. The positive outcome of this potentially confusing experience is a radical growth opportunity. Martin (1979) enjoys this "framework of considerable diversity" in which the trainee has to learn, apply and receive feedback on his own input; then to teach, see whether he has been heard and whether in turn his trainee produces the desired results and then feedback to his own trainers. Circularity of course reigns but the consistent epistemology supports and enriches the experience.

The transition from trainee to supervisor would proceed mainly via identification and modelling, cloning the teacher, were it not for the core experience of the supervision group—a highly valued part of the training programme in which, as Berman and Dixon-Murphy (1979) state, the trainees learn about themselves by getting feedback from others in the peer group. Therefore the crucial elements of supervision are the developing relationships between supervisor and trainees, and between the trainees themselves. A group encouraged to differentiate by continual discussion, evaluation and mutual feedback will diversify within a general consensus moving towards what Martin (1979) calls an increased capacity for therapeutic use of themselves in the clinical situation. It will not clone. Instead it will pass on the capacity to be a member of

FAMILY THERAPY SUPERVISION
ISBN 0-12-794815-5

a team with particular contributions from each member. The supervisor enables each trainee to make his or her transition by ensuring they know how to supervise at various stages. However much a trainee is told about how to supervise, it does not fall into place until he does it for him or herself. Knowing and doing go together. Tomm and Leahey (1980) underline the ability of the experimental task to drive home systemic concepts' relevance and usefulness. In supervising you learn what you know and how to articulate it clearly; thus the supervision group, through an increasing participation in the supervision process provides the opportunity for a particular kind of learning by clarification. As a cornerstone to this whole process the supervisor must develop a discipline of clear and relevant articulation with a trainee in a therapy situation. The trainees learn about therapy and teaching at the same time. Haley (1976) insists that practitioners not theorists are the goal, but would have the student think through and be able to explain himself to supervisor and peer as well as client.

I identify six possible stages of learning how to supervise within the Advanced Training Programme in Family Therapy.

Stage One: Identification and skills development

At stage one the trainee is being supervised in a supervision group. We have agreed a ratio of one supervisor to three trainees is most effective. La Perriere (1979) states: this ". . . approximates the treatment family in size . . . picks up and elaborates the themes . . . is a tool and vivid reminder . . . of the non-linearity of family therapy events". Here in the context of live supervision the trainee may have his first experience of being observed as a therapist. The supervisor intervenes by earphone or telephone to the trainee in the therapy room, or will consult in the observation room at an agreed time, or will call the therapist out of the therapy session. At this stage the supervisor is very like a teacher and the trainee may feel a strong identification with the supervisor's own style of therapy and way of conceptualizing about families and family therapy. The supervisor tries to make sure that his supervisee has seen him work, either through observation or videotape. He also provides the trainee with any material he has published. Initially identification is encouraged. Therapeutic skills are acquired most rapidly in this context. Success depends on a clear contract and trust existing between the trainee and supervisor.

Each of the methods of supervisory intervention described above requires different expertise; the trainee experiences their helpfulness within the supervisory relationship and observes other group members having similar experiences. Method is twice clarified in the two contexts of recipient and observer; learning proceeds quickly. It is the most economical method, Hayley

(1976) writes, which makes many cases and supervisor's comments available to all. However, only when the trainees understand how crucial are the issues of contract and trust can they move on to any of the next five stages. Mutual trust is essential before the trainee can step out and explore. The contract between trainer and trainee provides and defines safe limits within which this can occur.

Stage Two: Contributing to the supervisory process

In the second stage the trainee is more of an assistant to the supervisor. Basic trust has been established between each trainee in the group and the supervisor, and a group cohesion develops which can allow more interchange of ideas between all members of the supervision group and whoever is the therapist for that session. Every opportunity is given at this stage for the trainee to contribute his ideas but inevitably, and happily, the trainee can also rely on the more experience is seen as the most critical variable in the students' acquisition of clinical competence".

Stage Three: Supervising as a team without supervisor

At the third stage the trainee with another trainee supervises his peers or less experienced therapists. The practising supervisors are on their own. They can support one another as they identify and apply the principles clarified in their mutual or separate supervision groups. Garfield (1979) writes: "the supervisory experience is seen as the most critical variable in the students' acquisition of clinical competence."

Stage Four: On your own

Trainees are not convinced new learning has taken place until they act alone as supervisor, applying new methods and techniques learned on the Programme. Just as you have to be a therapist on your own to know you can do therapy, so you have to be alone as a supervisor to know you can teach. At this stage the trainee proves something to himself and moves to a different level of experience. Trainees develop self-reliance through establishing the ability to get across a point of view or instructions to the people they are supervising. Their interventions offer possibilities to the therapist in such a way as to be acceptable and engaging. This mirrors the way the therapist has to engage family members. Learning to communicate with conviction and enthusiasm in a non-threatening way is crucial if the essential congruence between therapist and supervisor is to be achieved and maintained.

Stage Five: Comparing experience with other supervisors

At this stage there is the opportunity of sharing the experience of being a supervisor with another supervisor. Most of the time supervisors will be working alone with their trainees, but supervisors also have the opportunity to meet or watch each other supervise. At this fifth stage more opportunity is offered for reflection and critical appraisal of the supervisory process. Shared responsibility makes for a more relaxed but nonetheless rigorous experience as ideas can be exchanged in context, more risks taken, new ideas explored and experiments made.

Stage Six: As staff member, supervision of other's supervision

The final stage is supervision of another supervisor. As a faculty staff member he can remain meta to the content and process of the supervision he is observing. The task of the meta person is to give feedback to the supervisor about his teaching style, his method and content. Management of the case can be ignored. Much can be learned about the process of supervision from taking this meta perspective. Visiting and observing other senior supervisors provides a similar opportunity.

There is a constant interplay between these various stages. Lessons learned at each stage contribute to the transition from trainee to supervisor. Personal style and individual preference are reflected in choices made about the functioning of supervision groups. But in learning to supervise, trainees become disciples of relevant and clearly articulated communication. The framework and content of the Programme are disciplines in which the trainee has to find his own style and method of communicating the content. Supervision provides the opportunity for spontaneous creativity; nevertheless the supervisor must be clear about the essential knowledge and skills that have to be acquired.

Teaching tasks for the supervisor fall into two parts: models for family therapy and the particular skills necessary for the practice of a particular model. Students are first led through hypothesis or formulations about the meaning of a problem, to strategies and interventions; the impact of which gives feedback and evidence for new hypotheses. It is important that a training scheme includes academic seminars in which the literature discussing these issues are explored. It is also useful to have a seminar format in which these issues are further examined experientially, with videotape and in discussion. Tomm and Leahey (1980) decided that lecture/demonstration is the method of choice for beginning medical students. Nevertheless Flomenhaft and Carter (1977) reported that the Philadelphia Child Guidance Clinic's programme wanted to avoid pitfalls of highly theoretical programmes by stressing interest in, practice of and ability to teach structural family therapy as criterias for staff selection. The Programme includes both a Reading Seminar and a Workshop in which this can be done. The supervision group can gain a great deal from this shared knowledge. The speed with which interventions have to be made dictate that lengthy discussion or explanations are rarely possible as therapy takes place. A supervisor gains considerably from having taught in these academic formats, and hence is himself fluent in the chapter and verse of what he is teaching.

A rigorous approach in supervision itself not only provides a secure base from which to teach but means the trainees get into a disciplined way of thinking about their actions as therapists. The relationship of trust is heightened.

My experience as a supervisor is in three settings; on the Family Therapy Training Programme in the Department for Children and Parents at the Tavistock Clinic; supervising live the clinical work of counsellors in a training programme for pastoral counsellors; and a day a month with a multidisciplinary and multilevel experienced group of 25 in a hospital child psychiatric unit. In all contexts the key issue is the art of supporting the trainee to take risks. Duhl and Duhl (1979) cites risk-taking as one of several basic theoretical constructs essential for learning. This requires learning to know when to push someone to do something new or untried as a therapist, or to know when he is indicating that he cannot do any more at this moment. The earphone is invaluable; only one trainee has denied its value and most are full of enthusiasm after an initial anxiety. Pre- and post-session discussion in the supervision group of a case provides invaluable space for rehearsal of new techniques and identifying areas where trainees need to develop skills. Martin (1979) utilized the discussion, the group process interpretations, to protect needed defence mechanisms of individual trainees, manifested as idiosyncratic reactions, thus highlighting the dilemma of personal growth as an aspect of professional training.

The supervisor is confronted by the dilemma of when to rescue and help, or when to teach by letting people make their own mistakes. Motivation to risk and learn new things often results from the experience of being "stuck" with a case. Nevertheless there is a balance between stretching the trainee and the supervisor demonstrating himself which is founded on personal style and the trainee's needs. The supervisor does not collude with ineffective therapy due either to inexperience or resistance to new material, by constantly offering something the trainee can use there and then.

Inevitably learning to be a supervisor mirrors learning to be a therapist or a client learning to change. The supervisor and therapist help to or expect to cause change but in some orientations Haley (1971) cites the client as totally responsible for change. Yet in each there is a shared experience, then a shift from something having happened between people to something happening inside a person; the change is established. In the end there is a privacy about the experiences that brings the certainty of having made the transition from trainee to supervisor.

My personal belief, as a supervisor tending towards an authoritarian style, is that giving a trainee an experience and then discussing it is more powerful than endless discussion about what to do. I try to offer a number of ways of intervening in a session as it seems that most people will tune into one of the ways outlined. Once engaged in this way trainees will develop an appetite and take off into their own learning with their own momentum. Thus learning has not been passive and for Duhl and Duhl (1979) the reward is competence in creative independent thinking and focus on unjamming deadlocked systems. Understanding how to whet people's appetites may be the crucial ingredient for enabling the transition from trainee to supervisor.

References

Berman, E. and Dixon-Murphy, T. (1979). Training in marital and family therapy at free-standing institutes. *J. Marital Fam. Ther.* **5**, 29-42.

Duhl, F. J. and Duhl, B. S. (1979). "Structured spontaneity;" the thoughtful art of integrative family therapy at BFI. *J. Marital Fam. Ther.* **5**, 59-76.

Flomenhaft, K. and Carter, R. E. (1977). Family therapy training; program and outcome. *Family Process* **16**, 211-218.

Garfield, R. (1979). An integrative training model for family therapists: the Hahneman master of family therapy program. *J. Marital Fam. Ther.* **5**, 15-22.

Haley, J. (1971). Approaches to family therapy. *Changing Families: A Family Therapy Reader* (J. Haley, ed.). Grune and Stratton, New York.

La Perriere, K. (1979). Family therapy training at the Ackerman Institute; thoughts of form and substance. *J. Marital Fam. Ther.* **5**, 53-58.

Martin, P. (1979). Training of psychiatric residents in marital therapy. *J. Marital Fam. Ther.* **5**, 43-52.

Tomm, K. and Leahey, M. (1980). Training in family assessment: a comparison of three teaching methods. *J. Marital Fam. Ther.* **6**, 453-458.

12. The Impact of Structural and Strategic Approaches on the Supervisory Process: A Supervisor is Supervised

or

How to Progress from Frog to Prince:
Two Theories of Change 1978–1980

Gill Gorell Barnes and David Campbell

Introduction

This paper concerns two family therapy trainers who wanted to experience live supervision in relation to different models of change for themselves, apart from the training groups where they had teaching responsibilities. As supervisors we believed that the effectiveness of therapy in training situations was related to the teamwork between therapist and supervisor. As we ourselves incorporated different theoretical models, moving first from a psychodynamic into a structural approach and then towards a more strategic view of therapy, we found that the models for therapist/supervisor teamwork also changed. This is an account of our early learning about two different approaches to live supervision in the privacy of a colleague team of two.

In making the transition from a style of family work that has its roots in analytic psychotherapy to one based on an interactional approach linked to systems thinking, the therapist not only has to take a number of theoretical leaps in his head but has to find ways of using his body, his wit and his tongue that are congruent with the new models he is following. One of us has described some of the theoretical work involved in relation to her own work elsewhere (Gorell Barnes, 1981) and we will focus here on the adaptations we were required to make in our actual behaviours and personal style as therapists rather than dwell on the struggle to change our theoretical perspective.

137

FAMILY THERAPY SUPERVISION
ISBN 0-12-794815-5

Method

We agreed that one of us (DC) would be the therapist for a newly referred family and that the other (GGB) would supervise. Joint experience of seminars led by Sal Minuchin meant that we were initially most comfortable in sharing a structural view of systems change and we agreed to maintain this perspective throughout our first shared piece of work. Supervision began behind a one-way screen. Therapy was interrupted by a knock on the door, by the use of the telephone or by the supervisor coming into the room. As there are still many family therapists who practise without a one-way screen, we were interested in the experience of live supervision in the room; so following the third session the supervisor joined therapist and family throughout the subsequent sessions. She sat in a corner of the room observing, initially moving to stand behind the therapist when she spoke, but subsequently finding she could address him effectively without leaving her chair.

Exploring various techniques of supervision led us to a more strategic use of the supervisor's intervention and to develop the technique for ourselves we decided to follow a different model of supervision with our second family.

In seeing a second family together we agreed to explore a strategic approach to therapy using the model of whole system rule change described by Palazzoli and her colleagues (Palazzoli et al., 1978) as we then understood it. In this situation the supervisor remained invisible throughout; rarely interrupted the therapy and acted as consultant to the therapist rather than director. She addressed the family only through written messages. These differences of method reflect the radical difference in theoretical approach as we then experienced it. Their implications are discussed more fully below.

Theory of change and congruence of style

A central premise of our shared work was that as therapists regarding the family as a self regulating system with rules formed over a period of time, we would be focusing on the transactions through which rules are formed and maintained. The behaviour of any member in a family inevitably influences the others so that each individual both affects the system and is affected by the communications received from it.

If we believe that effective therapy is best achieved by congruence between therapist and supervisor, or therapist and team, it becomes crucial that there is joint shared understanding of the differences in theories of change and their implications for how the therapy proceeds. We acknowledge here our debt to Gregory Bateson, a shared reading of whose work became part of the backdrop that helped us develop some joint understanding of potential levels of change within a system. The brief theoretical account we give here is incomplete and serves as a working guide to the clinical approaches we were exploring rather than being a proper exposition of two powerful, influential and fully documented theories of change.

Our ideas about strategies for change in family systems, normally defined respectively as structural and strategic work, are linked here to Bateson's definition of the levels of learning of which organisms or systems are capable (Bateson, 1972). Structural work is linked to a second level of learning, "Learning II"; in which through therapy a family are moved beyond the stimulus response patterns of the first level of learning, "Learning I". The therapy aims to repunctuate these sequences of experience and have them enact a variety of new responses within the same context. The family learns to learn and learns also how to transfer their learning to new situations.

Structural work addresses itself to change through the minutiae of interaction in subsystem sequences. These sequences which are in operation from the moment a child is born into a family (Stern, 1977) generate certain characteristics of the individual self which are in turn fed back into the system. While the family context remains the same certain behaviours whether verbal or nonverbal will be read within the family as cues or markers for sets of perceptions and expectations to be brought into play, which stimulate further predictable patterns of behaviour. Such expectations are normally determined without conscious thought, discussion and decision so that powerful, tacit but untested assumptions exist in the family. The way that the subjective experience of the system is punctuated can neither be true nor false in any absolute sense but represents the powerful view of reality within which the dysfunctional behaviour or "problem" is embedded (Bateson, 1972, op. cit.).

The therapist using a structural approach would aim to repunctuate sequences between family members so that experience takes on different meanings. This requires energy, focus, precision and intensity on the part of the therapist through repeated repunctuation of sequences that have rigidified thereby decreasing options for problem solving. By encouraging family members to enact new ways of talking and behaving with one another, a change in the overall context of meaning and expectation is achieved.

Whole system strategic work on the other hand does not require the therapist to work with the behaviours of the family to achieve a change in the system but aims at a change in the context of meaning within which the behaviours take place. Notions of step by step learning are thrown out of the session. Instead something akin to a therapeutic force binds the system, by addressing itself to the highest order rule the therapist can understand. Patterns are thrown out of the prior homeostatic balance while a simultaneous multiple reframing of the family behaviours is introduced. This removes negative connotations attached to behaviour and allows family members to view the same behaviour in positive terms which in turn leads to more adaptive solutions to the problem behaviour.

The strategic approach we were following does not therefore work primarily through change in subsystems but through addressing itself to the rules that govern the system as a whole. All therapeutic work may be seen as having elements of strategy (Haley, 1963) and much of the work described as strategic relates to individual or subsystemic interventions. (Haley, 1963; Watzlawick, 1978; Watzlawick *et al.*, 1967, 1974; Erikson, in Haley, 1973; Hoffman, 1971; Cade, 1979; Papp, 1980). We would like to distinguish the Milan approach as whole system strategy and relate it to Bateson's "Learning III". In this third level of learning a system may be freed from the bondage created through adherence to its own processes of second level learning by perceiving the issue of choice in a new way. The rules that govern perception and therefore learning as a whole are transformed. Bateson observes that such conversions are rare but are observed in religion, in psychotherapy and in porpoises: the essence of such a leap in logical type relating to the conflict of contraries generated and experienced at level II (Bateson op. cit.; Rabkin, 1976). We would like to offer a popular base for such experience in the fairy tales and legends in which such transformations are commonplace.

Princesses in fairy tales learn through circumstance to see the possibility of the prince in the frog, not simply to modify their own aspirations to a better interaction with frogs: knights in armour like Sir Gawain learn to risk the possibility of a marriage with a "loathly damozel" who alone can answer the questions he asks in ways that will save his life. The overall contexts and intrinsic possibilities that are contained within them are changed in fairy tales, often with the unstated injunction that the protagonists or "seekers after truth" must themselves give up old rules for making choices or decisions. Change through transformation, from frog to prince, implies that the original entity or view of reality held becomes a new entity with formal characteristics quite different from its predecessor. This shift is usually linked to foregoing a meaning system based on traditional social values of what is and what is not desirable.

In some crucial ways then, we see strategic therapy and structural therapy as approaching change from opposite sides, the strategic therapist aiming to upset the apple cart by transforming the belief system of which the problem is the expression, following which transformation change in behaviours will inevitably follow; the structural therapist overtly leaving the belief system intact and working actively within the session for changes of behaviour between people, following which the belief system will be extended within a system of traditional values but not transformed. Both methods aim for fundamental rule change, but the implications for the procedure and style of the therapist are radically different.

Each therapist will have to make a choice each time he engages a family about which way he is going to be effective and offer something which transcends the average run of advice the family will have already generated themselves or elicited from others. Knowing that all punctuation is arbitrary (even in topics as profound as which theory of change is "correct" for the would be family therapist) we have chosen to isolate these two approaches. Will the therapist move in close to the family and, from an assumed position of relative intimacy which permits risk and the taking of social liberties, start to change rules from the inside and recalibrate shared punctuation through change in subsystem transactions; or will he go for a more impersonal and neutral gathering of data in which by understanding the multiple paradoxes of the situation and feeding them back to the family with a no change recommendation he generates as with Bateson's porpoises the contradictions required for a leap to a different level of functioning; a new oscillation with more scope for revolution and creativity.

Following which Leader?

Our first assay was to work with fundamental rule change at a micro-level; to take a structural approach. Our knowledge of structural work had given us the experience of the therapist having to acknowledge the authority and the absolute right of the supervisor to interfere with his work. Haley (1973) has outlined the need for a training programme in directive therapy to teach students how to motivate someone to *do* what he is told. The trainee must learn to give directives, to make sure he has been understood, to anticipate a family's reluctance to follow him and to check to see if he has been followed.

As peers and colleagues with an equivalent amount of experience, we found that negotiation was needed between us before authority could be given and taken for directive work to be practised in this way. The therapist gave the supervisor authority within a frame of his own making. He laid down ground rules such as, "I don't want you to come into the room . . ." and, "Don't lead me astray because I want to remain in charge of the therapy". We labelled these constraints "Keeping to the structural pledge" and by positively reframing the limits of the supervisor's authority as essential to the therapists' creativity and learning within the agreed frame, (love me . . . love my technique) enabled the therapist to concede some authority. The supervisor was given authority to intervene in the therapist family system at the *micro* level of sequence change, "Congratulate the mother on her caring but point out that as she does it so well her daughter won't ever need to learn to decide anything for herself"; not at a *macro* level of theoretical reformulation ("I think, David, that you are avoiding attending to Gail's infantile rage in the face of this devouring mother"). The latter formulation, however correct, would place the therapist in a totally different frame for subsequent work in the session.

The first family

Mrs Temple referred her 15-year-old daughter Gail because she was depressed, sulky and uncommunicative. Her son, Lawrence, 19, was living at home, but father had died of a brain tumour four years before. Initially Gail was described by mother and brother as the "odd one out". However, it soon became clear that Gail was torn between an active struggle for independence from her mother and the wish to maintain proximity appropriate to a younger child. Lawrence was firmly tied to his mother without any wish to break away and was planning to work beside her in the family's retail business. Mrs Temple was an attractive, "flashy" woman and Gail, large for her age and self-conscious about her appearance, monitored mother's position within the system by recording her appointments including those with boy friends in her diary, regulating her own social life accordingly and occasionally accompanying her mother on "double dates" with a father and son couple.

The closeness Lawrence and his mother retained was highlighted during one interview when he said, "I never thought what life would be like when I leave Mummy".

Teamwork or Solo

The aim of the therapy was to help each family member move on to the next stage of development in which the adolescents would leave home and live independently. Over a four month period mother grew less critical of Gail and understood some of her own conflicts about being independent of her own parents' (the grandparents) values. A generational boundary between mother and her children was strengthened. This enabled Gail and Lawrence to develop a more supportive sibling alliance in the family and to face, together, problems of growing up. Although the family was united by the memory of their dead father, the children began to move further out by enrolling in college courses and developing their social lives. At the end of this period the family felt the problem had diminished and no longer wished to continue the therapy sessions.

The therapist wished to develop skills of enactment, interpretation, boundary making and unbalancing, while the supervisor had to learn to focus on the therapist's developing style in relation to the family system and to follow the rhythm, pace and direction *he* chose to lead through the therapy, rather than taking her own time and track. To use Minuchin's analogy of the "dance" of therapy, it was not clear at first which of us was leading, who was following, who was treading on whose toes or whether we were showing off our steps in turn, in competing routines with the family. We each had to learn to give up some of the autonomy we had previously enjoyed working on our own, in favour of tracking and trusting the process of the other, sometimes against our own judgement at the time. The supervisor's job had been defined as keeping the therapist functioning effectively as a "structural change agent". She therefore had to learn how to back up his skills and develop her own techniques of distancing and recovery after a supervisory intervention. She had to learn to replace her solo performance (the long exploratory intervention) with a quick "excuse me", before repartnering the therapist with the family. She found herself becoming, of necessity, briefer in intervention, more directive and process focused rather than being speculative and content focused. Lengthy discussions about "Why that intervention then" were curtailed until after the session.

Keeping the Pledge

Since it was the first time we had worked together in this way, ghosts of older, more familiar melodies and rhythms from the past kept taking us by surprise. In spite of the objectivity lent by the one-way screen, for example, the supervisor found herself cued into a positive identification with the teenage daughter in the family whom she saw as representing the memory of the dead father for the family as a whole. She told the therapist to work on this. Whether "true" or not this information was irrelevant in terms of the theory of change we were following and the supervisor was told in no uncertain terms that she was backtracking on the structural pledge. She had to forgo her instinct that the family should work on unresolved mourning issues. The therapist too found himself unintentionally backtracking on the authority inherent in the structural model of supervision. During the fourth session in which he had obviously had enough of the powerful mother in the family, he set up an excellent and positive alliance with the eldest son. Having established this two person male enclave, he then positioned himself so that he could not see any of the supervisor's cues for further change of direction. She finally came and stood between them saying, "There's no way set up for me to come in here but I'm going to anyway". These were the kinds of incongruence we had to iron out together as we went along, foregoing the competition of one person's choice against the other's, in order to become complementary to one another as a team following the "metaframe" of a structural alliance.

During the course of our work with this family we learned that some supervisory interventions were better than others. For example:

(1) It is better . . . when the supervisor can learn to enjoy and intensify the existing skills of the therapist and push them further as instruments of change. "That humour is really working . . . exaggerate her over-protection further till she can see it."

(2) It is better . . . when interventions are well-timed; not too early or late for

the therapist–family system. "Follow Lawrence's wish for mother to take decisions for ever," has to follow a verbal statement from Lawrence that the family are still reverberating to.

(3) It is better . . . when the behaviour to be commented upon is positively connoted before it is relabelled or intensified. (The "stroke and the kick" with acknowledgements to Sal Minuchin.)

(4) It is better . . . when interventions are succinct. "David, you're a man; back Lawrence up in this."

Supervising in the Room

We were interested to explore several ways in which live supervision could be conducted. In the first few sessions the supervisor sat behind a one-way viewing screen and interrupted the therapy by a knock on the door, or by using the telephone. During the latter sessions she sat in a corner of the room, observing the therapy, and moved to stand behind the therapist when she spoke.

We were particularly interested to use this approach since there are still many family therapists who must practise live supervision without the use of a one-way viewing screen. We found it made a considerable difference in the quality of supervision as well as the impact upon the family. Messages given privately to the therapist become a part of the therapist's armamentarium but do not change the context of the therapist's relationship with the family. However, when a supervisor speaks to the therapist in the presence of the family he is doing several things: (1) He is giving the therapist a directive to alter his behaviour, but (2) he is also changing the context of the relationships by putting therapist and family on the same level as "recipients of message".

We felt this experience of supervision "coming out of hiding" led us inexorably to use supervision more and more as a strategic tool. However, we learnt much from our attempts to achieve congruence in supervision using strictly a structural model of change.

The second family

The second family we worked with consisted of Mrs Arbour, her second husband whom she had recently married, and her two daughters by a previous marriage. Joanna, 15, was bright and affable, while Susan, 19, suffered from anorexia, negligible self-confidence and bouts of black despair. The family brought Susan for therapy after she began losing weight, dropped out of college and had a "nervous breakdown" which confined her to her room for weeks.

The early stages of the therapy were spent exploring the family's background, the inevitable link between Susan's depression and her father's suicide seven years earlier, and the triangulated relationship between Susan, mother and a stepfather who had been mother's chief friend and support during her father's illness and eventual suicide. The therapist's view was that Susan's powerful symptoms helped her avoid the loss of a very close relationship with her mother through the new marriage. By maintaining a high level of concern in the family Susan also protected her parents from facing the inevitable disappointments in a relationship which over many years had been idealized in the process of support and mutual suffering. Above all, the belief that the family was held in the grip of an evil force—anorexia, prevented the family from needing to change their relationships.

Changing Style from Learning II to Learning III

The approach we used with this family required a dramatically different relationship between supervisor and therapist. With the first family the supervisor viewed the family through the therapist's spectacles and suggested ways for him to interrupt systemic sequences from his position of intimate proximity to the family. For example, "Find out why mother chooses her daughter's clothes," or, "Ask mother and son to discuss how he should become more independent". With the second family the supervisor focused on the whole family as one system from which the therapist attempted to remain neutral and remote. At no point did he choose to become a part of the system nor did he actively suggest change of any kind. In drawing up the contract with the supervisor the therapist again outlined the style in which he wanted the supervisor to operate, and emphasized that he wanted help in maintaining neutrality and circularity. After the first interview we discussed specific hypotheses about the system and agreed to follow a particular line to gather further information about the hypotheses. We agreed that the therapist would leave the room or the supervisor would knock on the door to call him out when the therapist was "stuck" or the supervisor wanted to send a message to the family.

In practice there were usually three or four breaks during each session, initiated on both sides. These discussions provided the therapist some space to step back and consider the session from a broader viewpoint. He frequently confirmed vague impressions and went back into the session with a clearly defined hypothesis to explore. For her part the supervisor also confirmed her impressions and put them in the form of a statement to be read to the family at an appropriate moment.

Learning Neutrality

The effectiveness of working in this way is strengthened by the therapist maintaining a strict neutrality. This is a difficult skill to master and the therapist had many lapses along the way. Many times he would begin a debate with family members, moving towards an escalation or intensification, realizing too late how this was inappropriate. The supervisor played a major role in supporting neutrality by offering systemic comments and lifting the therapist from the one to one confrontation that did not belong to this model of change, to a meta position in which, by seeing such confrontations as part of a systemic pattern, he could use them to build an hypothesis about the family system and about appropriate interventions.

An example of this follows. During the seventh session the therapist went back to the family with a message from his colleague that Susan's anorexia allowed mother to show her strength by coping with life and death issues. The family particularly Susan, were furious with this observation and they each tried to disqualify the therapist in their own way. Susan challenged, "You mean I'm doing all this consciously"? Recognizing that another word of discussion would begin to weaken the message to the family, the therapist replied, "Well, I didn't write the message; how do you understand it"? With such a technique the therapist can continue to make meaningful intervention in the family system because he does not lose neutrality by entering an argument. Even though the family attempts to disqualify him individually, the power of the message from the team remains.

From Intensification to Abstraction

The supervisor's particular task, as bidden by the therapist, was to look for the behaviour maintaining the homeostasis, to find a way of identifying its value and then prescribe no change for the time being. For example, when mother began to talk about the possibility of her daughter moving away, of how she would love not to be preoccupied with her daughter's illness and the possibility of imminent death but just be "good friends with her", she then immediately began to talk of her own depression. In response the daughter escalated the discussion about her own illness into a statement of loyalty that read, "I will never put you in the position of having to face your own depression because I will always keep you preoccupied with me". The supervisor therefore sent a message to the family positively connoting the mutual vigilance and sacrifice of both mother and daughter, and the self-restraint of the husband for not attempting to change this balance. The message ended, "Only when new marriages show themselves of equal intensity and loyalty will they feel the vigilance can relax. Until that time the watch must be maintained".

Logical Adjustments: From Concrete to Abstract

The supervisor found the adjustment to this abstract level of pronouncement and positive connotation quite a difficult adjustment, previously being addicted to what trainees have termed the "Wellington boots and cornflakes school of therapy" (an English form of structural work that takes account of the climate). She took as her personal dictum a note in "Paradox and Counterparadox" which summarizes succinctly the rationale for working in this way.

> Russell's Theory of Logical Types postulates the principle according to which whatever includes all the elements of a collection should not be a term of the collection. In metacommunicating positively, that is, in confirming all the behaviours of the members of the collection, one metacommunicates something about the collection and thereby brings about that step up to a superior level of abstraction. (Palazzoli *et al.*, 1978, p.176)

This pulled together and reiterated a tradition of reading that therapist and supervisor had shared in different settings over the previous two years (Bateson, 1972, op. cit.; Watzlawick *et al.*, 1967, 1974). The supervisor was also helped by a verbal aside that Papp had made some three years before about the use of paradox, which can now be found in print (Papp, 1980).

> Experience has shown that paradox is neither always necessary nor desirable . . . our criteria for its use is based on an evaluation of the degrees of resistance to change in that part of the system that the system is regulating . . . where the resistance is responsive to direct interventions there is no need to resort to the use of paradox . . . we reserve paradoxical interventions for those covert long standing repetitive patterns of interaction that do not respond to direct interventions such as logical explanations or rational suggestions.

(These kinds of gems, often not fully understood at the time, can later return to throw a whole series of interconnected ideas into place.)

Repartnering

In Susan's family we worked within what we saw as the tradition of systemic paradox: initially accepting the family's view of events; positively connoting all the behaviours that were shown including the symptom as necessary to the system as a whole; framing Susan's "illness" as a sacrifice on behalf of the stability of a fragile (new) marriage; and connecting the symptom with the system in a number of ways that inevitably forced new information into it. By prescribing the continuation of the symptom within this changed frame and thus making conscious a series of expectations and behaviours that underlie the symptom, we sought to reduce the unconscious power of the game. By promoting discussion of the danger that might be incurred if the patient got better too fast, we invited the family to unite against the therapist, thus denying the symmetrical struggle within the system which had become its habitual way of preventing change.

Once the supervisor had found that this style of circular commentary seemed to be welcomed by the therapist and seemed to have an impact on the family, she began to enjoy herself and perceive that the method did in practice bear out the theory. She also discovered in the style of work rich dramatic and liturgical reverberations which any team working in this way will inevitably associate to other and much older forms of ritual. Papp (1980, op. cit.) has defined the persons behind the screen as the "Greek Chorus", but invisibility and circular pronouncements makes possible a range of "alter egos" from Sphinx or Delphic Oracle to Shakespearian Fool or Jester (by tradition the permitted commentator on the actions of the Great). Certainly the licence to comment with irony and humour as well as with gravity was felt by us to be an essential element in this piece of therapy, although we felt at the time we had introduced a rather British deviation to our intended purity of style. The spectators commenting upon the process from "downstage" as it were, includes the therapist in his strategic commentary reminding him that he too is part of a systemic pattern not in "charge" of it. For example, the therapist "showed himself" prepared to be "put down" at one point by the supervisor's observation that *only* Susan and her mother fully understood the importance of their close scrutiny of one another and that he, the therapist, must assume a humbler position with the new husband in learning to wait to understand its meaning. This took the onus for taking charge off him at a time when he was feeling impatient and frustrated. On two occasions the supervisor addressed Susan directly with written messages for her alone, confirming a view of herself for which she was receiving no (positive) feedback within the system, admiring her confidence in her ability to manage her own work and life as well as her diet and commending her chosen appearance as resembling "Twiggy" (a world famous and notoriously thin fashion model). This message was directed against a backdrop of mother's continued complaints of Susan's inadequate self-care which legitimized mother's own preoccupation with her. It demonstrated a secret siding of the supervisor with one part of the system which showed itself more ready to shift than another, by asserting to Susan that it was safe to have her own body and her own world view. Susan's smile and careful folding away of these messages on these two occasions, showed that she acknowledged at one level the element of "game" that was taking place. The therapist, however, was not involved with this message and was deliberately used as part of the "stupid" adult system which the supervisor was suggesting Susan could challenge in other more appropriate ways than by refusing to eat.

In this area of strategic address to one part of the system, overlap between the two methods of work was apparent. In maintaining differentiation between the two we would suggest that understanding Susan's "ready to shift" position as part of the larger Gestalt, distinguishes the strategic from the structural approach, as does the impersonal manner in which the message was delivered.

Chalk and Cheese

The two experiences of live supervision described here are vastly different. In the first we sought congruence between therapist and supervisor based on a hierarchical model of family functioning, of family therapy and of supervision. The supervisor worked towards improving the accuracy of the therapist's perceptions and the effectiveness of his interventions, and this was done by watching the therapist, the family and what happened between them. She added weight to the therapist's authority by speaking through him, encouraging the intensification of changes then and there.

In the second way of working, congruence between supervisor and therapist does not apply in a similar way. Instead, the aim is to help maintain the therapist's neutrality and broaden his vision so that what he sees and hears is perceived as part of a system. The supervisor did not speak through the therapist but alongside him and her input was used as a strategy in the battle to resist symmetry. The therapist was helped to elevate himself above a symmetrical battle or a linear view of family problems by using the supervisor's metaview of the family system and its functioning.

Through this experience we learned something about learning. Our decision to choose one way of working and stick to it brought a specific approach alive for us (first the structural model, then the strategic). The extent to which structural family therapy produced change in families and suited each of us as therapists became fully apparent when this approach was confronted by the theories of strategic family therapy.

The experience of having a trusted colleague to observe and experience the discipline of working toward a specific model plus the freedom of having a partner with whom you can make mistakes, gave each of us a sufficiently clear notion of the different conceptual schemes and related styles for us to develop these more systematically within our own training groups and also to develop our own variations. The account we have given here does not stand for the finished performance of a well rehearsed team but for the early stages of rehearsal. Only repeated drilling and hard work will provide any team with the degree of guaranteed reliability in the performance of the other within an agreed conceptual framework of change, from which spontaneous variations can safely develop.

References

Bateson, G. (1972a). *Steps to an Ecology of Mind*. Chandler, San Francisco.

Bateson, G. (1972b). Logical categories of learning and communication. *Steps to an Ecology of Mind* (G. Bateson, ed.) pp.250–277. Chandler, San Francisco.

Cade, B. (1979). The use of paradox in therapy. *Family and Marital Psychotherapy: A Critical Approach* (S. Walrond-Skinner, ed.), pp.91–105. Routledge and Kegan Paul, London.

Gorell Barnes, G. (1981). Family bits and pieces: framing a workable reality. *Developments in Family Therapy* (S. Walrond-Skinner, ed.). Routledge and Kegan Paul, London.

Haley, J. (1963). *Strategies of Psychotherapy*. Grune and Stratton, New York.

Haley, J. (1973). *Uncommon Therapy: The Psychiatric Techniques of Milton Erickson*. Norton, New York.

Haley, J. (1976). *Problem Solving Therapy*. Jossey-Bass, San Francisco, London.

Hoffman, L. (1971). Deviation-amplifying process in natural groups. Changing Families: A Family Therapy Reader. *Families* (J. Haley, ed.). Grune and Stratton, New York.

Minuchin, S. (1974). *Families and Family Therapy*. Tavistock Publications, London.

Palazzoli, M. S., Boscolo, L., Cecchin, G. and Prata, G. (1978). *Paradox and Counterparadox*. Aronson, New York.

Papp. P. (1980). The Greek chorus and other techniques of family therapy. *Family Process* **19**, 45–59.

Rabkin, R. (1976). Critique of the clinical use of the double bind hypothesis. *Double Bind: The Communicational Approach to the Family* (C. Sluzki and D. Ransom, eds), pp.287–306. Grune and Stratton, New York.

Stern, D. (1977). *The First Relationship*. Fontana Open Books, London.

Watzlawick, P. Beavin, J. and Weakland, J. (1967). *Pragmatics of Human Communication: A Study of Interactional Patterns, Pathologies and Paradoxes*. Norton, New York.

Watzlawick, P., Weakland, J. and Fisch, R. (1974). *Change: Principles of Problem Formation and Problem Resolution*. Norton, New York.

Watzlawick, P. (1978). *The Language of Change*. Basic Books, New York.

Part IV

Supervisory Methods Related to Specific Conceptual Frameworks

13. Training in Systemic Therapy at the Milan Centre

Luigi Boscolo and Gianfranco Cecchin

Foundation of the Milan Team

The Milan Team first began its research in family therapy in 1967, treating couples and families with the psychoanalytic model. By 1971, a rift occurred in the group's concept of the family and its treatment, and the team, then consisting of six members, splits into two groups. Two members continued to work with the psychoanalytic model, while the other four members (M. Selvini Palazzoli, original founder of the team, L. Boscolo, G. Cecchin and G. Prata) developed a systemic approach to the family, drawing inspiration from the work of Jackson, Haley, Watzlawick, and above all, Bateson.

The fruits of this study and research were the publication of several articles and the book, *Paradox and Counterparadox* (Palazzoli *et al.*, 1978), which contains the conceptual framework and method of therapy which forms the basis of the training described in this chapter.[1] In addition an ever increasing number of invitations to congresses treating schizophrenia and the family were received. There also occurred requests for workshops and training in the group's somewhat unique approach to the family. At the beginning of 1977, Boscolo and Cecchin initiated a training programme based at the Milan Center.

Limitations of the Training Programme

The programme, established in 1977, had to take into account several limiting factors. First, it must be realized that the Milan Centre was, and still is at the time of the writing of this paper, a total private organization, which naturally implies a certain restraint upon the size of its facilities and the amount of its equipment. The Centre is located in downtown Milan, and consists of two large rooms as well as several small consultation rooms. In one of the larger rooms we have created a classroom, and in the other, divided by a wall with

FAMILY THERAPY SUPERVISION
ISBN 0-12-794815-5

Copyright © 1982 by Academic Press.
All rights of reproduction in any form reserved.

a one-way mirror, we have created the therapy and observation rooms.

The number of our teaching and supervisional staff is now limited to two (the founders of the school and authors of this paper), although we hope in the future to incorporate some of our more promising students in the teaching staff. This naturally limits the number of groups which can be handled over a given period.

The case load is limited to families and couples which have been referred specifically for family therapy by private practitioners, colleagues, our own students, and, in some cases, public agencies (hospitals, mental hygiene clinics, family consultation centres). Thus the range of clinical problems treated in the centre is much more limited than it might be in a public mental hygiene clinic.

We must also consider the limitations imposed upon us by the very nature of our students. For the most part they are psychiatrists and psychologists working in public institutions, as well as some social workers. (The make-up of our first year's class was: 35% psychiatrists, 60% psychologists and 5% social workers.) Almost all of the students have a complete lack of experience in family therapy as well as of knowledge of systemic theories. The field of psychiatry in Italy is at present dominated by the social psychiatry and psychoanalytic movements (Freud, Lacan and Basaglia), which reflects the preparation of most of our students.

The time these students can devote to training is also limited. For the most part, they work full-time at public institutions scattered throughout Northern and Central Italy. They often have to devote a full day between travelling (often up to 250 miles) and time actually spent in a training session. We have, therefore, settled upon a formula scheduling training for half a day from once to four times a month, depending upon the availability of each student.

Trainees

As we have already mentioned, most of our students are psychiatrists, residents in psychiatry and psychotherapy, and social workers. They come from different geographical, cultural and educational backgrounds (the reader must remember that in Italy, a separation of 100 miles can signify cultures worlds apart), as well as from different professional circumstances. They operate in quite different contexts (psychiatric hospitals, mental hygiene clinics, school agencies, private clinics, private practice, etc.).

Their ages vary greatly, which, of course, has a bearing on their clinical experience and outlook. We may find a very well-read but young psychologist with few patients, or an older practitioner with a great deal of experience and know-how, but who has no time to keep up with the latest literature.

A significant variance in theoretical orientation could be observed at the beginning of training, the only common denominator being an almost universal lack of exposure to and knowledge of systemic family therapy.

Organization of Course

Our course in the systemic approach to family therapy is designed to last three years and consists of approximately 60 encounters. A student enrolls for one year at a time, and at the end of each year is required to submit a paper on family therapy which may be published with other students' articles by the Centre in the form of a pamphlet. At the end of each year, each student's record is reviewed by the supervisors. His general attitude, receptivity and participation in the classes at the Centre as well as the quality of his "term paper" are considered. Some factors considered are: Is he generally receptive to the ideas presented and investigated at the Centre? Is he able to implement these concepts in therapy and interventions made privately or with his fellow students? Will it be helpful and instructive to him to continue with his training and begin his second (or third) year at the Centre? In some cases, the answers to these questions are negative, and we advise the student to discontinue. With the passing of each year, the student is given more freedom and responsibility, and with the third year, the best students will be given the opportunity of assuming the role of assistant supervisors to students who are beginning.

The students are organized in groups of twelve, and come to the Centre at an average of once every two weeks for a class of four hours. The first hour and a half is dedicated to theoretical lessons and discussion or reading seminars based on the works of Bateson, Haley and Watzlawick. The second part of the class is devoted to practical experience based upon video tapes of family interviews and interventions or upon actual observation and actual participation in live family interviews and eventual interventions. The main issue throughout our training programme is the creation of a situation in which team work becomes the main learning experience.

Organization of a Typical Session in Family Therapy

Before going any further, we would do well to describe the format of a typical session in family therapy as it is carried out at the Milan Centre. This format has been evolved over a period of time, through trial and error, and we find it to be the most productive in creating effective interventions for the family and in stimulating the therapists to think in a more circular manner.

We work invariably in teams, and have discovered that teamwork is probably the best method for achieving a systemic epistemology. All of us who have come in contact with the systemic model are aware of how difficult it is to renounce the linear-causal way of thinking, and this is especially true of the therapist working by himself. On the other hand, members of a team working together can offer, almost simultaneously, different punctuations of the relationships and behaviours under observation, and can be corrective to one another so that circular views can more easily occur. This teamwork is fundamental to the format for the family session which we have devised.

Every session with a family is preceded by a team discussion (*the pre-session*) in which all the known data concerning the family is elaborated upon and evaluated. At this time hypotheses are formed which will be tested during the encounter with the family.

The session is conducted by one or two (usually two, and usually a hetero-sexual couple) therapists, while other members of the team observe the session from behind a one-way mirror. If the therapist(s) encounters difficulty or shows signs of being confused by the family's behaviour or manipulation, the observers may call him out of the consultation room in order to discuss their observations and give him some "objective" hints. During this time, the therapist tries merely to elicit information from the family and create observable interaction between various members of the family.

At the end of this interview, the family is asked to wait, and the therapist meets with the other members of the team in order to *discuss* new data that has been elicited during the session, and decide upon the eventual intervention to be made.

In the *conclusion of the session*, the therapist rejoins the family in order to make a brief comment and prescription, which has been decided upon during the team discussion. The observers are careful to note the reaction of the family to the actual prescription.

When the family has taken its leave, the team once more unites in the *post-session discussion*, which, in our opinion, represents the most creative moment of our work. This is what we call the "orgy of hypotheses period", borrowing the term from Bateson, during which team members engage in a free-floating discussion and consideration of first-hand impressions, intuitions and simple hypotheses. These are often linear-causal views of a limited part of the family system. Different punctuations are made of the same relationships and phenomena, and gradually more general hypotheses are made which include and conciliate the different views expressed. For example, one team member may make an observation or hypothesis concerning the relationship between father and son. A second member may make a different punctuation of the same relationship, or may comment upon the relationship between mother and grandmother. A third may enlarge the context to explore the relationship between the family members and the referring doctor or agency, etc. This process generates a series of ideas and hypotheses leading to the formulation of a more general hypothesis. This process can be described as a movement upward in a hierarchy of logical types ("Steps to an Ecology of Mind", Bateson, 1972), starting from the lower level of first raw impressions, observations and simple hypotheses which concern only part of the system and moving upwards towards a new stage of a more general hypothesis.

Two explanations are better than one, as Bateson (1979) states in "Mind and Nature", and they can produce a third explanation of a logical type which, when confronted with still another explanation of the same level, produces another idea of an even higher logical level, and so on. When the team reaches the stage of forming the more general hypothesis, a sense of consensus is experienced, a sense that everything has fallen into pattern.

Obviously, the productivity of team work depends upon, among other factors, the sharing of the same epistemological model, the time the team has worked together, and the absence of serious interpersonal conflicts. In our experience, team work enhances the capacity of thinking in cybernetic and systemic terms.

Team Work as the Basic Training Experience

This same format is used in our training sessions. We first create a teacher-student situation, and gradually work up to the formation of teams. This development can be traced through three phases.

The first phase, which lasts from two to three months, is the period of maximum activity for the teachers. One of the teachers acts as the therapist, while the other acts as the observer. The students watch both therapist and observer. Although they have no direct involvement in treatment decisions, they are asked first to simply observe and then eventually to participate in discussion, making hypotheses and formulations of the first logical level.

In the second phase, the students are divided in two groups. The therapeutic group (T-group) is involved in the direct therapy of the family. One or two members of this group have direct contact with the family, solicit information, make eventual interventions, etc. The other members of their team and their teacher (who now enters into the role of supervisor) remain behind the mirror and act as observers, interrupting the session when necessary, making suggestions and hypotheses, participating in the discussion concerning the intervention, etc. The second group, the observation group (O-group), also led by a supervisor, is also behind the mirror, but limits itself to observation, and makes no comments during the session. During the period of team discussion, each group meets separately and forms its own hypotheses.

When the T-group has completed the session by taking leave of the family with some kind of intervention or prescription, the two groups finally meet together to discuss the case. The T-group first gives an account of the hypotheses made and how it reached a conclusion concerning its intervention. At this point, the O-group explains its own hypotheses and what type of intervention it would have made. From the differences between the two sets of hypotheses[2] and interventions, new ideas are developed with new solutions which may be useful in the next session with the family. By this process, learning, in our view, is greatly stimulated.

We try to ensure that every student has the chance to deal with families in different roles: as a therapist, as a member of the therapeutic team and as a member of the observational team. With every new family, the members of T-group and O-group change position so that every member may participate in group discussions at different functional levels. Classes which are treating three or more families can give the opportunity to each of their members of having these three experiences during the same period of time.

During this phase, our purpose is to stimulate and focus the observation of the T-group upon the relationship between the therapist and the family, and the observation of the O-group upon the relationship between the therapist and the T-supervisor. Needless to say, being at a meta level, the O-group is often able to produce better ideas and solutions.

During the third phase, which begins some time during the second year of training, depending upon the development of the group, the T and O-groups begin to work independently of their supervisors, meeting with them only during the post-session discussions.

The Therapy of a Family as a Training Experience

Here we can give the description of a specific family therapy as we used it as a training experience. The C family, composed of the father, 57-years-old, M.D., the mother, 53-years-old, high school teacher, daughter Vera, 26-years-old, M.D., and daughter Maria, 15-years-old, high school student and designated patient, was referred to the centre in November 1978 by the family's physician. The younger daughter, Maria, was suffering from severe anorexia which had begun about six months earlier. She had been hospitalized for several weeks and then referred for psychotherapy, which she had attended for several sessions with no results.

First session

The training group chosen to treat this case was in the second phase of training as described above. The group was divided into two subgroups, the T- and O-group. Before the first session, the T-group met briefly to decide which of its members would act as therapists; two female therapists volunteered. From observation through the one-way mirror, we could observe the family: Maria, who appeared very sad and was, indeed, very skinny, was sitting off to one side of her mother; very attractive, and appearing to be sure of herself, Vera, the older sister, was sitting closely between her two parents. Before beginning the session, the members of the T-group suggested a simple hypothesis and plan of action: Vera seems to be important — examine her position in the family system.

The interview was conducted in the almost casual circular style of what we call "gossiping in the presence", and some interesting information was produced. Vera had been "happily" married for the last two years, and now had a six-month-old bouncing baby girl. Since the birth of the baby, both father and mother C visited Vera often to give her a hand with the new arrival. Another reason for their frequent visits was to discuss the problem of a fasting Maria. On one hand, mother C could give advice to Vera about the baby, and on the other, Vera could give advice to her mother about Maria. The amount of the telephone bills of the two houses had also greatly increased in the last months.

During the interview, Maria had very little to say, and father C talked a lot, but said little — in fact, he seemed to count very little in the family. While his wife and Maria remained in Trieste where Vera also lived, he worked in a town a hundred miles away, and during the week lived apart from his family. According to information gleaned during the discussion, Maria could not stand her father recently (she had always been "Daddy's girl") and couldn't get along with either Vera or Vera's husband. As for the baby, she could not care less about it.

During the team discussion following the initial interview, the T-group concentrated attention upon the involvement of Vera in the original family after the birth of her baby, as well as upon the possible feelings of "betrayal" of Maria. In a certain sense, the newborn, Anna, had become the new "baby" of the family, displacing the adolescent Maria, and placing her in the position of having to grow up fast or of regressing to competition with the newborn. From her attitude and behaviour, it seemed obvious that she had chosen the second alternative. However, the anorexic behaviour of Maria had the pragmatic effect of increasing Vera's involvement with her mother rather than her separation from the original family, and had perhaps delayed Vera's assumption of responsibility within her own family, that is, with her husband and child. The T-group decided that their intervention would be a request to the family to come back again with Vera's husband.

The simultaneous discussion of the O-group came to similar conclusions, but concentrated more on the hypothesis that the parents seemed to need the presence of their children in order to enjoy a good relationship. In some way, the birth of Anna, and the more or less simultaneous "outbreak" of anorexia in Maria had brought them closer together. (This was discussed as an example of homeostasis vs change in the family.) Two groups had been formed within the C family, with the mother and Vera forming the more important and "prestigious" couple, and the father, Maria and perhaps Vera's husband taking a secondary position which did not enable them to form any coalition or alliance.

The intervention formulated by O-group was as follows (remember that for the moment, at least, the O-group had had no direct contact with either the family or with the T-group — their observations and ideas of interventions were at a purely hypothetical stage):

In Maria we see a girl with character, intelligence, and love for her family (here the group had discussed the value of positive connotation) who showed all the indications of growing into an independent, sociable and beautiful girl. Suddenly, instead, she decided to stop eating, to become homely and isolated. Why? Because she felt that her parents weren't yet ready to stay without their children. When Anna was born, she saw a great danger for her parents—the danger that Vera would become totally involved with her baby and husband, and forget her mother and father. They would feel abandoned in a period in which she, Maria, was also beginning to grow away from the family because of social and school interests. With Maria's decision to stop growing, she was able to get Vera back into the family—she had to support her mother in this new crisis. We think that Maria should keep on doing the same thing, at least until the next session.

This was the hypothetical intervention formulated by the O-group. As we have already mentioned, there is no contact between the T- and O-groups at this stage, and the actual intervention made by the T-group was as follows:

Usually we come to a conclusion after a first meeting with a family. In your case, however, we need a second meeting to clarify our ideas. At this second meeting, we need the presence of Vera's husband, Giovanni.

Vera resisted this request, saying it was impossible, Giovanni had to watch the baby, etc. but the family finally agreed that they would ask him to come to the next session.

After the family left, the T- and O-groups met and exchanged their views. The different hypotheses and interventions were discussed and confronted. A certain agreement was reached about the validity of both hypotheses. The T-group found O-group's hypothetical intervention interesting, but felt it would be more effective if used after the second session. For the moment, they preferred the intervention they had made; making no comment about Maria's behaviour, etc. but insisting upon the presence of Vera's husband at the next session. They felt this would have a powerful effect upon the family. After having asked so many questions about the "marriage" between Vera and her mother, the convocation of Giovanni could be received in different ways by the different members of the family: to Vera, "Let's see how you're able to put these two marriages together"; to Mr C, "Since you can't take charge of the situation, let's see what Giovanni can do"; to Maria, "You see, someone does understand that Vera's supposed to be married and out of the family", to Mrs C, "Let's see if you really accept the fact that your daughter's married and has someone else to turn to"; and to Giovanni, "How come you don't have anything to say about all this?"

A long (and very productive, in the view of the supervisors) theoretical discussion ensued concerning the superior effect of doing over saying, of action over explanation, and why, in some cases, explanation can diminish the effect of action.

Second session

A month later, the family arrived accompanied by Giovanni. He and Vera were sitting quite close together, the parents were in adjacent chairs, and Maria had placed herself between the two couples, with some space separating her from their chairs. Her appearance was as before; she was thin, pale and seemed extremely isolated.

Giovanni seemed very embarrassed and his attitude seemed to say, "What am I doing here, what do these people want from me?", and Vera had a very protective attitude towards him. In the beginning of the encounter with the therapists, the discussion, dominated by Vera and Giovanni, was kept on the level of small talk—everything very polite and very general. The therapists had difficulty in breaking this barrier of chit-chat to bring the conversation to more substantial matters. They were called out a number of times by their team mates, but to no avail. The family was too powerful in imposing its own style of communication (later pointed out as being one of the family's many forms of defence).

The T-group decided to send in a reinforcement in the person of the T-supervisor. For ten minutes he succeeded in changing the level of the discussion, and asked Giovanni some specific questions: how did he see the relationship between his wife and mother-in-law? Was Vera more involved with her mother now or before the birth of Anna? What was the difference between now and before their marriage? What did his father-in-law think of him?, and so on.

One question in particular resulted in an answer which proved to be useful for an eventual intervention. Giovanni was asked what he thought about the readiness of Mr and Mrs C to live without the close presence of a daughter. Both he and Vera responded that they did not think the parents could adjust to this possibility. At this point, feeling that this was the best moment to call the session to a halt, the two therapists and supervisor left the family for the team discussion.

The T-group decided to incorporate the intervention suggested by the O-group at the last session with some changes:

As you see, we've had to discuss your case for a long time. We've been trying to understand why a girl like Maria should decide to become thin, homely, sad, and to give up all her friends to stay at home with her mother all the time. After a long discussion, we have discovered a possible explanation. We think she decided to do this because she felt her parents weren't ready to live without a daughter to worry about. Because of her "sickness" she's brought Vera closer to her mother, and has also brought her parents closer together. We are pretty sure that Maria will continue her "work" for a long time, but, in the meantime, we want to see you again in a month.

The therapists thanked Giovanni for having come and for having helped them, and told him that the next time, he would not have to come. To Vera, the therapists gave a prescription. At the end of every week, she was to write down an evaluation of her impressions of the capacity of her parents to live alone (without the presence of a daughter). This evaluation was to be in the form of a graduated scale from one to ten, and should be kept secret from the other members of the family, recorded in a notebook, and brought to us at the next session.

In the post-session discussion, the O-group expressed concern about the position of the two female therapists in the family system. They had noted that the parents were turning to the two therapists as possible surrogate daughters (in that daughters had always represented a sort of insulating field between the elder C's), and felt this might explain their apparent paralysis during the earlier part of the interview.

The discussion then turned to the possible implications of the supervisor's intervention in the session, and what kind of messages this might have given the family. Had the family seen the therapist-supervisor system as a hierarchical system (which they lacked in their own family) and, if so, what effect might this have had upon them — negative or positive?

The T-group, instead, focused upon the effect of the inviation of Giovanni upon the system. It appeared to have scared the younger couple and pushed them together as, during the session, they had appeared to be strongly allied. After having asked so many questions concerning the strong involvement of Vera in her original family, the prescription to stay at home for the next session while his wife was requested to return, could only have had a strong effect. There was the implied message, "Since your wife is so involved with her parents and sister, and since you seem to be aware and approve of it, she should come the next time, but you don't have to bother". (Also implied was, "We're not doing anything you don't know about, so no need to worry — stay home and take it easy.")

The team meeting ended with a naturally developed theoretical discussion of the therapeutic meaning of asking circular questions (gossiping in the presence) which led to the conclusion that the asking of the question (which introduces new information in the sense of structure and difference into the system — the famous "thought-provoking question") is more important than the receiving of an answer.

The therapy of the C family continued in a similar vein for four more sessions — three at regular monthly intervals and a final session after a one-year interval, with the constant interplay between family, therapists and supervisors upon which we base our training programme.

Some Common Attitudes which Interfere with Learning

In the three years since we have begun our training programme we have discovered certain attitudes we often find in our students which have a tendency to interfere with the learning process. We shall describe these attitudes as well as the measures we have developed to counteract them.

A common phenomenon which often occurs in the relatively inexperienced therapist when placed in direct contact with the family is the appearance of "stage fright", a natural tendency to be anxious which leads to an inability to take positive action. As a consequence of his nervousness, the therapist becomes more dependent upon his team mates and supervisor behind the mirror. Unable to act, he expects to be called out for advice at any moment. His attitude becomes frozen, and he sticks to the hypothesis made during the pre-session discussion, regardless of new information produced during the interview.

If there are two co-therapists, they often sit close together, and if one is called out for consultation, the other usually follows immediately as if attached by an invisible string. It is as if the relationship between therapists and the observers were predominant, making the engagement between therapist and family more difficult.

In order to eliminate the occurrence of this phenomenon, we introduced the use of what we call "the thirty-minute ritual". This consists of an agreement made before the session stating that the observers will call out the therapists for discussion only after thirty minutes have passed, no matter what happens during that first half-hour. The effect is usually that the therapists begin to appear more spontaneous, more creative, and, in some sense, more experienced. With this method, we are able to avoid a common escalation through which the more we call out the therapists, the more "stupid" they become, and the more "stupid" they behave, the more we call them out. The O-group is usually in the best situation to observe this phenomenon when it starts to occur.

Another barrier to learning which we encounter rather frequently is the tendency of students to look for a solution or intervention which can be applied to all cases: a kind of "kit therapy". This desire reveals itself in a certain tendency towards applying a successful intervention to different cases having some common factor or basic similarity. We see this tendency at the Centre and see it in practice with cases our students are treating independently, and, most often, when the same intervention is applied to different contexts, the results are disappointing, and, in some cases disastrous. This tendency towards over-simplification and the consequent failures in application brings about a sense of impotence and dissatisfaction with the method.

To counteract this tendency, we give particular emphasis to the context of the therapeutic situation when discussing the individual cases being treated by our students outside the Centre. We have found this consideration of context to be frequently lacking when a therapist is treating a patient in a public institution. He may acknowledge the systemic approach by including parents, brothers, sister and so on in the patient's therapy, but he often fails to enlarge the context to include his own position within the institution as well as the position of the institution in relation to its patients.

We can give the example of one of our students, a school psychologist, who found himself in a quandary after having made a prescription to one of his patients modelled upon an intervention made at the Centre two months earlier. We had treated a family of three with an eight-year-old son. The boy refused to go to school and remained close to his mother all day long. After a few sessions, basing our thinking upon precise information and impressions gathered during previous sessions, we prescribed that the child continue to remain at home for the moment in order to keep his mother from being lonely and depressed during this moment of crisis for the couple. This intervention, given in the context of a private and highly recommended centre, assumed a certain degree of authority, and effected the system in such a way that within a few weeks the boy had resumed attendance at school.

This same intervention, applied to a similar family situation, but within quite a different context (everyone knew that the job of the psychologist was to *keep children in school*), had quite a different effect. The family remained unchanged and the psychologist was reprimanded by his superiors and risked losing his job. The child remained at home, the parents became angry and protested to the school principal, his superiors threatened to fire him, and the teachers sarcastically congratulated him, telling him to keep it up so that their teaching loads would be reduced.

Conclusion

Our main purpose in our training programme is to develop in our students a systemic approach to therapy. In order to do this, we must create a context in which there is a continual flux between linear and circular thinking, simple linear hypothesizing and circular hypothesizing. Team work is essential to achieve this result and is the basic tool of our training program. However, our purpose is not in producing family therapy teams, but therapists who, working singly or in teams, treating families or individual patients, will be able to make valid and useful hypotheses, always aware that the map is not the territory, and able to make effective interventions without unwittingly becoming part of the problem through their very efforts of trying to solve it.

Notes

1. We wish to thank Elizabeth V. Burt, our translator, for her collaboration in the writing of the English version of this paper.
2. It should be clear that when we talk about hypothesis, we are talking about "maps" which introduce a pattern in the territory, without ever being "the territory".

References

Bateson, G. (1972). *Steps to an Ecology of Mind*. Ballantine, New York.

Bateson, G. (1979). *Mind and Nature*. Dutton, New York.

Palazzoli, M. S., Boscolo, L., Cecchin, G. and Prata, G. (1978). *Paradox and Counter-paradox*. Aronson, New York.

Palazzoli, M. S., Boscolo, L., Cecchin, G. and Prata, G. (1980a). Hypothesizing — circularity — neutrality: three guidelines for the conductor of the session. *Family Process* **19**, 3-12.

Palazzoli, M. S., Boscolo, L., Cecchin, G. and Prata, G. (1980b). The problem of the referring person. *J. Marriage Fam. Ther.* **6**, 3-9.

14. Teaching a Strategic Approach

Brian W. Cade and Philippa M. Seligman

The Programme and the Setting

This chapter will describe a training programme that has grown out of the mistakes and the successes of the programmes of previous years, which will almost inevitably be changed by further experiences and feedback.

The programme is an Advanced Course in Family Therapy offered by the Family Institute, Cardiff,[1] an agency set up within the structure of a well known British charity, Dr Barnardo's. The agency developed out of the enthusiasm of a small, multi-disciplinary, multi-agency steering committee interested in promoting the practice and teaching of and research into family therapy. It was established as a clinic within the Barnardo's organization in 1971, offering a free service to the community.

Its staff (at present, five full time and two part time) represent the three major helping professions, though all are employed as family therapists, the hierarchy being based on experience rather than professional discipline.

The training programme is open to practitioners in any of the helping professions usually with at least two years relevant post-qualifying experience, including work with families. Occasionally a less experienced or qualified person may be offered a place because of their obvious potential.

The programme is divided into a clinical component comprising two days each week over a six month period, and an academic component during the second part of the year during which a dissertation of approximately 10 000 words is to be prepared and submitted. The two days of the clinical component are divided between the live supervision of cases supplied by the agency, a more formal two and a half hour supervision group, and a theoretical seminar given by a staff member. Towards the end of this half year component each trainee is also expected to prepare and present a seminar to the staff and to his or her peers.

Although the various staff at the Institute use a range of theoretical approaches from which to work with families, the main framework for the course derives from structural/communications theories. The therapeutic approach taught is primarily structural/strategic with a considerable accent on the use of directives,

FAMILY THERAPY SUPERVISION
ISBN 0-12-794815-5

both straight and paradoxical. We do not undertake to teach from a psycho-dynamic or experiential/growth framework and our main focus is on development as a therapist and the acquisition of a range of skills and techniques rather than on the trainee's own personal growth or family of origin.

The final assessment is based on the continual observation and discussion of each trainee's clinical work, via the one-way mirror, videotape recordings and weekly clinical and theoretical discussions, and on the academic quality of the dissertation.

In the authors' experience there have been many difficulties in moving trainees towards a systemic, interactional view of problem formation and maintenance. In Britain, particularly, professionals are largely taught to diagnose in the more traditional linear frameworks focused predominantly on the individual and his inner world or his social conditioning. Where family therapy is considered it is often seen as an extra possibility though of limited application. Watzlawick has commented (Watzlawick and Weakland, 1977) that "family therapy . . . is in our opinion not simply a new, additional treatment *method*, but first of all a new way of conceptualizing human problems".

It is the belief of the authors that there is a discontinuity between the more traditional, monadic, intrapsychic or social conditioning frameworks and the interactional framework developed from cybernetics and communications theories. We further believe that eclecticism in frameworks can lead more to confusion than to flexibility and creativity. Using the principle embodied in Occam's razor,[2] we have attempted to evolve a core deductive interactional framework of simplicity, capable of being applied to the myriad of complex family systems and from within which a therapist can make use of a wide range of techniques and modes of intervention.

As Albert Einstein commented,

. . . nature is the realization of the simplest conceivable mathematical ideas. I am convinced that we can discover, by means of purely mathematical constructions, those concepts and those lawful connections between them which furnish the key to the understanding of natural phenomena. (Burnstein, 1973)

Our programme attempts to shift trainees from a Democritian view of the world consisting of "things" to a Heraclitian world of process and relationship; to shift them for example, from a framework in which people *are* depressed or inadequate or aggressive, to a framework in which people *behave repeatedly* in what can be described as depressed, inadequate or aggressive ways *in particular contexts*.

The programme is also concerned with the development of a theory about therapy and about the nature of change, drawing heavily on the Brief Therapy Centre, Palo Alto's concept of "more of the same". It attempts to encourage flexibility and creativity with an accent on the creative potential of humour. We believe that therapy is a serious business that seriousness can often obstruct.

The Theoretical Framework

Central to the framework is the acceptance that there is no such *thing* as "reality". As Bronowski (1978) remarks ". . . none of our explanations can be true . . . in some sense there is no ultimate truth accessible to us . . . we have to decide what is relevant and what is irrelevant".

All of our frameworks are only models that abstract from the total possible interpretations of limitless data, transferring what we consider "significant" relationships or processes to where they can be highlighted and studied. No model can exactly replicate what it attempts to represent and in fact need not in order to be useful. As de Bono (1971) has observed,

> The difficulty lies in deciding at what level of organization it is best to explore the functioning of a system. If the level is too detailed and the units are too small, then the overall function of the system may not be disclosed at all. On the other hand, if the level is too high one may only be able to describe the system in broad functional terms that are of no practical use whatsoever . . . ideally one would like to choose a level of explanation that not only explains observations adequately but also allows one to make useful predictions.

The problem is finding criteria, which must be related to purpose (e.g. therapy, description, research), for what to include and what to discard, for judging when the model has sufficient factors for it to become functional.

We have thus attempted to evolve a model that initially over-simplifies and selects the broader features of the relationships in a system which, in a sense, is a framework about frameworks. Thus, right from the start, we attempt to instil a relatively easily assimilated model with its different language in order to more quickly help trainees think interactionally and systemically, providing a core framework on which more sophisticated thinking can be built, and from which creativity in therapeutic thinking can develop.

The model is based on axioms such as the following:

(a) We all view the world through a belief system that, amongst other things, defines what is "safe" and what is "unsafe" in relationships. We will all, where possible, choose to make our more significant relationships with others having a similar belief system about what is "safe" and "unsafe" in relationships, and equal levels of confidence in dealing with them. This will be true in spite of *apparent* differences in personality and levels of maturity (however defined).

(b) All relationships, or sets of relationships, develop "rules" (inferable by observation) governing permissible ranges of behaviours having regard to shared belief systems about what is "safe" and what is "unsafe" in relationships, and to the degrees of involvement required by the range of functions of the relationships.

(c) All systems will organize somewhere on a continuum ranging, at one end, from those that are flexible and able to change their "rules" where pressures from internal (e.g. family developmental stages) or external (e.g. social or economic changes) sources demand structural changes, to those, at the other end of the continuum, where any pressure for structural changes causes high levels of anxiety and a homeostatic negative feedback, often involving symptomatic behaviour, to negate the change.

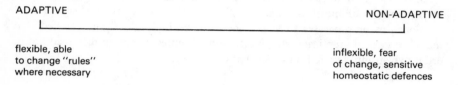

ADAPTIVE   NON-ADAPTIVE

flexible, able   inflexible, fear
to change "rules"   of change, sensitive
where necessary   homeostatic defences

As a rule of thumb we teach that families at the left hand end of the continuum, if they come into therapy, have the ability to use insight promoting or educative inputs to facilitate change. In the centre range structural/strategic approaches can be used, though the more rigid the family, the more resistant and therefore the more demanding on the therapist's power and personality. At the right hand end of the continuum lie those rigid families that may be totally enmeshed or disengaged or in schizophrenic transaction (see Palazzoli *et al.*, 1978), highly skilled at resisting therapeutic inputs, where a paradoxical approach is indicated.

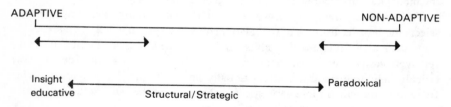

ADAPTIVE   NON-ADAPTIVE

Insight   Paradoxical
educative   Structural/Strategic

(d) The behavioural manifestation of a family's structure and "rule" system will be the repetitive sequences that occur in respect of particular functions (e.g. the disciplining of children, the negotiation of procedures around sex, etc.). From such sequences can be induced the various splits and coalitions in the family's structure and also the ways of dealing with "problems", the attempted solutions that tend to be continually applied and increased in intensity even in the face of their failure to affect the problem (see Watzlawick *et al.*, 1974).

(e) The nearer a family is to the more rigid end of the continuum, the more any input that attempts to change a part of the system (e.g. the symptom bearer) will produce an equal and opposite negative feedback that keeps the overall "rule" system of the family unchanged.

(f) Symptoms tend to occur around transitional stages in a family's developmental cycle as the input of new information (e.g. a baby, the onset of puberty, a death, a loss of status) requires the renegotiation of the structure and "rules". Problems may be maintained where "solutions" appropriate to an earlier stage continue to be applied. As suggested earlier, the more rigid the system the more threatening will be the need to incorporate the new information and thus the greater the likelihood of some acute "symptomatic solution".

From a framework based on such axioms, each trainee can be helped from the start to form systemic hypotheses based on structure and process avoiding simplistic, cause-effect punctuations or the attribution of characteristics (such as strong/weak, motivated/unmotivated, depressive/well) as existing *within* individual members.

From the beginning, the course also concentrates on the acquisition of therapeutic skills together with operational "rules of thumb" ·such as: "Helping" parents to "see" that their problem child is a function of other family, particularly marital, tensions will ensure their resistance or failure to keep the next appointment.

Where the therapist's behaviour, however "correct" within the framework through which the problem is being viewed, produces no change, the tendency to continue or to intensify the "correct" solution is likely to produce "more of the same" problem behaviour in the family. In such circumstances the therapist's behaviour should become the focus of attention rather than an intensification of attempts to more clearly "understand" what is happening in the family. Thus therapist behaviour should be constantly the prime focus for consultant supervision sessions.

A family's or individual's belief system must be respected, however bizarre, until such time as the therapist has made a strong enough "connection" to be able to begin to challenge it (whether by confrontation or by the use of positive connotation). Belief frameworks can usually be best widened after the therapist has been able to enter into them long enough to validate the family or individual (though not long enough to become trapped). Belief systems when challenged tend to harden.

Asking people how they feel about things tends to gather minimal operational data, it is best to concentrate on questions about what they do. Forming hunches about people's feelings (e.g. "You must at times be very frightened at how angry you can get with her," or "If I were you I guess I would be feeling very depressed and hopeless about the possibility of change," or "You must be wondering what on earth I can do to help after so many other therapists have failed") if correct can much more quickly validate and make people feel that here is someone who may really understand them.

"Rules of thumb" such as the above are presented not as absolutes but as a way of beginning to develop in the trainee a feeling for therapeutic thinking and planning rather than more traditional diagnostic thinking. They are made aware of the pragmatic effects of their ways of intervening and forced continually to re-think about how their behaviour can be best shaped to the maximum effect. Their use of posture and gesture etc. is also given considerable attention.

As suggested earlier, we also attempt to encourage flexibility and creativity through developing the use of humour and the power of the absurd. One of our most creative groups always started each supervision session discussing the previous evening's "Monty Python's Flying Circus", a television show full of "the absurd" and of shifting logical types. Talking of creativity, de Bono (1971) discusses the necessity of "re-arranging available information so that it is snapped out of the established pattern and forms a new and better pattern". He goes on to suggest the making of "deliberate arrangements and juxtapositions of information that might never otherwise have occurred . . . to allow information to arrange itself in new and better patterns . . .". Koestler has said (1975), "We all know that there is only one step from the sublime to the ridiculous; the more surprising that psychology has not considered the possible gains of reversing that step".

Thus, during case discussions, we encourage the occasional throwing in of absurd, humorous, sometimes seemingly irreverent ideas for interventions. We find this can often have the effect of freeing the therapist and the group from mental "sets" in which they have become "stuck". Of course trainees vary in the extent to which this comes easily to them, and many of them have been already trained into seriousness. As commented by Fred Duhl of the Boston Family Institute at a workshop led by the authors, "We put in years of discipline before we learnt to have fun, the question is can we cut this process short for trainees . . . we try to give in a year or two what we learnt in many more".

The Teaching

Each programme begins with an intensive five day course introducing the framework described above and preparing the trainees for the first interviews that will have been scheduled for the following week. This "orientation week" includes theoretical seminars, a great deal of role-play simulating first interviews and also an introduction to the administrative requirements of the agency. This first week concentrates both on the acquisition of basic engagement and information-seeking skills and on the formulating and testing of a systemic hypothesis to guide the therapist's behaviour into productive channels as quickly as possble. Time is also spent, via role-play, rehearsing the essential "rules" of live supervision.

The trainee must be taught quickly to present himself to the family as a confident expert, yet, at the same time, he must learn to accept the supervisor's instructions and guidance during the session. This juxtaposition of helper/ helped roles is clearly modelled for the trainees by the staff group of the Family Institute who work using a team approach with peer group "live" consultation.

In order that the trainee is able to introduce the one-way screen and the video cameras to a family in a positive and confident way it is obviously necessary that he himself feels fairly positive about and confident in the system. Role-play is used to teach the trainee how to behave confidently. The style of teaching is directive, orientated towards practical skills and, in keeping with the conceptual framework of the trainers, is concerned that the *process* as well as the *content* is congruent with the therapeutic framework.

Despite the rehearsals dealing with nightmarish catastrophic expectations, which fellow trainees gleefully, and with seeming malice, invent, and despite clear instructions about how — and how not — to introduce the "hardware" with reassurance but without defensiveness or the communication of anxiety; despite our best endeavours, the first "real, live" interviews have a degree of unpredictability.

One trainee began his introduction smoothly enough. "Before I ask you about your family I'll just tell you something about how we work here." Pause, hard swallow, "Er . . . you may not have noticed but . . . well, perhaps you have noticed . . .," waves his arms towards the screen, rolls his eyes towards the microphones as the family begins to shift posture. "You see there's a camera — well, two actually. And that mirror . . .," tone rising and voice picking up speed, "well that's really a one-way screen and there's a — er — some colleagues who are watching — er — helping — and we can't see them." By now the family, who had been nodding in amicable agreement soon after he began, have begun to frown uneasily. . . .

For many trainees the experience of live supervision and observation by (and of) their colleagues is a new one. They have, perhaps, worked alone, unquestioned and unseen for years and stage-fright is a natural response to having their work performance observed for the first time. Over the first few weeks we see a transition which can be described as moving from "My God! They're watching me!" to "Thank God they're there!" There is often an initial resistance which may be overt and explicit or covert and very subtle. Examples include continuing with a conversation for some minutes after the supervisor has "buzzed" on the intercom phone, sitting out of reach of the phone, looking irritated at the interruption, mishearing the message, etc. One trainee, asked by the supervisor to come out for a consultation, replied, "Just a minute. We're talking about something important". Another listened, expressionless, to the instruction and then turned to the family saying, "My colleague says — and she *may* be right — that. . . ." Another persisted in putting the phone to his slightly deaf ear and eventually exclaimed, "It's no good phoning me — I can't hear you"! Luckily our screens are well enough sound-proofed to allow some hilarity at such moments.

Live supervision is a dual-purpose tool. It has, in the use of "off-stage" consultants, an infinite variety of therapeutic uses and it offers an obvious source of richness as a teaching aid. Each trainee is given the following set of clearly defined "ground rules" for the supervisory process, which are included in a handbook given at the beginning of the programme.[3] They are as follows:

Live supervision

Live supervision is a term describing the process by which someone guides the therapist while he works. The person supervising watches the session from behind a one-way mirror, and intervenes while the session is in progress to guide the therapist's behaviour or to provide inputs designed to advance the course of therapy. In this way the advantages of the observers are maximized: the therapist is given immediate feedback to enable corrective measures in his/her behaviour, and the observers can use messages to balance the inevitable pitfalls of therapy and the attempts on the part of families to frustrate the efforts of the therapist. While this method of supervision may at first be quite new to the trainee, our experience suggests that it enables the trainee to learn techniques of therapy more rapidly and economically.

Ground rules

The following rules of live supervision operate at the Family Institute.

Supervisor and trainee agree that there will be free interchange between both sides of the screen. This interchange may occur in any of the following ways:

(a) The trainee may leave the interview to consult with the supervisor at any time.

(b) The supervisor may call the trainee out of the interview for a consultation.

(c) The supervisor may phone through to the trainee to make a comment, offer a suggestion, or give an instruction.

(d) The supervisor may enter the room to deliver a message in person.

The supervisor will attempt to time and to frame interventions so as to maximize their help to the flow of the session. Some interventions need to be made immediately so as to capitalize on the here and now process of the session without time to fully explain them until later.

The following ground rules apply to consultations during interviews (regardless of whether the trainee comes out or is called out):

(a) Consultation begins with trainee stating where he/she feels he/she is with the session.

(b) All observers are encouraged to offer comments and suggestions while the interview is in progress. However, during the actual consultation, the supervisor is responsible for guiding the consultation to the therapist.

(c) Ideas should be about what to *do* in therapy, not diagnosis or criticism.

(d) Whenever possible, consultation should be brief.

(e) A summing-up consultation should always occur 10–15 min before the end of the session.

Supervisor and trainee, before settling down to work, agree on defined limits within which both will operate. If the supervisor uses "must", it must be done. It is a signal for the trainee to carry out the suggestion. This has to happen, because the supervisor, too, has a stake in what happens. In fact, the supervisor is ultimately accountable for the outcome of the therapy. If the supervisor does not use must, the trainee may discuss alternative interventions.

The procedure for establishing the overall direction of the therapy is routine talks during the half hour slots before and after each session and during group supervision.

Group supervision

Each team meets for two hours weekly. These group supervision sessions are geared to reviewing the progress of cases and planning future treatment strategies. They are also intended to look at particular treatment interventions/issues in greater detail where time allows. To facilitate this process, each trainee should select a short excerpt of video tape from a recent session, and present it at group supervision. The video will serve as a basis for working on particular treatment strategies and interventions. Other action techniques such as role play may be used.

Telephoned interventions must obviously be brief and concise in order not to overload the trainee and will generally be suggestions that help him develop a theme he is already working on — unless certain that the trainee will understand the implications of an intervention that suggests a radical change in direction, these are best made by calling him out for a consultation.

The trainee is instructed never to meta-communicate to the family about the phone message but just to continue with the interview incorporating the suggestion. This is unless instructed otherwise where it is felt that an observer message will help the flow of the session (e.g. "Tell the family that your colleague has just rung to say that he does not feel you have fully understood how concerned the two of them are about their child". Such an intervention relayed from the supervisor through the therapist can often validate and help engage parents who are beginning to feel defensive in relation to a therapist's implied criticism of them).

An entry into the room by the supervisor can either be to help the trainee through a difficult situation and onto a more constructive track, or as part of a devised strategy in order to give particular impact to an intervention (Breunlin and Cade, 1981). Obviously either kind of entry must take into consideration, as far as is possible, each trainee's ability to deal with the impact of the intervention and to build on rather than undermine or even disqualify it. However, obviously there will be times that a trainee will feel as though "thrown in at the deep end before learning to swim".

Examples

A trainee was attempting to encourage a couple who had presented with sex problems, to talk about what it was that had first attracted them to each other. The question was evaded by the couple who said that they had "sort of drifted together", then went on to elaborate on what they did not like about each other. The trainee appeared to be groping for direction and soon came out for a consultation. After discussion the trainee was given a number of suggestions including the instruction to intensify things by pushing the couple harder to say why they had chosen each other and what they found attractive about each other. She returned to the room and was again diverted, merely receiving vague and rather negative replies. The couple's voices remained low and monotonous, the pace of the session was slow, the mood depressed. The trainee was obviously still struggling and unable to carry out the ideas discussed during the consultation.

At this point the supervisor entered, walked intrusively to the centre of the room and said, "I just *had* to come in because I see it but I don't believe it". Speaking loudly, rapidly and with dramatic hand movements, she continued to express amazement that this attractive young couple were so unable to say anything nice about each other. Acting flirtatiously, the supervisor mentioned some of what she saw as the attractive features in both husband and wife and said how terrible it was that they no longer knew how to flirt with each other. "No wonder you can't make it together in bed."

Then suddenly she became very serious and concerned and said, "We understand how bad you feel about such a serious problem and how hurt you must both be feeling, but if you can no longer see anything attractive in each other. . . ." the supervisor gave a hopeless shrug and made a quick exit. The couple flushed and looked at each other in stunned silence for several minutes. From then on they were more animated, more positive and more relaxed in discussing their problem with the trainee, who found herself able to carry through what she had previously found difficult to do.

A trainee, working with a reconstituted family having problems with an eight-year-old boy, was told by his supervisor that he was dwelling too much on negatives. It was planned that he should explore with the parents the ways in which they could best demonstrate to the children that their new marriage was a secure one. Once in the session he was soon focusing again on negatives. A telephone call reminded him of the agreed strategy. A call was put through each time the trainee veered away from the agreed plan. Towards the end of the session he was much more easily controlling the interview in a productive way.

Another family came into therapy for help with a difficult eight-year-old. During the third session, the parents were discussing how they had become full-time parents and that they had not been out alone together for some years. They both agreed enthusiastically that, if they were able to spend some time together free of the children, particularly of the eight-year-old, it would allow them to "re-charge their batteries" leaving them less tense and irritable.

However, the couple continually resisted a trainee's attempts to persuade them, during the session, to arrange an evening out. They were convinced that nobody would be able to cope with the children and that they would return to a "wrecked house". Even the fact that an older cousin of the children was available and prepared to babysit could not influence them. The trainee was finally pulled out by the observers, and sent back with a strict instruction to look despondent and to report that he had just been "hauled over the coals" by his colleagues who had called him insensitive for not hearing the family's pleas that, at the moment, they were unable to undertake such a difficult task; he was being unrealistically optimistic and the family were right to resist trying to bring about changes before they were ready for them. The family immediately sprang to their therapist's defence, expressed some annoyance at the observers for *their* lack of understanding, and proceeded to plan the evening out. At the next session, with some pride they reported a successful and enjoyable evening and that the children had caused the babysitter no trouble at all, even the eight-year-old had gone to bed when told.

An important component in this model of learning is the trainee's experience of being part of an observing team whose role is to assess the progress of the interview taking place in terms of the therapy rather than in terms of diagnosis (though, of course, this must also be happening). It also gives opportunities to sharpen powers of observation, to test out ideas and hypotheses immediately by discussion and to join in the process of creating and planning interventions. Initially we find trainees tend to become "glued" to the screen, particularly where a session is somewhat affect-laden, thus often becoming as "bogged down" as the therapist.

In our staff teams, we use, sometimes unconsciously, a range of tactics to help the team stay meta to the therapist/family system. We have found that humour, often at the apparent expense of therapist or family, can often, paradoxically, help the team be of the most help. Coffee breaks and discussions of football results or a young wife's legs can all be ways that the observing team keeps itself from becoming too involved in, and thus constrained by, what is happening inside the therapy room. It can often take a trainee group by surprise when initially experiencing this seeming irreverence, that is until they are able to recognize the extent to which the family's welfare remains the primary focus.

Also, as suggested earlier, we attempt to use the more creative potentials of humour to enable team members to break free of mental "sets" into which we can all become easily trapped. Many of our more useful interventions have begun as jokes or "silly" suggestions which have, like a free-association, given us access to different perspectives.

Thus, as it were, we invite trainees to join us at the "cutting edge", to join us in our search for more effective ways of helping families. We have found ourselves unable, or unwilling, to totally separate out our own experimentation and development from the training programmes. Obviously allowances must be made for differences in a trainee's experience and outlook, but our feeling is that, to keep the two areas apart, can only lead to a more sterile training programme, although, of course, there will always be risks and uncertainties in inviting trainees into less "well charted" areas.

In some earlier training programmes we used to include formal sessions devoted to a trainee's personal growth, with a particular focus on his family of origin. This we no longer do though, of course, we are sensitive to the possible effect on the process of therapy of a trainee's personal experiences both past and present. However, consistent with our strategic/problem solving approach to therapy, where "blocks" occur, we concentrate on teaching the trainee, using video-feedback and role play, how to behave differently with the family. Just as insight promotion or enlightenment are not primary aims in our approach to therapy, neither are they primary aims in our training. That skills, development and personal growth as a therapist should inevitably be adjacent threads in any training programme seems self evident. However, we believe that it is consistent with our framework that we do not confuse our role as trainers with the different role of therapist. This position has been somewhat justified by the findings of Walrond-Skinner researching into some of our earlier training programmes using repertory grids to measure the "changing construing processes and element organization of a family therapist in training" (Walrond-Skinner, 1979). She concluded that "a considerable amount of personal growth takes place in a student even after a short behaviourally oriented training programme".

Summary

We have described the two main features of our training programme. The first is the deductive framework from which we argue that reasonably accurate predictions can be made about the features of a system and also the possible effects of systemic interventions. It is the test of the usefulness of a model that it can be used to make predictions about the outcome of particular inputs. Secondly, we have described some of the basic ground rules for both the therapeutic and the supervisory approaches used on the course.

Notes

1. Unfortunately, owing to the economic recession this course has had to be discontinued. It is hoped that it will be resumed in the near future.
2. William of Occam was an English philosopher of the fourteenth century who believed that the fewest assumptions should be made when explaining any phenomenon. Working from the principle that "it is vain to do with more what can be achieved with fewer", he dissected every framework as though with a razor. As explained by Russell (1979) ". . . if everything in some science can be interpreted without assuming this or that hypothetical entity there is no ground for assuming it".
3. In constructing these "ground rules" we were strongly influenced by the Philadelphia Child Guidance Clinic's training methods. In particular see Montalvo (1973).

References

Breunlin, D. and Cade, B. W. (1981). Intervening in family systems with observer messages. *J. Marital Fam. Ther.* **7**, 453-460.

Bronowski, J. (1978). *The Origins of Knowledge and Imagination*, p.69. Yale University Press, New Haven.

Burnstein, J. (1973). *Einstein*. Collins, London.

de Bono, E. (1971). *The Mechanism of Mind*, pp.236-8. Penguin Books, Harmondsworth.

Koestler, A. (1975). *The Act of Creation*, p.32. Picador, London.

Montalvo, B. (1973). Aspects of live supervision. *Family Process* **12**, 343-359.

Palazzoli, M. S., Boscolo, L., Cecchin, G. and Prata, G. (1978). *Paradox and Counter-Paradox*. Aronson, New York.

Russell, B. (1979). *History of Western Philosophy*, p.462. Allen and Unwin, London.

Walrond-Skinner, S. (1979). Education or training for family therapy? A reconstruction. *Family and Marital Psychotherapy: A Critical Approach* (S. Walrond-Skinner, ed.), pp.200-224. Routledge and Kegan Paul, London.

Watzlawick, P. and Weakland, J. (eds) (1977). *The Interactional View*, p.12. Norton, New York.

Watzlawick, P., Weakland, J. and Fisch, R. (1974). *Change: Principles of Problem Formation and Problem Resolution, the Terrible Simplifications*. Norton, New York.

15. Provocative Supervision

Maurizio Andolfi and Paolo Menghi

Premises

In this chapter we describe a modality for live supervision which we have called *provocative*.[1] Its purpose is to render the strategy worked out by the therapeutic team more incisive[2]; in particular it ensures that the model of supervision is congruent with the model of therapy, therefore it is important that the similarities between the two are understood. The model of intervention which we have worked out is primarily intended for working with *rigid family systems* (Andolfi *et al.*, 1980), that is, with those systems which interact with the therapist in such a way as to enmesh him in the relationships at highly contradictory logical levels.

These families enter therapy with the expectation that the therapist will help them to reconsolidate the system's previous equilibrium. "Basically, the family wants the therapist to perform an impossible task: to help them *to change a situation while adhering to the same rules of interaction that previously served to maintain the existing situation*" (Andolfi *et al.*, 1980). Clinical experience has shown that these contradictory expectations on the part of the family often create a situation in which the therapist attempts to cure a family group whose members unite to demonstrate the futility of his efforts. "As a result, a rigid therapeutic system is formed, and family-therapist interactions tend to crystallize in increasingly static and predictable roles and functions" (Andolfi, 1980).

All differences and conflicts among the members of these families are disguised by the one issue on which they unanimously agree: that the sick member, the only one who needs treatment, is the identified patient. His behaviour in the sessions tends to reinforce three basic characteristics of all such family transactions: the patient's symptomatology is of central importance to the system, apparently filling the family's entire world; many patients' communications (even those that are fully appropriate) are denied validity; consequently, all efforts made by the family or by outsiders to modify such behaviour are doomed to fail.

181

FAMILY THERAPY SUPERVISION
ISBN 0-12-794815-5

The family's request, which is based on these premises, can be formulated as follows: "Help us to cure him by telling us what to do to make him normal". If the therapist fails to see the incongruity between the request for treatment and the more or less explicit definition of the patient's disturbance as unchangeable, any move he makes will prove ineffectual. He will inevitably become trapped in the homeostatic mechanisms that have so effectively maintained the identified patient in his passive yet central role as the sick member of the family. If the therapist ignores the paradoxical message transmitted by the family system and openly accepts a therapeutic role, the question of the patient's curability will eventually become a battleground between the two factions. On the one hand, the therapist will try to force the system to effectuate real change; on the other, the family members will engage in a collective campaign to demonstrate its own good intentions and the failure of the therapist. The identified patient will be completely excluded from the whole process, and his inadequacy will thus be reconfirmed once more.

The approach we have developed during the past six years at the Family Therapy Institute in Rome consists in considering the message transmitted by the family as a *provocation*, and trying to formulate a therapeutic strategy that constitutes a counter-provocation as a *response* to this message.

According to Stanton (1981), this strategy conforms to a model of *relative contrasts*, in which the therapist tries to stay one step ahead of the family and, until later stages, almost invariably pushes for more homeostasis than the family is comfortable with. In a sense he "one ups" them, and in their resistance to his directions, they start to change in an opposite direction.

The objectives of supervision

Provocative supervision is a response to the problems encountered with rigid families which draw the therapist into their own habitual models of interaction, preventing him from working for change. "Such families, in their interaction with the therapist, tend rapidly to form *therapeutic systems* which are equally rigid" (Andolfi, 1979). When this occurs, the therapist risks reinforcing the same transactional modalities which have brought the family to seek therapy. If he presents himself openly as an agent of change, he will become easily *predictable* and he will be unable to control the relationship within the therapeutic context. Without this control he will be unable to breach systems grown rigid over a long period of time. The primary aim of our intervention is, therefore, to forestall the formation of rigid therapeutic systems.

While this risk is greater in the early stages of therapy, even in successive phases the therapist may commit the error of becoming predictable, by demonstrating that he is more interested in overcoming the interactive difficulties of the family than is the family itself.

Provocative supervision is geared to *modulate in time the therapist's level of unpredictability*, thereby helping him to maintain control of the therapeutic relationship during the entire course of therapy.

While the therapist intervenes in the family's equilibrium between homeostasis and tendencies for change, the supervisor intervenes in a similar way vis-à-vis the therapist. A parallel situation is created between the T-F and S-T relationship[3], and the progress of the entire therapy depends on the way the latter functions.

If the therapist has become too involved with the family to carry out effective interventions, the supervisor can use provocation (ultimately aimed at the therapist-family system) to attack the therapist's function. By interrupting the therapist's action, the supervisor *blocks an interactive modality*; as a result, the complementary functions assumed by the family members become untenable. Let us try to explain with an example. If S says to T that it is better to interrupt the therapy rather than continue to "go to bed" with Mrs Rossi so that Robertino will suffer less from his father's absence, he is communicating at various levels. On the one hand he is warning T of the danger of functioning as a substitute and of confusing the needs of the mother with those of the child; on the other hand, he is preventing Mrs Rossi from filling her personal emptiness with surrogate functions, generously offered by T.

Even an experienced therapist who feels he needs help to bring his intervention back to an adequate level of unpredictability, may make requests to his supervisor which would in reality make his behaviour more predictable (and therefore easy for the family to neutralize). The reasons for this are clear if we consider that the therapist-family encounter leads to the formation of a *new system*, which is structured according to new rules which evolve through a process of reciprocal negotiation. The more rigid the family system, the more difficult it is for the therapist to avoid being trapped in the pre-existing family rules. When this happens he may make contradictory requests to the supervisor, such as, "Help me to foster the differentiation of the family members (explicit request), while protecting their need for cohesion (implicit request)"; or, "Help me to separate myself from the family (explicit request), while keeping it dependent on me (implicit request)". In such cases the supervisor must confront implicit and explicit requests, thereby highlighting their contradictions. At other times, as we shall see from the examples below, the supervisor provokes the therapeutic system by attacking the family, but the final result is identical.

Further, *supervision must regulate the dynamic equilibrium between participation and separation* to favour the progressive individuation of the single members of the family. For this reason the use of *space* during the course of therapy is of fundamental importance. Whereas a static space would eventually favour a parallel immobility in the therapeutic system, its dynamic utilization underlines and amplifies the processes of participation and separation.

Space and timing in supervision

The therapeutic relationship evolves through various *phases* corresponding to successive phases of the intervention. As the therapy progresses the supervisory process strategically modifies the dynamics of this relationship: from the *formation of the therapeutic system* (when F and T meet), to the *variations* of this relationship over time, to its *scission* when F and T separate.

The fundamental phases of therapy are articulated dynamically in the space in which the members of the therapeutic system interact. The therapist represents a pathway connecting family and supervisor. He alternates between two units which are spatially separated by a one-way mirror. During the sessions the supervisor can communicate with the therapist through an interphone (Fig. 1) and make immediate suggestions; or the therapist can leave the therapy room—either spontaneously or at the supervisor's request (Fig. 2)—to exchange information, to interrupt an unproductive phase, or to put the final touches to a strategic intervention. In other circumstances the supervisor may temporarily leave the observation room to enter the therapist-family system (Figs 3a, 3b) to provoke a change in the context. The family may also move from one place to another, or one or more members of the family may be invited to join the supervisor behind the mirror (Fig. 4).

The rhythm with which various spatial modifications are called for is important: the supervisor must find the optimum frequency for his interphone calls, for the therapists' exits, for his entries into the therapy room, and for changing the positions of the family members. An accelerated rhythm breaks the continuity of the intervention, a slackened rhythm permits the crystallization of unproductive situations. It is the supervisor's task to gauge moves according to therapeutic requirements. Each of the spatial modifications described aims at *interrupting an unproductive context and/or promoting the therapeutic strategy.* The choice of one form or another is made on the basis of whatever will best guarantee the re-establishment of the level of unpredictability required at that moment in therapy.

In this spatial disposition (Fig. 1.) the relationship S-T takes place through the

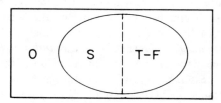

Fig. 1. S: supervisor; T: therapist; F: family; O: observer; ————: one-way mirror; ⬭ : therapeutic system.

interphone: S can suggest interventions to be carried out immediately, while also recommending the most appropriate emotional colourings — dramatic, aggressive, bored, warm, etc.

The interphone is placed at a distance from the therapist so that he has to get up to answer, temporarily altering his distance from the family system and interrupting the sequence of communication. Since the family is unable to predict either the contents or the objectives of the call, there is an atmosphere of expectation with increasing stress. It is up to the therapist to use this to advantage by giving a personal interpretation to the advice he has received.

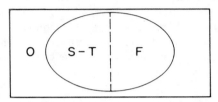

Fig. 2. S: supervisor; T: therapist; F: family; O: observer; ———: one-way mirror; ⌒: therapeutic system.

The therapist can leave the therapy room to go to the observation room (Fig. 2.) either *spontaneously* or *at the request* of the supervisor through the interphone; in either case the therapist's exit *reactivates the unpredictable element in a context which has become too predictable,* either because the therapist has become enmeshed in the family rules or because his intervention has not been sufficiently incisive. In the first case the aim is to enable T to recover lost ground; in the second, to plan together a more effective strategy. Leaving the room enables T to detach himself from his emotional involvement with the family. In this way the unity of the therapeutic team is temporarily recomposed, thus reassuring the therapist who may have fantasies about being abandoned or judged by the supervisor. Observing the family together gives the therapist and supervisor a common perspective and recreates an emotional bond between them. The family, without the presence of an "outsider", acquires greater cohesion, which enables it to reorder its ranks with a view to the next therapeutic move, which appears menacing precisely because it is unpredictable.

T represents an element of continuity for the family and offers them a relationship which can be developed and deepened; for that very reason he runs the risk of becoming enmeshed in the family rules. S, on the other hand, carries out his function of reinforcing T's unpredictability by maintaining an invisible presence. He is perceived by F as the person in the best position to maintain control over the relationship: his mere entry into the therapy room therefore causes stress.

Since *the entire therapeutic system operates within a unified space,* any confrontation between two sub-units takes place in the presence of the third. This creates a high level of exposure for all, in particular for the therapist, whose expectations with regard to S are contradictory: on the one hand he wants help from him; on the other, he fears any such request will underline his predicament in the eyes of the family. For this reason S must be sure to give authority back to T before making his exit.

We have found that to maintain the effectiveness of this spatial disposition, it should be used parsimoniously during the course of the therapy, otherwise the effects become progressively weaker and the intervention turns into an ill-defined co-therapy.

Two variants of this scheme have been contemplated, and can be used separately or during the same intervention. Both enable T and F to have greater objectivity in observing the functions which have evolved during the course of the therapeutic process.

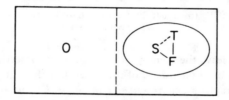

Fig. 3a. S: supervisor; T: therapist; F: family; O: observer; ———: one-way mirror;
⬭ : therapeutic system.

S interacts directly with F, temporarily substituting T (Fig. 3a.). This enables T to observe F in its interaction with another therapist. T then has the possibility of interacting in turn with S, or with F in the presence of S.

In the next scheme (Fig. 3b.) S provokes F indirectly, through T, in F's presence. This further increases the stress for the entire therapeutic system and acts as an example of direct confrontation.

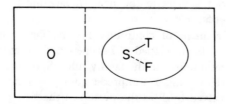

Fig. 3b. S: supervisor; T: therapist; F: family; O: observer; ———: one-way mirror;
⬭ : therapeutic system.

In the spatial disposition of (Fig. 4.) the family is split up during the session, with some members watching the behaviour of others from the observation room. The supervisor interacts directly with part of the family, encouraging them to observe the interactive modalities of specific sub-units among themselves and with the therapist. To observe and to be observed is an unusual modality which breaks habitual patterns. It enables the family and the therapeutic team to experiment with different relationships. Although this may cause stress, it leads to the acquisition of new equilibriums between the need for cohesion and the capacity for differentiation.

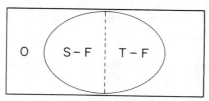

Fig. 4. S: supervisor; T: therapist; F: family; O: observer; ———: one-way mirror; ⬭ : therapeutic system.

Examples

The parents of Cristina, the eight-year-old identified patient, have been invited to attend the sixth session without their daughter. The aim of the therapeutic team is to alter the focus of the intervention from the identified patient to the parents as individuals, avoiding any explicit reference to their relationship as a couple. They would feel threatened were there any discussion of this relationship, which seems at present largely functional to their own non-definition. Though an explicit intervention on the couple would be premature, the team does not exclude the possibility of acting on them indirectly, by working on each one in the presence of the other. Exposing each partner in front of the other while forbidding them to interact during the session should stimulate a subsequent confrontation between the two, based on a clearer reciprocal individuation, without having to go through the identified patient.

In the following extract we should like to illustrate a series of specific suggestions made by S to T on the interphone (Fig. 1). Though the rhythm of the calls was in fact less frequent than in this abridged example, it shows how to increase tension during the session, so that the logic of the intervention as worked out by the therapeutic team becomes more and more stringent.

The couple are speaking about Cristina's last drawing. The mother seems interested in it and from time to time expresses disappointment at her husband's indifferent replies.

S: (calls T on the interphone) Ask the husband, then the wife, to draw on the blackboard the drawing Cristina did at home.

Since Cristina serves as a go-between in her parents' marital conflicts, asking the parents to reproduce her drawing is a way of starting to explore each partner's individuality — without depriving them too abruptly of the protection afforded to them by speaking of themselves through Cristina. It represents a first step towards individuation.

> *T:* (handing the chalk to the husband) Draw your daughter's drawing for me. Perhaps you can use half the blackboard, so that your wife can try after you.

At first the husband is reticent, but then he sets to work while making comments on the drawing. In the meantime T asks him questions intended to elicit clear personal definitions.

> *S:* (on the interphone) Now ask the father to interpret Cristina's drawing. First draw the daughter's drawing, then interpret it: two steps towards a progressive revelation of emotions.
> *T:* (turning to the father) What does your daughter's drawing say to you?
> *Husband:* Well it's difficult for me to interpret Cristina, even if she does resemble me.
> *S:* (on the interphone) Put the question another way: what do you think your daughter wanted to communicate to you, her father, with this drawing?

S intervened immediately to forestall the father's eventual flight from a question which seemed too revealing: not what he thinks, but what he thinks the daughter has communicated to him.

> *T:* Precisely because your daughter resembles you, you are the person best able to help me understand! What can Cristina have wanted to say to you with that drawing?
> *Husband:* Well . . . perhaps that she would like more attention from me, that I should be more tolerant towards her . . . something like that. In fact she's a very lonely child. Often I can't understand her, talk to her. Perhaps at her age it's normal . . . I don't know . . .
> *S:* (on the interphone) Ask the husband to draw a picture he might have drawn at the age of eight.

The request continues referring to Cristina's drawing, but goes direct to the father's emotions. T conveys S's suggestion to the husband. The husband sets about drawing, but stops after a few strokes, leaves the drawing and starts to speak, overcome by strong emotion.

> *Husband:* I was alone at an institution . . . I was only eight years old and I felt like an orphan. My parents thought that by putting me there they had got rid of a problem, that they could finally think of putting aside a few filthy coins. I felt that no-one was in any way interested in me . . . my shoes became tighter and tighter as

I grew bigger . . . in one of them there was a nail, always that same nail, nobody ever thought of having them repaired and I . . . always had that suffering inside me . . .

The wife participates intensely, and seems very upset at seeing her husband openly express emotions which he had never revealed when they had been alone together. Afterwards it will be easier for the wife to speak of her emotions, when discussing their daughter's drawing. The objectives of the session have started to be realized. The supervisor's interventions enable them to pass from *speaking around the problem to acting* (by means of the drawing), *from using Cristina to speak of themselves to speaking of themselves directly.*

In the following example the supervisor's entrance (Fig. 3a.) transforms a context permeated by a general sense of impotence into a situation in which the symptomatic function of the patient, a heroin addict, is seen as correlated to the function of other family members.

The supervisor provokes the patient by bringing to the session a metaphorical object (Angelo, 1980), a syringe, which becomes the reference point for the entire system in this session.

Alberto, the identified patient, has been silent with an expression of guilt and shame for a good half of the session, preventing his parents and elder sister from shifting attention away from him. Everyone, including the therapist, seems almost paralysed by his behaviour.

The supervisor, after asking permission from the therapist and the family on the interphone, enters the room in an attempt to unblock a context which is decidedly unproductive.

S: (comes up to Alberto showing him a syringe) Who do you help most with this?
Alberto: (after a long silence) I don't understand.
S: (putting the syringe in his hand) Who do you help most with this? (He goes to sit next to the therapist. A tense silence comes over the room which lasts several minutes.)
Alberto: My father.
Father: So you help me!?
S: (takes the syringe from Alberto's hands and gives it to the father) How?
Father: (irritated) How what?
S: Your son has said that he thinks he is helping you. How do you think that your son wants to help you?
Father: I really don't think I need his help! . . .
S: (giving the syringe to the mother) Perhaps your husband has it in for me . . . he doesn't seem to have any intention of helping me understand.
Father: Well, on the contrary . . .
S: (interrupting) You've had your turn . . . let's hear your wife.
Mother: Perhaps . . . Alberto thinks that my husband . . . well, you know, at home I've always taken care of everything . . . He never understood even when I needed him . . . (starts to cry).

S: (hands the syringe to the sister) Let's hear what you have to say.

Sister: (shaking the syringe in the air) In the first place he helps papa by making him understand that when he uses this . . . it's the same as when papa drinks!

The following example is composed of two successive parts. The first fragment illustrates how an unproductive context can be blocked by directly provoking the therapist in the presence of the family (Fig. 3b.).

The pragmatic effects of this strategy can be seen clearly in the second fragment which occurred a few sessions later. Here the therapist has regained full control of the therapeutic relationship and is able to carry out, in a creative and self-assured way, the strategy agreed on with the supervisor. The context has changed radically, and everyone now feels personally committed to reactivating the family drama.

The Calo couple are quarrelling openly during the session. The motive is Marco, their eldest five-year-old child, who for over a year has been behaving strangely: he alternatively wears skirts and trousers; he plays with dolls, and wants to go to bed with mama's pyjamas. Is it mama's or papa's fault? This is the perpetual question which the two are constantly struggling with, perhaps to avoid another question which would undoubtedly be more menacing: what function does Marco's symptom have in their relationship, and what does it say about their own sexual identities?

In the vain attempt to evade the request of acting as arbiter, the therapist ends by falling into the role of a babysitter, taking care of the children while the couple continue to fight. A quarter of an hour of shouts and insults are not enough for her to realize that her apparent neutrality is reinforcing the quarrel. The central position she maintains in this first session in fact substitutes her for the patient, in the role of maintaining the habitual behaviour between the parents. In striving not to make alliances with either one or the other, she is unaware of the couple's complicity in avoiding any real confrontation. From time to time they look questioningly at the therapist and with a knowing smile seem to be saying, "What have we come here for, since the only thing she can do is play with the children?" The supervisor enters the therapy room without any warning, rapidly greets the couple and sits in front of the therapist. His glances and his gestures are directed exclusively at her, leaving the couple out.

S: It bothers me to accept the definition that they (indicating the couple but continuing to look at the therapist) are here because they don't agree. My problem, however, is not with them but with you, who are apathetically accepting this definition.

The problem then is not the quarrel, but the use which the couple make of it to cover their reciprocal protectiveness and dependence. This message is intended for the couple, but it is communicated to the therapist. The supervisor attacks the reinforcement which the therapist—through her attempts to be a neutral mediator—brings to the definition of the problem.

> *Husband:* But we . . .
> *S:* I don't want to speak with you, I want to speak with Ms Conforti.

The temporary exclusion of the couple blocks possible arguments, implicitly urging the two to participate for the rest of the session at a different level.

> *T:* I agree with you but it's very difficult.
> *S:* You don't agree with me! Otherwise you wouldn't let them (indicating the couple) fill the room with anger and rancour, which they throw around like a boomerang.

The therapeutic strategy is reinforced by the disagreement between the supervisor and the therapist, which turns out to be as effective as it is unexpected.

> *T:* It seemed to me that there was a possibility . . . to speak in a different way.
> *S:* Do you see that you don't agree at all? Up till now I haven't felt that there was any possibility, perhaps there was too much chaos in the room.
> *T:* (turning towards the supervisor) How can I prevent this from happening?
> *S:* Switch channels and see if you can find some reason why it would be useful for them to return here, instead of wasting time with useless discussions.

Provocation now makes way for an alternative. The therapist will have to channel the aggression accumulated towards the supervisor in order to interrupt futile sequences.

> *T:* But they (indicating the couple) link their difficulty to contingent problems, for this reason it's difficult.
> *S:* Well, for them it's understandable . . . (to the wife) For how many years have you been married?
> *Wife:* Seven.
> *S:* Seven years, they've been playing this game for seven years, so they have every right. But I can't approve of your accepting it! They have the right to link things as it suits them, but not you! (He gets up and leaves the room.)

The apparent acceptance of "rights" for the couple is very provocative, all the more so since these are denied to the therapist.

The supervisor's unexpected entrance, and his open disagreement with the therapist in front of the couple, bring about a sharp change of context, which forces the therapist and the couple to come out into the open. The therapist will be compelled to break through the couple's protective circuit (quarrelling), rather than reinforce it; the couple will have to interrupt their futile game to present a more substantial request for change. In this case the provocation, ultimately intended for the family, has the therapist as its intermediate target. Since she does not seem able to shake the family's defences, to which her own are linked, the supervisor tries to break her defences to enable her—in a kind of chain mechanism—to start to break down those of the family. The input transmitted to the therapist is, in fact, the same input that she should transmit to the family: supervisor-therapist-family are three links in the same communicational chain.

Although this strategy might have been inappropriate for a novice, it was highly effective with an expert therapist, able to use in a creative way the stress caused by the supervisor's challenge. Lastly, it is evident in this example that the experience of therapeutic effectiveness is a powerful learning experience for the therapist.

A few sessions later the Calo couple show a considerable change in their relationship with the therapist, who is now altogether in control of the session. In this case the therapist leaves the room (Fig. 2) in order to *construct* with the supervisor *a strategy* intended to provoke the family's network of reciprocal functions which seems to sustain the child's symptoms.

The supervisor and the therapist decide together to invite the whole family to tell a story about a child who does not know how to answer the following: who has the penis in the family, papa or mama? The aim is to make explicit the relationship between the function of Marco's symptoms and the functions of his parents, in a context in which the couple can express their conflicts concerning their own sexuality.

The therapist returns to resume the session.

T: Now I want to play with you. We must move the chairs and sit on the floor, (all sit, laughing). Let's play a game like this, the grown-ups will tell the children a story . . . I'll start.
Mother: Then who'll follow?
T: You decide . . . Once upon a time there was a child who didn't really know whether it was his papa who had the piddler or whether it was his mama . . . Who'll take over now, mama or papa?
Mother: Marco, you must listen.
Father: (turning to Marco) Then . . . this child who didn't know whether his papa had a HE-piddler or a SHE-piddler, what does he do to find out what his papa has? He says, "If I go to see papa when he undresses I'll understand. And if I want to know without seeing him undressed what'll I do?"
T: Should mama continue?
Marco: No . . . me . . . I already know, it's a HE-piddler!
Mother: Who has it?
Marco: Papa has it!
Mother: Then this child, who isn't sure at all, puts on his mama's clothes and his papa's clothes, but he puts his papa's clothes underneath and his mama's clothes on top.

Marco: No!
T: And he's so good at putting mama's clothes on top and papa's clothes under that he confuses everyone's ideas. He also knows that if he wants to keep everyone happy, it's much better to wear a skirt and pants.
Father: Not only that, but since he wears a skirt and pants he can be a man when it suits him and a woman when it suits him, isn't that so?
Marco: Well . . . yes!

The next example illustrates how useful it can be to divide a family during the session, using the one-way mirror as a diaphragm (Fig. 4.). Besides permitting the therapist to explore specific sequences at the subsystem level, while blocking inopportune interactions on the part of other members of the family, it encourages the family to *listen* instead of denying the *need* for differentiation of its members. In the fragment described, the suggestion of a game to be played during the session permits a kind of restructuring of the therapeutic system: part of the family plays the game with the therapist while the rest of the family and the supervisor watch from the room.

Such restructuring, which seems simple because motivated by a game, conceals a high level of provocation because it challenges the credibility of the definitions presented by the family members.

Annalisa, a ten-year-old child, is brought for therapy because in the past few months she has been surprised while stealing at home and in a department store. During the first session the parents express discordant views: whereas the father tends to exaggerate the importance of his daughter's behaviour, the mother completely justifies the child. In a short time the following network of relationships comes to light: the mother feels insecure in her educational function and incapable of confronting her husband, who interferes and criticizes her. The husband feels sure of himself only when he can deny his wife's competence; he foresees a future full of uncertainty for the child, whose symptomatology seems to confirm and stabilize both positions. S and T agree in this case to attack the functions of incompetence of the mother and interference by the father, at the same time motivating the child to behave normally during the session.

The family is divided as follows: the mother, Annalisa and Ruggero, her six-year-old brother, organize a game in which they all participate, while the father, from the observation room, observes his wife in her relationship with the children. He is to subsequently describe in detail her qualities (qualities which he claims that he would be very happy to "discover").

Electrified by the proposal the children immediately invent a game. The mother and the therapist are customers in a restaurant, while the children play the part of waiters and then organize a show with dancing and singing for the clients. The children enjoy themselves very much and their mother seems radiant. The husband, forced by the evidence to dwell on his wife's self-possessed and competent ways, mutters in a surprised way behind the mirror.

T and S have made the spatial division more incisive. T encourages the mother to let herself go without any fear of her husband's critical gaze; S, with the attention he gives the game, shows the importance he attaches to this observation and provokes the husband, by ironically congratulating him on having chosen such a capable and self-possessed woman.

In the second part of the session, when the family is reunited, the context appears definitely changed: the wife's attitude is less submissive towards her husband, who is now compelled to define himself instead of hiding behind sterile criticisms. The game has enabled the wife to recover her competence, so that she can start to give up the role of the yielding, dominated wife, which had previously reinforced the husband's need to be in control, thus perpetuating a truly vicious circle.

Conclusions

Provocative supervision can be considered either *didactic* or *strategic*, according to whether interest is directed towards training the family therapist or towards making the therapeutic strategy incisive. However, we feel that these two objectives cannot be separated since they co-exist in reality, even if in different proportions: didactic supervision is also strategic, and the latter must necessarily be instructive as well.

It is evident that the degree of stress brought about by supervision must be calibrated according to the therapist's level of experience. The stress and confusion caused by the supervisor's input are necessary stages in the evolution of the therapeutic system, as it moves from one level of integration to the next through a process of progressive differentiation of the individuals. This stress can only be fully accepted and understood by a therapist who has rejected much of the conditioning derived from stereotypes of professional relationships. In fact a therapist who is starting out is usually unwilling to accept interventions which require utilizing his own unexpressed potentialities. Rather, he prefers to use a familiar repertoire, which is less likely to expose him to uncomfortable situations. An experienced therapist, on the other hand, is able to put to advantage stress arising from unexpected input: instead of feeling incapable, he is able to integrate the new input into the intervention, thereby *learning directly on the job* how to use new and more differentiated parts of himself. This is what we propose to achieve in our training programmes, which consist of two co-existing activities: *group work* and *direct supervision*. The latter is offered by the trainers after the first year of study and continues, parallel with group work, for the next three years, either with the entire group or in sub-groups of two to four students.

One of the principal objectives during this period is to teach a provocative approach. In the first stage this is transmitted to the student through theoretical and practical work with the group, where the trainer, though guaranteeing full support to the student, assumes a very provocative position.[4] "Rather than protecting students from the embarrassment they feel at individuating themselves in the group, he forces them to reveal themselves by using various techniques of activation" (Andolfi and Menghi, 1980).

In the second stage the provocative approach, which the students have already experienced in person in analysing the systemic functioning of their own group, is introduced again — as we have shown in this article — during the process of supervision. In both cases supervision is aimed at fostering the progressive individuation of the therapist: first within the *learning* system, then in the *therapeutic* system. In the therapeutic system supervisor, therapist and members of the family must experience new and more varied ways of relating based on *choice* rather than on *necessity*. As the system evolves in an equilibrium between homeostasis and transformation, every individual must gradually progress from the position of *being forced to exist* ("I can't exist unless someone commands me") to that of *having permission to exist* ("I can be myself, but only in the role granted to me") to arrive at *being able to exist* ("I can exist freely, liberated as much as possible from the conditioning of others"). That is, the individuals must progress from co-existing at the *functional* level to choosing to co-exist at the *personal* level (Piperno, 1979).

The outcome of therapy can therefore be evaluated on the basis of the type of relationships which have been established during therapy, which may be either flexible or rigid and, even more, on the basis of the mode of termination. Supervisor, therapist and members of the family must reach a point where they can make a mutual decision to separate. In fact, before this can happen it may become necessary during therapy to establish a new set of reciprocal relationships among the members of the therapeutic system; this new system may be more or less consciously perceived as a lasting relationship, with each member again taking on rigid functions.

Supervisor and therapist must therefore be the first to perceive themselves as distinct and self-sufficient entities, and to be capable of changing their own ways of relating during the course of therapy. The possibility of the members of the family to differentiate from each other and to separate from the therapist is directly proportional to the therapist's ability to vary his ways of relating over a period of time. This ability becomes the most important metaphor for the family in its own search for new solutions.

Notes

1. The elaboration and experimentation of this model of live supervision have been carried out at the Family Therapy Institute, Rome.

2. The therapeutic team which is directly responsible for the progress of the therapy consists of the therapist and a supervisor. Usually an observer is associated with them (sometimes even two) with the function of controlling the entire therapeutic system. We are at present working on a study of the observer's functions in our model of provocative supervision.
3. T = Therapist, F = Family, S = Supervisor. These initials are used to show the various components of the system under discussion.
4. The relationship between trainer and students is based on an equilibrium between provocation and support.

References

Andolfi, M. (1979). *Family Therapy: An Interactional Approach*. Plenum Press, New York.

Andolfi, M. (1980). Prescribing the families' own dysfunctional rules as a therapeutic strategy. *J. Marriage Fam. Ther.* **6**, 29-36.

Andolfi, M. and Menghi, P. (1980). A model for training in family therapy. *Dimensions of Family Therapy* (M. Andolfi and I. Zwerling, eds), pp.239-260. Guilford Press, New York.

Andolfi, M., Menghi, P., Nicolo, A. M. and Saccu, C. (1980). Interaction in rigid systems: a model of intervention in families with a schizophrenic member. *Dimensions of Family Therapy* (M. Andolfi and I. Zwerling, eds), pp.171-204. Guilford Press, New York.

Angelo, C. (1980). The use of the metaphoric object in family therapy. *Am. J. Fam. Ther*, 69-78.

Piperno, R. (1979). La funzione della provocazione nel mantenimento omoeostatico dei sistemi rigidi. *Terapia Familiare* **5**, 39-50.

Stanton, M. D. (1981). Strategic approaches to family therapy. *Handbook of Family Therapy* (A. S. Gurman and D. P. Kniskern, eds), pp.361-402. Brunner/Mazel, New York.

16. Supervision of the Double Axis Model of Therapy

Chris Hatcher

Introduction

General characteristics of family therapy supervision

A great deal has been written, primarily from an analytic base, about the individual supervision of individual therapy. Considerably less information has been available about supervision of any kind of family therapy. This chapter will look at some of the general characteristics that distinguish family therapy supervision, and will then present the double axis model of therapeutic and supervisory process, developed in the Family Therapy Programme, Langley Porter Psychiatric Institute, University of California, San Francisco. In my own survey of therapists, agreement emerged on the following general characteristics:

(1) Family supervisors employ more direct observation of data. Whether by audiotape, videotape, live demonstration interview, one-way mirror, or co-therapy, the family supervisor clearly communicates his viewpoint that verbal report of the trainee is too susceptible to errors of omission or bias. While supervisors of other therapies may occasionally use these direct data techniques, the family supervisor favours their use all or about all of the time. He further does not believe that verbal report is something that can be trained to sufficient accuracy. Accomplished as well as beginning family therapists are to present their work directly.

(2) Family supervisors are more active in offering observations. They talk more, both in asking questions about what the trainee has observed as well as making statements about what they see. We are not necessarily referring to directing or dominating the supervisory session, although that can become an issue. We are saying that the family supervisor, like the therapy that he is teaching, is more *interactive*.

(3) Family supervisors are more likely to be focused on present interaction than past. Consistent with their theoretical positions emphasizing process analysis, they are far more concerned with who is doing what to whom, than with content

197

FAMILY THERAPY SUPERVISION
ISBN 0-12-794815-5

analysis or history taking. They frequently return the trainee to a missed interaction and stress the importance of devoting considerable concentration on the entire family's present behaviour. When family supervisors do live family demonstration sessions, they usually do not want the historical background, preferring to draw their impressions from what the family displays in the interview.

(4) Family supervisors are more likely to be focused upon the interpersonal than the intrapersonal. Traditionally, family therapy has primarily focused upon interpersonal or transactional issues (Hatcher, 1978). Its major contributions have been in the development of communication analysis, communication opening techniques, and in illuminating group responsibility in the creation of an identified patient. Issues of personal responsibility versus family and group responsibility have received far less attention. To spend a large portion of a family session exploring an issue intrapersonally with one member would be an uncommon event for family therapists.

(5) Family supervisors are more likely to offer a specific intervention idea or technique. While not neglecting overviews of the family's dynamics, his attention to process naturally leads to the development of specific interventions. In general, the family supervisor will offer an intervention as an illustration of his strategy with the family. He considers it to be all right for a trainee to ask how the supervisor would have responded in a given situation, and all right for the supervisor to respond. He will begin to delay these offerings if he feels that the trainee is not developing his own ideas, but begins with a more co-operative, shared exchange premise about the supervisory sessions.

(6) The family supervisor is somewhat more likely to support the trainee's use of self-disclosure with the family. He will assist the trainee in understanding his role as a very real member of this family. The trainee must learn to provide support and empathy without losing his own boundaries in the situation. The trainee is encouraged to strategically use self-disclosure of feelings or of a past event in his family, as a model of communication and an impetus to movement. Family supervisors trained from the perspective of the humanistic movement clearly anchor one end of the self-disclosure continuum, but even those trained from a more traditional perspective actively discuss and employ this technique.

(7) The family supervisor is somewhat more likely to employ group, as well as individual supervision. A common rationale for this does not exist but four to six heads are considered to be better than one, while twenty heads are considered too many. Whether it is because he is more comfortable in a group setting, he wishes the trainee to deal with the "family" of trainees, or stresses the utility of several observers to complex family process, the family supervisor likes to use both formats. Further, he is more likely to support a "democratic" process within this group supervision, encouraging each member to express ideas and to be listened to. The analogy to family therapy process is clear.

(8) The family supervisor is more likely to have an explicit agreement with the trainee approving work with the trainee's family of origin. He views this as an essential part of becoming a family therapist, but does not label it as therapy. While engaging in this work, the family supervisor will share experiences from his own family of origin and attempt to relate them to this behaviour and growth as a family therapist. If a family of origin issue appears over and over again, he will establish a boundary and recommend that the trainee consider work with a therapist on this issue. However, even if the trainee is in therapy, the family supervisor will not retreat from an issue if it is impacting on a family in treatment.

The preceding eight points represent one view of some general characteristics of family supervision, and provides us a common base with which to begin to look at our programme at the University of California, San Francisco.

The Supervisory Context

In order to set the stage for the supervisory model utilized, it is necessary to briefly examine the overall training programme and the setting in which it exists. In contrast to some of the other programmes referenced in this book, the Family Therapy Programme, Langley Porter Psychiatric Institute, University of California, San Francisco, is based in a department of psychiatry in an urban university heavily committed to graduate education and research. Our faculty consists of 17 members, two of which are full time and the remainder are part time. The programme is committed to exposing students to different theories and styles, and every major approach is represented. The trainees are enrolled in the mental health training programmes of the university and are subsequently selected for participation. In the family programme, they generally start having completed beginning training in psychotherapy, are with the programme part time, from one to two years, and carry other graduate work concurrently. An exception to this is the psychology post-doctoral fellow in family therapy who works exclusively in the programme for one year. The programme provides teaching, research and clinical service to the outpatient department and to an inpatient adolescent unit.

There are three characteristics to the U.C.S.F. (University of California, San Francisco) programme which we feel gives a distinctive focus. First, most historians in family therapy agree that application came first, followed by attempts to conceptualize and frame what was happening. As compared to other, older psychotherapies, we still do not have a unified and well developed theory. There are several excellent and even testable, models, but not a fully developed theory. Bell (1978) has pointed to family therapy's middle age. The grey hairs and the "remember when" stories are here. There is a tendency to accept things as they have been, with flashes of recognition that we just do not have the sense of coherence and unity hoped for at a younger age. While general systems theory would represent the best label for the U.C.S.F. programme, we are committed to having trainees see family therapy practised from a variety of perspectives and personal styles. The programme strives to teach the trainee to think critically, noting common, as well as distinctive elements. We are assisted by the fact that our trainees have already completed their beginning clinical training. Even so, this is not the easiest way to proceed, but the end product is felt to be a more adaptive and inquiring professional.

Secondly, there is a major investment in the importance of intercultural and subcultural family systems. This includes not only the substantial U.S. populations having strong cultural and ethnic heritages from other countries, but also the regional and subcultural differences. For example, a family growing up in New York City and a family growing up in Los Angeles have very different experiences and develop some very different behavioural expectations. Effective family therapy requires sensitization and education to these issues. Obviously, no trainee can learn all of these varied experiences and expectations, so we aim to train the therapist to be a respectful student and detective of a value system that may be quite different from his own. This investment directly involves us in the sharpner-leveller cognitive dimension. The sharpners are those that tend to emphasize differences, while levellers tend to emphasize common elements. The pitfalls of moving too heavily in either direction are evident. Our training and supervision is somewhat toward the sharpner side, and that it is important to represent this in the family therapy field.

Thirdly, we do attribute importance to intrapersonal issues and responsibilities, and do provide training on ways to work on this in the family therapy setting. As previously referenced in the discussion of general characteristics of family therapy supervision, the focus tends to be almost exclusively upon interpersonal issues. Part of this focus comes from early family therapists' recognition of its neglect in other therapies, but part of it comes from a later political motivation to define family therapy's separateness and uniqueness from other therapies. Family therapy is now known and recognized as a major treatment modality almost everywhere, so there are few political battles left to fight. The concept of group responsibility in the creation of an identified patient is in every major review text of psychotherapy. An equally important phenomenon, however, is the individual who takes a mostly intrapersonal issue and attempts to make the group responsible for it. Family therapists criticize traditional individual therapists for their lack of awareness about interpersonal issues, while traditional individual therapists criticize our lack of attention to working with intrapersonal issues. It is time for family therapists and teachers to recognize the logic of that criticism, and we have been developing procedures in this area which are detailed in previous publications (Hatcher, 1978; Hatcher and Himelstein, 1976).

Trainee Experience

The trainee enters a combined programme of group seminar, supervision and teaching, four or five session topic workshops, family cases and individual supervision. The seminar is one and a half hours per week, with about half of the sessions devoted to group video tape review of trainees cases and half devoted to a family development teaching format. The trainee sees an average of two to three families per week with an individual supervision ratio of one hour to each hour of therapy during the first four months. After that the ratio becomes 1:2. Faculty would prefer to maintain the 1:1 ratio, but this has not been economically feasible within the university. The trainee participates in two to three weekend or one day a week for four to five weeks' workshops by faculty. A great deal of live demonstration of different types of families and ways to work with them is done here, with the trainee often being asked to participate. Further, a three day international symposium is held each year on a selected topic in family therapy or relationships. This is explained in an explicit contract between trainee and faculty which includes trainee responsibilities, and the need to do family of origin work as well. Further descriptive material of programme design and course content is available elsewhere (Hatcher, 1979).

Conceptual Framework, The Double Axis Model

The supervisory process, as well as the therapy itself, is guided by the double axis model. As can be seen in Fig. 1, the vertical axis represents the family's past to future relationships. The horizontal axis represents their relationships outside

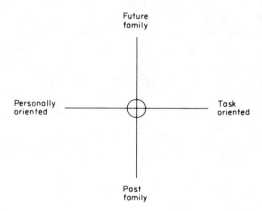

Fig. 1. The double axis model of therapy.

the family. On the right side are the task-oriented relationships where a business or similar function is the primary reason for the existence of the relationship. On the left side are the personally-oriented relationships where shared interests, values, or experiences are the primary reasons for the relationship. The intersection of the double axis is the family's current state, or inner core.

There are six stages in the use of the double axis model. While stages overlap, they serve as a guide for both supervisors and beginning family therapists as they approach the beginning stage.

Stage 1

The initial task (Fig. 1) is to explore the family's current state, or the inner core of the axis. A great deal of attention is paid to observation of data. The trainee begins to learn to separate out his observations of actual behaviour, his feelings stimulated by the various family members, and his hypothesis about past and future behaviour in the family. In our experience, trainees tend to mix the first two and make the third a factual conclusion. It requires substantial attention on the part of the new trainee to learn accurate behavioural reporting. Of particular behavioural importance are the communication patterns of transmission, reception and clarification. Are messages well sent and well received in the family, and if not, how are those discrepancies clarified? As this is accomplished for the family within the therapy session, a parallel process is being worked out between trainee and supervisor within the supervisory session.

In the midst of this, care must be taken that trainee feelings about the family be viewed as a useful resource, neither as a liability to be suppressed, nor as the sole guide for therapy. This can be a difficult area for the trainee as he is exposed to models from other therapies that promote the former or latter positions.

To pursue our goal of gaining some separation between the three, extensive use is made in supervision of videotape review and stop action simulation. A basic honesty and directness must be established in this stage also. The therapist must openly describe the programme, his status as a trainee, the purpose and use of video and other supervisory procedures, and the evaluation period. Most trainees are uncomfortable with their lack of experience; most families are uncomfortable with some aspect of their family functioning. Honesty in the former provides for a relief of tension and promotes a similar experience for the latter. This principle of self-disclosure is continued in the supervisory relationship. A stronger bond is formed if the supervisor is able to volunteer some of his own specific insecurities and difficulties as a trainee, as well as issues which still tax him in doing therapy.

Stage 2

In Stage 1, the trainee has learned about communication patterns of transmission, reception, and clarification within the family. He now proceeds to

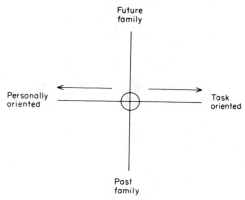

Fig. 2. The double axis model of therapy.

explore members' task oriented and personally oriented relationships outside the family (Fig. 2). Primarily, this assists him in seeing if behaviour observed within the family is evidenced in other social relationships. For example, does the father have similar difficulties making himself understood in one or more of his task oriented relationships? Does the son have similar difficulties in making activity plans in his personally oriented relationships? If the answers are yes, this defuses the immediate pressure upon the family and assists in "descapegoating" the family relationship ("If you would just change, everything would be fine") or the identified patient ("We only have problems with you"). If no, proceed to Stage 3. This outward exploration helps to identify family members as focusers or dispersers. Focusers seek almost all of their emotional gratification from a single relationship, while dispersers spread these needs out among several relationships. A focuser-disperser marriage is one of the most emotionally unstable combinations. In a similar sense, if triangulation patterns are present within the family, they are very likely to be found in outside relationships too. For high-tension families, it is frequently easier for them to begin to understand a triangulation process if it is done in the context of an outside relationship. As a logical extension to triangulation by the family, transference/counter-transference issues must be attended to, as the trainee-therapist may be an object of triangulation also. Consistent with this outward movement on the horizontal axis, the trainee and supervisor begin to see how much of their new relationship is task oriented versus personally oriented, and how that affects their expectations of each other.

Stage 3

In Stage 3 (Fig. 3), the trainee goes down the vertical axis to the past. Unfulfilled expectations are the major cause of family dysfunction. The ways in

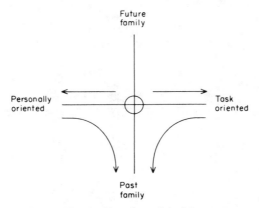

Fig. 3. The double axis model of therapy.

which those expectations were formed and life scripts subsequently created are important. Insight is certainly not everything, but family members do hide significant past events from each other, and the open discussion of these events has a very positive effect for most families. If the resulting reaction is very negative and unworkable, go back to Stage 2. The family has shown the trainee that they are not sufficiently supported in the current relationships line to accommodate Stage 3. The prime benefit of such past exploration is not so much the drawing of an accurate picture of the past, as gaining a picture of what is phenomenologically carried into the present. Here the trainee learns to employ projective expression. Family art work is used, primarily because few families are well defended in this medium. If a member is accomplished in art, an alternative projective medium in which the member is less likely to be defended is employed. The most common dynamics displayed by a partner or parent are feelings of anger and rejection by their father or mother, anger and rejection that they take out on their partner or children, semi-consciously demanding that they heal these past wounds. In a similar way, this stage usually activates the trainee's thoughts and feelings about his family of origin. Each of us has at least one event or area in which we feel our parents let us down. Trainees routinely report that such feelings and memories are more difficult to avoid in family cases, than in individual cases. The supervisor can easily be seen as a parental/authority figure with the possiblity of disappointing again and the possibility of healing also.

Stage 4

In Stage 4 (Fig. 4), the trainee goes back up the vertical axis to the family's current state. Information has now been obtained about current process in the

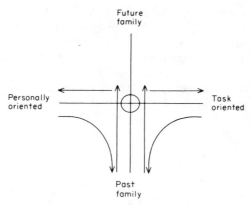

Fig. 4. The double axis model of therapy.

member's process outside the family, and experiences from the past phenomenologically carried forward into the present. The trainee should know that he will still have to return to these areas in later therapy, but working through each has been essential to etablishing goals for the therapy. An explicit agreement is obtained from all members about the goals. This begins with consensus on one very basic point: "What we're doing right now as a family isn't working". If this is not obtained, individual members have other agendas about their interest or what they want to use family therapy for. Frequently, an individual member or small alliance group has established good protection, and does not wish to risk a realignment of the pain and emotional energy amongst the conflicted members. Pressing into a goals agreement without dealing with such an issue will persistently keep the family magnetized to the intersection of the double axis, advancing slightly and then being pulled back. With consensus, goals are established with the trainee/therapist and the family expressing opinions. The family has the largest role in setting goals, but must logically acknowledge some trust in the trainee/therapist's abilities. Experimentation strategies are initiated with the family understanding that this carries the capacity for both positive and negative change. Just as the family must begin with a basic consensus, so must trainee and supervisor: "What we're doing right now isn't going to get us anywhere". This is not easy. The trainee has established a degree of comfort for himself in gathering information and conceptualizing dynamics. A reluctance to leave this comfort is naturally present. Since his experience base in family therapy is low, he, too, must acknowledge a degree of trust in his supervisor's guidance. If not, directions agreed upon in supervision will not be present or pursued enough in the therapy session. Further, the supervisor, trainee and family enter a value arena in establishing the goals for therapy. The experienced supervisor, even with his naturally distinctive cultural or subcultural background, has learned that families differ widely in their conceptions of what positive or ideal change might be, with attempts to impose another value system being usually unsuccessful. The trainee often carries an implicit assumption that *really* successful family therapy keeps the family together, walking happily into the sunset. He is disappointed when the family does not set their goals high enough, or fails to see certain pathological patterns. If this values conflict is unresolved, the trainee will pull himself back to Stage 3, seeking to show the family how negative values were acquired in their past.

Stage 5

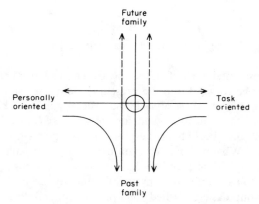

Fig. 5. The double axis model of therapy.

In Stage 5 (Fig. 5), the trainee goes up the vertical axis with the family into the future, experimenting with alterations in communication, role structures, alliance patterns and boundary setting. Here he is likely to run into the major blocking patterns: family myths or super rules. In a family myth, every member of the family is in some way invested in preventing change. This is distinguished from a minor blocking pattern, previously described in Stage 4, where one or two members are providing resistance. When the therapy first touches on the family myth in a conscious way, considerable anxiety is generated and the entire family goes running back down the vertical axis to the previous safety of the axis intersection. If unprepared for this by his supervisor, the trainee will also become anxious, often assuming that he has made a major mistake and wonders if he can really do this kind of therapy. In fact, he is just beginning to make progress, but such anxiety is a major test of the trust that the supervisor actually knows what he is doing. Meanwhile if the family myth is to be maintained, the family must enlist the trainee/therapist or expel him. This is the core challenge to therapeutic change. There seems to be some consistency of development in coping with this from beginning to advanced family therapists. From a well known analogy, the beginning family therapist tends to use wrestling to overpower the family myth with his own strength. Later, he learns judo to use the strength of other members to overpower the family myth. Finally, he learns aikido maintaining his position, but evading entrapment until the defensive power of the family myth is exhausted. Even trainees who know this analogy still seem to follow this path and the supervisor must maintain a sense of patience as the trainee develops. As the therapy begins to succeed, the trainee is very impressed. Because of the nature of family therapy training, he has most likely seen his supervisor in live demonstrations and, now, he is able to do some of this family therapy himself. The trainee, like the family, has moved up the vertical axis into uncharted territory. This produces a natural tendency to attach undue importance to any evidence of stability or control over this new area. This tendency can lead to an imprinting on the supervisor's techniques and/or therapy style. The supervisor's ego may be activated by such behaviour, but he must guide the trainee out of this imprinting and back to utilizing his own uniqueness.

Stage 6

There is no figure for Stage 6. Because in termination, the family moves up the vertical axis and off the page. As the issue of termination begins to come up, the big concern of the trainee is: "Are they ready?" The question is never really answerable, but can be viewed more easily from the perspective of the supervisor-trainee relationship. The supervisor, pleased with the trainee's progress and anxious to refine this progress, asks: "Has he learned enough?" The trainee, pleased with his progress and wanting to celebrate, asks: "When will I be good enough? When will he stop finding things to correct?" Both trainee for the family and supervisor for the trainee need to see these expectations as primarily generated by a need to maintain their "acquired family". Experienced supervisors are well aware of the difficulties for the trainee who has unworked-through separation material from his personal life. A less discussed issue is that of the trainee who has not experienced significant emotional loss in his personal life. Such a trainee will experience little difficulty in following termination schedule and separating from the family and supervisor. Frequently, this means a lingering sense of incompleteness for the family and some unexpected, often cryptic, remarks in the supervisor's final evaluation of the trainee. A mutual sharing of family of origin history of separation and loss is highly useful in identifying such a problem, but not necessarily in managing it. The supervisor cannot have the trainee go out and experience an emotional loss so he can come back to do better therapy next week. Therefore, the trainee must learn to listen and learn *from* the family in a now slightly shifted arrangement of roles in therapy.

Summary

This chapter has first explored some of the general characteristics of family therapy supervision, showing them to employ more direct observation of data, to be more active in both observations and techniques, to be more focused on the interpersonal than the intrapersonal, to support self-disclosure, to employ both group and individual supervision, and to work with the trainee's family of origin. The double axis model of therapeutic and supervisory process, developed at the University of California, San Francisco, was presented as a stimulus for further thought and discussion.

References

Bell, J. (1978). Family context therapy—model for family change. *J. Marriage Fam.*, **4**, 111-126.

Hatcher, C. (1978). Intrapersonal and interpersonal models: blending Gestalt and family therapies. *J. Marriage Fam. Counsell.* **4**, 63-68.

Hatcher, C. (1979). *Family Therapy Programme Brochure*. Langley Porter Psychiatric Institute, University of California, San Francisco.

Hatcher, C. and Himelstein, P. (eds) (1976). *Handbook of Gestalt Therapy*. Aronson, New York.

Part V
Contextual Issues in Supervision

17. Multilevel Training and Supervision in an Outpatient Service Programme

Karl Tomm and Lorraine Wright

Introduction

The Family Therapy Programme in the Faculty of Medicine at the University of Calgary was established as a mental health resource for families with children, mostly under 14 years who present with emotional or behavioural problems. The original goal was to develop a family therapy service which would provide a base for teaching and research activities. The Government of Alberta provided the initial grant in 1973 and continues to maintain fiscal support while the University provides the facilities. The programme has grown into a large outpatient service with an active caseload of 150-200 families at any one time and approximately 600 referrals per year. We are fortunate to have this large volume of families as a rich clinical resource for the learning experiences of our trainees.

A family interviewing method and a family systems conceptual orientation is applied in *every* case. All members of the household are invited to participate in the initial session and are encouraged to attend subsequent sessions whenever feasible and appropriate. Even when individual or marital interviews are provided (19 and 20% of all sessions respectively), they are conducted within the context of a family systems conceptualization.

Emphasis on direct observation, problem clarification, differentiation of problems at various system levels, circularity and feedback pervade both the therapeutic model and the training programme. Thus there is considerable consistency between the therapy process and the training process. Just as individual growth of the family member is not a primary focus in our family therapy approach, personal growth of the trainee is not a primary focus in our training programme. However, just as individual growth of a family member *does* occur indirectly when there is a positive outcome in the resolution of family system problems, so individual growth of the trainee occurs as a result of supervision in developing clinical skills for work with families.

211

FAMILY THERAPY SUPERVISION
ISBN 0-12-794815-5

Training Facilities

The excellent physical facility provided by the University in the Health Sciences Center of the Faculty of Medicine is an important component of our training programme. The architectural design of the physical space and the use of technical equipment has significant influence on the training activity in our setting. Considerable care was taken in the design to enhance the therapeutic and training capabilities of the Family Therapy Unit. For instance the interviewing rooms are decorated with paintings and plants much like a comfortable sitting room in a family home. The chairs were selected not only for comfort but easy mobility to allow spontaneous or therapeutic changes in seating arrangements during sessions. Blackboards in each room allow young children to show what is on their minds in the context of the family process. Therapists also use the blackboard from time to time to summarize or illustrate ideas about relationships.

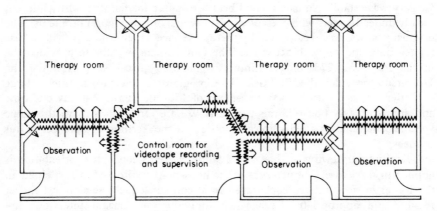

Fig. 1. Design for training flexibility: possible camera and observer viewpoints.

The suite of four therapy and three observation rooms are designed to provide a high degree of flexibility for the use of one-way screens, telephone intercom and videotape equipment (Fig. 1). Each therapy room has a one way screen so that the interview can be observed and supervised. Alternatively the observation rooms may be used as therapy rooms at peak periods of use. The therapy rooms may also be used for videotape recording. Remote control videotape cameras are visually and acoustically insulated by being built into triangular "book shelves" in the corners of the rooms. The technician in the central control room may record up to four interviews at one time. All rooms are connected with a telephone intercom. One room is also wired for an earphone. Each room may be "closed" for a private session by drawing the curtains and locking the videotape ports with wooden covers. With this degree of flexibility, the usual logistic problems of scheduling rooms for observation and supervision or arranging equipment for videotaping are minimized. We feel that these facilities have greatly enhanced the training in our programme.

Content of Training

Family assessment

The family assessment process includes two major procedures: data collection and problem delineation. A tripartite family assessment framework has been developed to outline specific categories for data. The three parameters of the tripartite framework include family structure, family functioning and family development. The family functioning parameter has drawn heavily from the Family Categories Schema (Epstein *et al.*, 1968).

All problems that are identified are listed according to level (individual, marital subsystem, whole family system, etc.) on a front sheet in the clinical record. This provides a summary that keeps the therapist aware of all the important problematic issues that have been raised in regards to this particular family.

Circular pattern diagramming

One of the idiosyncratic features of our assessment process is the concrete application of the cybernetic concept of feedback by using circular diagrams to conceptualize problems. Circular pattern diagramming is usually applied to summarize a dyadic relationship. Certain "stable" characteristics of two family members and recurrent sequences in their interaction are carefully selected on the basis of their "connectedness" to form a circular diagram. The resultant circular pattern is regarded as an ongoing, self-perpetuating structural element in the relationship. The use of these diagrams has facilitated our efforts to teach students to use circular rather than linear concepts. "Homeostasis" for instance is immediately apparent when the circular diagram is complete and events are seen to come full circle.

The basic components and links of a dyadic circular diagram are indicated in Fig. 2. The behavioural output of each interactant becomes the communicative information to provide the basis for the perceptual input for the other. Interpersonal linkages between behaviours are made on the basis of cognitive and/or affective inference of intrapsychic process. These inferences are explored by examining the meaning that one person's behaviours have for the other. The behaviour output of each interactant usually has a feedforward regulatory *intent*

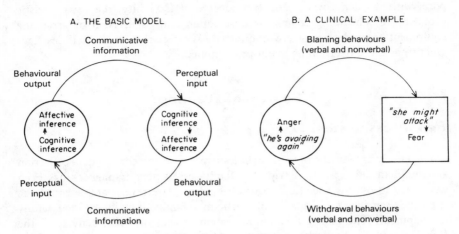

Fig. 2. Circular pattern diagramming.

but in fact has a positive cybernetic feedback *effect* that maintains or escalates the circular process (a more detailed discussion of the background theory is available in another paper, Tomm, 1980).

The circular pattern in Fig. 2B describes the common blame-withdrawal pattern that characterizes so many marriages among our clinical families. The wife in one particular family (represented by the circular enclosure on the left) kept blaming her husband (represented by the square enclosure) for various things that he should have but did not do. Her tone of voice, facial expression, pointed finger etc. conveyed considerable anger (affective inference). At the observational level, his withdrawal behaviour (no comment, changes subject, looks away, disinterested tone etc.) was clearly linked to her blaming and vice versa. What was less obvious was the meaning they attributed to each other's behaviour. Exploration of his cognitive and affective set revealed that he was fearful of her violent outbursts (e.g. she had once even attacked him with a knife). By withdrawing he tried to avoid conflict and to calm her down. Superficially she perceived his withdrawal as avoidance of responsibility and felt justified in her anger, but further exploration revealed that this was associated with a significant fear of loss. Repeated blaming represented her attempts to get him more involved and prevent further loss. Thus each inadvertently contributed to maintain a homeostatic pattern in the relationship, when each thought he was in fact trying to modify the other's behaviour.

By striving to identify such circular patterns the student is oriented to making *connections* based on meaning, to discovering missing links and to understanding why the status quo is perpetuated. When a student or therapist recognizes the circularity in graphic terms it is easier to keep it clearly in mind and to avoid taking sides inappropriately. He is also more readily able to help the family members shift from linear perceptions (that activate feedforward regulatory responses) to circular perceptions (based on cybernetic feedback).

Our efforts to conceptualize problems as circular process is not limited to the dyadic level. The alignments and splits of triads are also circular. Repetitive individual response patterns reflect circular intrapsychic process. Ultimately one strives to identify a circular pattern which includes all family members and explains the homeostatic impasse in the whole system.

Family treatment

Having assessed the family, the task of the clinician is to facilitate change that will be therapeutic. Change is seen to occur as a result of new connections in patterns of thought and behaviour. In our treatment approach we attempt to replace maladaptive interaction patterns with more adaptive ones. We try to achieve this by using various intervention techniques to interrupt and break problematic interaction patterns and encourage the emergence of constructive exchanges between family members. We also attempt to alter affective blocks by helping family members recognize the possible consequences of specific behaviour patterns and restructuring their perceptions of events. Recently our emphasis has shifted to focus more heavily on introducing new information into the system to alter patterns of thought. This information may be in the form of (a) new ideas, (b) new *connections* between existing ideas or (c) both. Thus the primary focus now is increasingly on altering patterns of thought with the expectation that changes in patterns of behaviour will follow. The current transition in treatment emphasis has been inspired in part by the innovations of the Milan group (Palazzoli *et al.*, 1978) and is being guided by the theories of Bateson (1972, 1979).

For teaching purposes, a specific family therapy model has been outlined and described for the Calgary programme. It organizes therapist activity at three levels: overall functions, general competencies and specific skills. The four major therapist functions are engagement, problem identification, change facilitation and termination. Each function includes several therapeutic competencies which in turn are described by a cluster of detailed skills. Two types of skills are described. Perceptual-conceptual skills refer to the therapist's ability to pick up and make sense of family data. Executive skills refer to his overt action in relation to the family. These skills are paired so that when a trainee does not display a specific executive skill, the supervisor may explore to see if he has in fact developed the perceptual-conceptual skill on which it is based. Almost 300 specific skills have been differentiated and documented in the form of instructional objectives to guide both supervisor and student (Tomm and Wright, 1979). They provide a more precise focus for the supervision process.

Levels of Training

Due to varying degrees of professional experience, clinical skill and academic achievement, four general levels of competence in family therapy have been differentiated for our programme. Levels 1 and 2 include students in the "Block Placement Programme" while levels 3 and 4 make up the clinical staff that comprise the "Family Therapy Team". Different learning experiences are available at each of these levels.

Level 1 is the novice therapist, e.g. an undergraduate medical or nursing student who is taking an in-depth elective in family therapy. Level 2 is the developing clinician who is usually a postgraduate student in psychiatry, family medicine, psychology or social work. (Mental health professionals who have been practising in the community and already have individual and/or group psychotherapy skills, but who join the programme as trainees to develop more expertise in family therapy, are also included in this group). Level 3 is the career family therapist who has had extensive training and experience in family therapy. All the "front-line" clinical staff in our programme are level 3 family therapists and most are also qualified in social work or psychology (usually with a Masters degree). Level 4 is the family therapy consultant and professional trainer who is recognized as having a high degree of expertise and is qualified at the doctorate level.

Assigned versus sapiential authority

These levels are organized in a hierarchical structure so that anyone at a higher level may be assigned to supervise anyone at a lower level. Level 4 consultants hold faculty appointments and carry the heaviest teaching responsibilities. Level 3 therapists carry a full caseload of families and supervise level 2 and level 1 students. A level 2 trainee (e.g. a psychiatric resident) may supervise a level 1 medical student in order to gain supervisory experience. Same level (peer) supervision occurs informally or may on occasion be arranged deliberately (e.g. a more senior level 3 therapist may supervise less experienced level 3 staff members).

It is important to emphasize that it is clinical and training responsibility and authority that is structured in this organizational hierarchy, *not* information, understanding or learning. For instance, when in the course of therapy a family member discloses suicidal intent the urgency with which the therapist is expected to seek supervision or consultation varies inversely with his level of competence. Specific clinical indications to seek supervision have been outlined as a guide for therapists at each level. The supervisee is expected to act on and follow through on the recommendations or directives of the supervisor. Thus a clear complementary relationship exists between individuals at different levels in

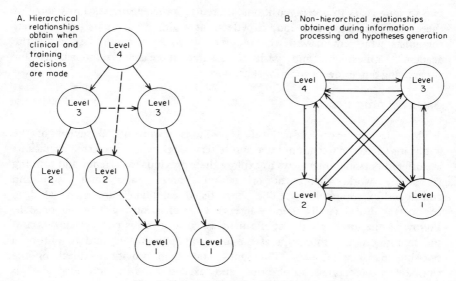

Fig. 3. Assigned vs sapiential authority.

regard to responsibility and authority (Fig. 3A). On the other hand when it comes to understanding clinical problems, the importance of specific data or the usefulness of a particular hypothesis takes priority over the level of the person who introduced the data or hypothesis (Fig. 3B). For instance, if a level 1 therapist proposes a more systemic and more complete hypothesis explaining the suicidal threat than the hypotheses offered by more senior therapists, the more "useful" explanation should take priority in planning therapeutic intervention. To promote the possibility that this sapiential authority will take priority over assigned authority, an atmosphere of mutual trust and respect must be maintained in the programme. Toward this end, senior staff regularly expose their clinical work not only for modelling but also for feedback by junior staff and students.

Level 3 training

The most intensive training offered in our programme is actually provided for our level 3 family therapists. Although these staff members are not considered students, they initially undergo intensive training and supervision in our particular assessment and treatment approach and then continue to be closely supervised on an ongoing basis for as long as they remain employed by the programme. Our experience has been that qualified professionals apply for these positions because of the unusual learning opportunity and then often leave after two to four years to accept positions offered by other agencies. Thus some of these staff positions function, in effect, as training positions. Those staff therapists who remain with the programme do so because they enjoy the academic atmosphere and wish to assume increasing responsibility for supervising our students and new staff.

Selection processes

The selection process for level 3 positions starts with a review of the applicant's letter, curriculum vitae and letters of reference. Preferred applicants are offered personal interviews to explore their previous experience and training in family work, theoretical orientation, career goals, motivation and colleagueship compatibility. The short listed candidates are then asked to conduct a clinical family therapy interview which is observed by senior staff. Following the interview the applicant is asked to give his conceptualization of the family process, to comment on his own interventions and to outline a possible management plan. The senior staff then provide feedback on the candidate's perceptual, conceptual and executive skills and evaluate his receptivity to feedback. Finally the most promising candidate is offered a staff position on a probationary basis (for six months) with the task of learning and incorporating our particular cybernetic-systems approach. During this time these new staff members receive live and videotape supervision and attend the regular theory seminars (organized for level 2 students). On successful completion of the probationary period the supervisory requirements are reduced but level 3 staff continue to receive regularly scheduled as well as *ad hoc* supervision of their interviews.

These career family therapists also receive training in the development of supervisory skills. They are assigned the task of supervising level 1 or level 2 students and are provided with back-up support in the form of supervision seminars and direct "supervision of supervision". During the supervision seminars, verbal reports are given of each student's progress in assessing families and in intervening as part of a "family-therapist system". The opportunity is also provided to discuss and delineate problems at the next interface, i.e. between the supervisor and the supervisee. In keeping with our emphasis on direct observation a level 4 senior supervisor intermittently observes the level 3 supervisor actually supervising the level 2 student. During this process the senior supervisor not only observes the interview to form his own impression of the family and of the student's skills, but also assesses the process and content of the level 3 supervisor's feedback to the student. Supervision of supervision (like therapy) requires the ability to evaluate relationship systems at multiple levels simultaneously (Fig. 4). Difficulties in the supervisor-supervisee relationship may be construed as problems in assessment due to confusion between issues of assigned versus sapiential authority. On the other hand the supervisor may complain that the student is uncooperative when in fact he does not understand how to implement a specific therapeutic intervention. Thus care is taken to differentiate the level of the problem(s) in the training process (much as in the family assessment process) and the career therapist-supervisor receives feedback on his supervisory skills.

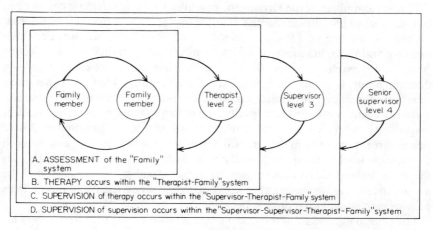

Fig. 4. Supervisory differentiation of problems at multiple system levels.

Level 3 family therapists may also act as preceptors in courses provided for undergraduate medical students. One course, "The Family in Health and Illness", is designed to provide undergraduate medical students with basic skills of family assessment. These future physicians are not expected to develop family therapy skills but are expected to become more aware of the possible relationship between problematic behaviour and some somatic symptoms (in a family member) and the interaction process of the whole family. Thus level 3 therapists have considerable opportunity to develop supervisory and teaching skills.

Level 1 and 2 training

As mentioned earlier formal training for *students* occurs in the "Block Placement Programme". These students are placed in the programme for varying blocks of time, from two to twelve months. Block placement students are expected to be committed to the programme for a minimum of half time but preferably full time, for the duration of their placement. Thus when students are introduced into the programme they find themselves immersed in patterns of conceptualization and practice which are heavily systems oriented. This immersion experience seems to have a beneficial impact on altering the more traditional linear and individual approaches which they may have learned prior to joining the programme.

Apart from the occasional outside professional who makes direct arrangements with the programme, these students are selected by their respective professional training programmes (although we reserve the right to refuse any particular student). For instance, psychiatric residents are selected by the Residency Training Committee of the Division of Psychiatry. Our programme has an open commitment to provide six months' training for each psychiatric resident during his second year and no additional selection procedure is carried out. For those degree-granting programmes in which family therapy training is an elective (social work, psychology, nursing, etc.), the student is also selected by his own discipline but a senior staff member of the Family Therapy Programme interviews the student to confirm his suitability prior to joining the programme.

Each student is assigned to a specific career family therapist who functions as his primary supervisor from the time he is assigned to the programme. Often two or three students from the same discipline are grouped together and assigned to the same level 3 therapist. Working in a small group has been advantageous for both supervisor and supervisee. A larger number of students may be accommodated (using group rather than one-to-one supervision) and the students provide each other with mutual support.

The clinical experience of the student begins by observing the interviews of his supervisor through the one-way screen. Gradually he is invited to sit in with the supervisor and participate in the interview itself. Depending on his progress in skill development the supervisor may remain out of the therapy room and supervise the student from behind the one-way screen. Through this step-by-step process (with different families) the student gradually absorbs the therapist's role by modelling himself after his primary supervisor. A level 1 student seldom moves beyond this stage. Nearly every interview he conducts is observed and supervised live. Level 2 trainees, however, progress more quickly and depending on their skills are eventually given the autonomy to select and carry their own cases with supervision provided by intermittent case discussion or videotape review.

Methods of Training

Direct clinical experience of interviewing families is essential for developing competence in family therapy. However, it is unfair and inappropriate to assign distressed families, who present themselves in good faith for skilled professional help, to students who have not yet developed at least some clinical competence. Didactic teaching and passive observation simply do not provide the opportunity required to develop executive skills in family therapy. Simulated role playing is an insufficient substitute to develop the interviewing skills required. Hence there is a dilemma; the student needs to have at least some clinical competence to be allowed to work with real families, yet this competence cannot be acquired without clinical experience. One way around this is to accept only those students who already have clinical experience in other therapeutic modalities. Another is to develop a pattern of service delivery in which the student's clinical work is very closely supervised. We use both approaches by differentiating levels and delineating different degrees of clinical responsibility. The following is a description of the types of learning experiences provided.

Seminars

Although supervised practice remains the backbone of our training programme, the initial orientation takes the form of assigned readings, seminars, observation and role playing. The seminars are held on a regular basis for two hours, twice a week for several weeks and once a week thereafter. These seminars tend to be didactic and cover basic systems theory, the assessment framework, the treatment model, specific intervention strategies and detailed skills. They are augmented with videotapes of selected interviews to illustrate interaction concepts and demonstrate particular interventions. Role playing exercises of simulated families are used to help students experience and identify the force of a system and to practise specific skills (e.g. refocusing, posing other-cognition queries, stimulating interaction). A library of videotapes is available for students to review at their leisure.

Students are also invited to attend the inservice training events for the clinical staff of the programme. Each week a brief academic presentation on a topic of current interest in family therapy or the mental health field generally, is followed by open discussion. Staff members may present relevant clinical issues for exploration, review journal articles or books, or report on conferences they have attended. Students are also encouraged to present at these weekly academic seminars on topics of personal interest.

Screenings

The single major teaching event in the programme is the Friday morning "screening". All staff and students are expected to participate in this in-depth assessment of a specific family and to evaluate the therapeutic process. Particularly difficult cases are usually dealt with in these sessions. The morning starts with an organized case presentation by the primary therapist. After some preliminary discussion the family is interviewed (usually by one of the consultants along with the primary therapist) while the remaining staff and students observe from behind the one-way screen. Feedback to the interviewers may occur during the screening by using the telephone intercom or an intersession discussion. (The intersession discussion is a brief interlude during the course of an interview when the therapists leave the room to consult with the observers before returning to continue the therapy.) After the interview there is a major in-depth discussion of both the family interaction process and the therapeutic process. We have found that this postsession discussion is more focused and productive when it starts with a formal review of specific facets of the interview. For instance, prior to the session particular observers are assigned assessment tasks such as basic data regarding differences, dyadic circular patterns, triadic patterns, key therapist interventions etc. These observers are expected to summarize observations related to their task during the postsession. In this way the observers become more involved and participate actively during the screening. This Friday morning training event is an important occasion for our staff and students to develop greater concensus in the use of terminology and in clarifying assessment concepts and intervention strategies.

Live supervision

When a student demonstrates a reasonable level of perceptual and conceptual skill he is encouraged to become directly involved with families to develop executive skills as well. Such involvement is supervised *live* until the student is recognized as having considerable competence at which time supervision may become *remote*. Live supervision refers to a process whereby the supervisor is present and observing during the actual interview. Usually the supervisor is behind the one-way screen so that he is less liable to take over and do the interviewing for the student. Remote supervision does not require the presence of the supervisor but depends on a verbal report of the interview or on the review of a videotape at a later date. The verbal report method is discouraged in our programme because the information presented by the trainee is inevitably edited and the supervisor loses the opportunity to form his own impressions from the raw data. Live supervision usually entails presession, intersession, and postsession discussion as well as intrasession input.

A typical live supervision session starts with *presession discussion* of the case. This may include a review of the family assessment, the problems identified, the overall treatment plan, specific intervention strategies and/or specific goals for this interview. Emphasis is, of course, given to the skill development of the therapist. For example, if in previous interviews a trainee has shown difficulty in exploring problems in a focused manner, then during the presession discussion (e.g. of an initial interview with a new family) the trainee may be given the task of remaining focused to obtain a clear and precise understanding of the presenting problem.

Intrasession input refers to suggestions or directives from the supervisor while the therapist is interviewing the family, through the use of a telephone intercom or an earphone. The intercom that has been installed in our interview and observation rooms is much like a telephone receiver and is not an open speaker that allows everyone in the room to hear the message. When the supervisor calls the therapist, the interview is very briefly interrupted while the therapist answers the 'phone and the message is conveyed. Families are, of course, always informed that the interview is being observed (and supervised) and usually readily accept these interruptions. This is particularly true when the therapist explicitly shares at least part of the message—a procedure which we now strongly encourage. The earphone is less intrusive but technically more difficult to use. It consists of a hearing-aid like device which contains a miniature radio receiver. One or more interviewers may wear an earphone and family members are usually not aware when the supervisor is speaking to them. The advantage of both these intrasession methods is that the supervisor's comments provide immediate corrective feedback and his suggestions can be implemented in the course of an ongoing session. Depending on the level and skill of the therapist, intrasession input may be provided in the form of specific "one liners" (e.g. "ask them how things are different since the heart attack") or in the form of a more general hypothesis (e.g. "explore the possibility that the fear of a heart attack now serves the function of avoiding confrontation with father"). A study within our programme of telephone intercom feedback has revealed that the length and form of the supervisor's statement is significant in regard to its usefulness during the interview (Wright, 1979).

When a trainee is unable to sustain a focus despite the supervisor's intrasession calls, the supervisor may request the trainee to come out of the room for *intersession discussion*. Sometimes the trainee becomes overwhelmed by the information presented by the family and requires an opportunity for more extensive discussion to understand what is happening and how to refocus the inquiry. It is of course necessary to adapt this supervisory process to the immediate process of the family. Occasionally an intersession discussion may be required to ease from focusing on one task to another primary task. For instance, if a specific family event is enshrouded with a considerable amount of sadness which the therapist does not deal with, the supervisor may suggest that the therapist shift his focus to uncover this affect and explore the related cognition. Some trainees have difficulty coping with intense sadness in family interviews. If this becomes evident as a consistent pattern the supervisor must identify it as a problem for that trainee and provide focused supervision to help the trainee develop the necessary skills to cope with that type of family resistance. If the trainee remains too confused by the whole situation the supervisor may join the trainee in the interview to demonstrate what the supervisor was suggesting.

Following the session the supervisor and trainee concentrate their *postsession discussion* on how the supervisee went about trying to meet the specific goal of remaining focused during the inquiry. Thus the live supervision process maintains a problem-solving focus with regard to the trainee's skills.

Videotape supervision

Videotape supervision is a particularly useful method for developing perceptual and conceptual skills. The major advantage of the videotape is that it may be stopped and replayed again and again. More time may be taken to carefully understand and evaluate the content and context of what is being said (as well as the accompanying non-verbal messages). Through review of videotape, trainees become more consciously aware of non-verbal process which lead to certain "intuitive" judgements. This helps in sharpening perceptual skills. A microscopic analysis of the session also allows the trainee to review his interventions and think through alternative interventions that could have been used at key points of the interview. Often videotape feedback is necessary to confront a trainee on certain idiosyncratic patterns of his interviewing style which he is not fully aware of (e.g. the tendency to avoid sadness). When a trainee has difficulties in his communicative style we encourage him to ask the technician to focus one camera on himself, another on the family and record a "split screen" tape. The student is then able to observe his own non-verbal communications (such as facial expressions, gestures and posture) in the context of the family's interactions. One student immediately recognized how "mousey" he must have appeared to the family and promptly began to change his interviewing style.

Case discussion and review of records

As noted earlier, supervision by verbal report is discouraged. However, there are times when an interview was neither observed nor videotaped but important events did transpire. Then typical case discussion does take place but only on an *ad hoc* basis. Once a supervisor gets to know a trainee's specific style and typical difficulties in therapy, it is often possible to identify the recurrence of a previous theme and through discussion readily reorient the trainee.

Another important method of providing supervisory feedback is through the review of the trainee's clinical record keeping. Intermittent audit of records is a well established method of maintaining quality control. The first clinical task students who are beginning are assigned, is to record their observations while watching their supervisor work. By reviewing the type of information trainees enter into the record and how it is formulated, the supervisor gains insight into the student's perceptual and conceptual skills. For instance, if on reviewing a student's problem list, the supervisor notes that problems are identified only as individual ones and are described in a linear fashion (e.g. mother is angry and blames too much) the supervisor encourages the student to reconceptualize the problem at a higher systemic level. The mother's problem may have been part of the maladaptive interactional pattern, e.g. father withdraws—mother feels angry and blames—father feels guilty and withdraws etc. Thus an individual problem may be raised to the level of being a marital subsystem problem. Other aspects of the record are reviewed to see if the trainee introduces a treatment plan that follows logically from the problems that have been defined. In other words, a treatment plan for a circular maladaptive pattern in the marriage would be different from a plan for a linear individual problem.

Caseload Review

The supervisor has the responsibility to intermittently review the whole caseload of families of each trainee. To assist in this process, data is systematically collected concerning each therapist's intakes, interviews, closures etc. Information is available on the number of sessions each family has been seen, the frequency of whole family versus marital and individual sessions, the time interval between sessions etc. Thus each trainee's overall pattern of practice may be reviewed and those cases with unusual patterns are readily identified. This can often be beneficial in assisting the therapist identify problems that he may not be aware of. For example, a male therapist seeing a single parent mother individually for several sessions may inadvertently suggest "suction" into a surrogate spouse role. The supervisor would draw this possibility to the therapist's attention and encourage him to bring in members of the mother's social network to facilitate more natural supports.

Consultation/cotherapy

An additional training method for level 3 and level 4 staff is the use of co-therapy, consultation and team supervision. Consultations may be provided by level 4 family therapists, psychiatrists, neurologists, paediatricians, psychometricians etc. depending on the issue that requires clarification. Typically the consultant provides his feedback and recommendations to the family in the presence of the primary therapist who then continues the ongoing case management. If necessary, however, the case may be transferred, or a second therapist be co-opted to remain involved in an on-going basis in a co-therapy role.

Evaluation

The most convincing evaluation of the outcome of training would be to demonstrate an improvement in a trainee's effectiveness in treating families.

However, it is impractical to obtain pretraining baseline measures of student effectiveness with families. As implied earlier it is unethical to allow beginning students to work with clinical families without supervision. We do ask our level 3 trainees to generate and retain videotape recordings of their early interviews for comparison with their later work, e.g. at the end of their probationary period. The programme also maintains an ongoing consumer satisfaction survey. All families seen for one or more interviews are sent a questionnaire three to six months after the case is closed. Trainees are given the opportunity to review the comments of the family and to evaluate them in the light of their therapeutic efforts. Return rates for these questionnaires are in the order of 60% and we now have feedback from over 1000 families. Approximately 74% of these families report improvement in the presenting problem but 9% report deterioration. These deterioration reports require further investigation and we hope to examine these cases in more detail in the future. Included in the questionnaire are invited comments on various competencies of the therapist, e.g. "Did the therapist help clarify relationship problems?"

A more rigorous research approach has been used in a smaller study to evaluate the effectiveness of teaching skills in family assessment. Using brief segments of videotape and short answer questions, pre- and post-tests were devised. These tests have been used to evaluate not only student learning as a result of our regular training programme but also to compare the effectiveness of differing teaching methods (Tomm and Leahey, 1980).

The most direct and specific evaluation of the trainee is the supervisor's written report of the trainee's skills. These reports serve to summarize and document the informal ongoing feedback on skill development provided to the student during the supervisory process. Specific comments are made regarding strengths and weaknesses in each of the therapeutic functions or competencies. The students are also asked to evaluate their own experience in the programme. Student feedback has been in the form of verbal report, written report and most recently by questionnaire. The latter encourages more differentiated comments on the seminars, screenings, live supervision and so on. All of this evaluative feedback contributes to the ongoing development of our training procedures. Along with many other inputs it facilitates the evolution of our programme at the University of Calgary.

References

Bateson, G. (1972). *Steps to an Ecology of Mind*. Chandler, San Francisco.
Bateson, G. (1979). *Mind and Nature: A Necessary Unity*. Dutton, New York.
Epstein, N., Segal, J. and Rakoff, V. (1968). *Family Categories Schema*. Unpublished manuscript.

Palazzoli, M. S., Boscolo, L., Cecchin, G. and Prata, G. (1978). *Paradox and Counter-paradox*. Aronson, New York.

Tomm, K. (1980). Towards a cybernetic-systems approach to family therapy at the University of Calgary. *Perspectives on Family Therapy* (D. Freeman, ed.). Butterworths, Toronto.

Tomm, K. and Leahey, M. (1980). Training in family assessment: a comparison of three methods. *J. Marriage Fam. Ther.* **6**, 453-458.

Tomm, K. and Wright, L. (1979). Training in family therapy: perceptual, conceptual and executive skills. *Family Process* **18**, 227-250.

Wright, L. (1979). Live supervision—analysis of "phone-ins" and the implications for training family therapists. Unpublished manuscript.

18. A Contextual Comparison of Three Training Programmes

Elsa Broder and Leon Sloman

Introduction

A basic tenet of family therapy is that an individual does not exist in isolation but is part of larger systems, the most significant of which is the family. The supervisor and his supervisee function in the context of the various institutions of which they are a part. In this chapter[1] we will examine the interrelationship of supervisee to various institutions and how exchange of information alters the content and process of supervision.

The authors teach in different settings but subscribe to a common philosophy that espouses systems theory as it applies to family adaptation. To us, family therapy implies both a way of conceptualizing and a way of acting. It may include work with an individual or a subsystem such as parents or siblings. Our techniques vary but we always have the goal of helping the family reach a higher level of homeostasis as exemplified by a more flexible and stable family system (Sloman, 1980; Speer, 1970).

In teaching we believe that it is important to observe the student's work directly. This enables the supervisor to draw attention to what the student has failed to observe or misinterpreted. Therefore, our supervision generally has an observed component either with the use of a one-way mirror or tapes, preferably videotapes.

We prefer to supervise the students in groups believing that this way of teaching has distinct advantages besides the obvious monetary and time efficiency aspects. Families can be role played and sculpted. A greater number of families can be seen extending experience and providing an opportunity to learn from observing how others in the group handle various therapeutic situations. As well, one can, in some ways, compare the group to a family in that supervisors, like parents, can encourage open communication, autonomy and mutual support, so promoting the growth of the members.

There has been a rapid expansion in the number of family therapy training

229

FAMILY THERAPY SUPERVISION
ISBN 0-12-794815-5

opportunities available. These programmes are directed at candidates with a wide diversity of therapeutic skills from the most rudimentary to the very sophisticated. Political forces influence the development of such programmes. As Sluzki has pointed out, what organizations say they want and what they do in practice is often poles apart (Sluzki, 1974). This can place the supervisor and his supervisee in an ambiguous situation which complicates the teaching and learning of family therapy.

To illustrate some of these issues, we will describe supervision in three different systems involving: (1) psychiatric residents,[2] (2) probation and aftercare officers (PACOs) and, (3) trainees of a family therapy training programme; Clarke Family Therapy Training Programme: (C.F.T.T.P.).

We plan to discuss points of similarity and difference between these programmes and the implications that we see for the supervision of family therapy.

Family therapy training of psychiatric residents

In most psychiatric centres the prevailing attitude towards family therapy training has been characterized by a reluctance to accept major involvement, so that in many university settings family therapy has grown like an unwanted stepchild. This is despite the extensive contribution to family therapy made by psychiatry.

At our University most of the family therapy training is done in child settings. Hence, while child psychiatry residents will have the opportunity of gaining experience during two of their four years of training, the average adult resident will have only six months in which to gain experience. The goals of training, therefore, have to be adapted to a time frame. Six months does not give enough time to train a family therapy practitioner. One can only aim to teach family therapy as an orientation with the focus on assessment rather than treatment. Yet there is a growing interest as shown by the increasing number of adult residents wishing to continue their family therapy training at the end of their six month rotation, or requesting to come for a year rather than the mandatory minimum of six months.

Residents have come to child psychiatry expecting to develop an expertise with children. They may find it difficult to integrate their learning in child psychiatry with that of family therapy where the child is viewed as only part of a system. How readily they can integrate the various points of view partly depends on their own personal comfort in taking an active role, in functioning in a group, in their ability to think on their feet and on how well they have resolved conflicts with their own family of origin. It can also be highly confusing for a resident to discover that a single piece of behaviour may be formulated in many different ways (Scheflen, 1978). It is important for the supervisor to interweave the various components of the child psychiatry curriculum with family theory. A supervisor that feels individual psychopathology and development are totally incompatible with family systems theory will contribute heavily to the dilemma of the students, leaving them to flounder not knowing how to integrate all the various "bits" of knowledge that they have acquired and possibly feeling guilty because of their desire to put it all together. There is no reason, to our way of thinking, why family theory needs to be presented as contradictory. Great harm is done by people who teach only about the larger system and ignore or say it is irrelevant to consider, for example, the inner life of the child or the effect of biology on the system.

Our university curriculum dictates that we emphasize the importance of diagnosis, but the issue of diagnosis can be a thorny one. One would be hypocritical if one were to both teach individual diagnosis and also indicate that it is not truly relevant. Although psychiatrists in general accept the importance of diagnosis, many see it as a hostile act to force one member of a family to carry the stigma of a label for what is essentially a family problem (Haley, 1975). Although diagnosis may be equated with labelling, in the truest sense it is closer to formulation and should lead to a treatment plan (G.A.P., 1966). At times, there is a magical faith in diagnosis as if once a diagnosis is made then everything will be solved.

Residents and programmes often tend to be examination orientated and family therapy only comprises a small fraction of a heavy curriculum. Residents must be taught psychopharmacology, neurophysiology, neuroanatomy and psychopathology, to name but a few, and not mentioning the whole range of therapies and intervention techniques. The focus, at times, changes from the biological to the psychological and then to the social. Each change entails a conceptual shift. The move from linear to circular thinking in learning a family therapy orientation entails yet another shift. For example, diagnosing brain damage or schizophrenia, or administering drugs, within one conceptual model, could lead to a labelling of the identified patient. However, within a family systems orientation, one might reframe the situation as a family problem. Deciding which model should take precedence at any given moment may not be a simple matter, even for the supervisor. The conceptual conflict is encapsulated in the question of whether one can have "a brain-damaged family". It is little wonder that a resident may come to feel confused or overwhelmed.

Residents' medical training has instilled in them the importance of taking personal responsibility for their patients' welfare, particularly, when the patient happens to be seriously ill. The Moons were referred for family therapy after their eldest daughter, Carol, had a psychotic break and because their therapist felt the illness was the result of disturbance in the family. Indeed, communication was indirect and ambiguous. There was frequent disqualification of expression of thought or feeling. Carol's vacuous stare and vague response seemed to protect her from appearing to defy her parents, although all were left frustrated and confused.

The resident who did the reassessment felt strongly that Carol was still suffering from a schizophrenic illness and that a major tranquilizer should be prescribed. Family therapy, he felt, was contraindicated because of the degree of disturbance of the girl and mother's fragility, as indicated by a previous history of mental breakdown. The supervisor insisted and began to work with the family. Although, at first angry, the resident came periodically to watch the successive sessions, possibly hoping that family therapy would fail. Gradually, the family began to change with clearer communication and more open expression of feelings. Carol became more oriented, less indirect, and more involved with what was happening. School work improved. The resident was initially surprised and grudgingly admitted that something positive was happening. Some months later, the supervisor was amused and pleased to note that the resident had become a strong advocate for family therapy, even where the indications were somewhat questionable and was striving during the remainder of his year to gain as many family skills as he could.

Residents working with severe family disturbance associated with schizophrenia, fire setting, or anorexia nervosa may express strong reservations about the use of family therapy. Some residents dwell on the element of risk in doing family therapy with a particular family. For these residents, an approach which puts a positive connotation on the patient's symptoms and views it as an expression of a family problem rather than an illness (for example, Palazzoli *et al.*, 1978) is perceived as a denial of medical responsibility and, therefore, implies a failure to take these responsibilities seriously.

Residents are taught to think critically. They may reject family therapy because it does not appear "scientific". This is, in part, because there is still no consensus as to how to diagnose families (Fisher, 1977; Keeny and Cromwell, 1977; Tseng *et al.*, 1976). In addition, an integrative theory of family functioning that can provide a theoretical basis is not yet available. Much of the literature on family therapy has been purely anecdotal with small samples and an absence of controls. Most residents, though, are aware that there is the same difficulty with research in individual psychotherapy. On the positive side, family therapists, like individual and group therapists, are becoming more rigorous in their attempts to evaluate treatment effectiveness. Family therapy is now coming to acquire a sound data base (Gurman and Kniskern, 1978). However, there is still the need to dispel the myth that family therapists are hostile to the need for hard research (Gurman and Kniskern, 1978).

In summary, today, psychiatry continues to have an ambivalent stance towards the rapidly growing field of family therapy. Family therapy in some instances is still considered as secondary to biological psychiatry and psychoanalysis. It is this tension between the resident's training in family therapy and the rest of his psychiatric and medical education that creates specific problems for the trainee.

Family therapy training of probation and aftercare officers

In Canada, the philosophy regarding how the individual juvenile delinquent should be managed has been gradually changing from policies espousing reform through incarceration, to one of guidance and management in the community (Broder, 1977). This has led to a closure of many training schools with an increased number of officers working in the field. Probation and Aftercare Officers (henceforth referred to as PACOs) have been expected to act *in loco parentis*, providing guidance and authoritative direction (Juvenile Delinquents Act, 1970).

Present policy formulated at senior levels encourages work with the family of the delinquent, extending the mandate in law (Children's Probation Act, 1978). However, there are no clear guidelines to indicate how this is to be accomplished. Parents can refuse to be involved, claiming they have not broken the law. They can even refuse to keep the child at home (Child Welfare Act, 1978). Because those in middle management have little knowledge of family systems they are at a loss as to how to implement the change in focus. Many, as well, are frankly hostile to this new philosophy feeling it mollycoddles the child and represents an abdication of responsibility.

Approximately four years ago, three PACOs approached one of the authors, who was a consultant to their Ministry, asking if they could observe her therapy with families and obtain some supervision. For the first year they came in their own time. Then, with the change in policy, senior management asked the author to conduct a family therapy training seminar to run once a week for three hours for a small group of PACOs who requested such teaching. The author agreed to take on the task if the PACOs were willing to come regularly and discuss with the others their work with families.

Most PACOs have had little formal training in personality development, psychopathology and theories of change, but have a wealth of practical experience in dealing with large and small systems. They are accustomed to considering, for example, the clash between peer group norms and the wishes of the family. They must also face the contradiction between the pressures resulting from their role as representatives of the legal system, and their desire to be helpful and therapeutic. They have been exposed to the all too pervasive view that provision of enough love and attention will make most problems go away. Many have tried to work with the family and have come to recognize that family work is not as simple as some had been led to believe. Considerable training and supervision is required to enable one to become effective.

A small group of eight began to meet weekly with the consultant who quickly discovered that a curriculum, loaded with abstract theory, was not meaningful. The PACOs preferred a practical focus that had immediate relevance. Concepts couched in behavioural terms (for example, the work of Alexander and Parsons, 1973; Barten and Barten, 1973; Haley, 1976; Stuart, 1971) were considered helpful while psychoanalysis and general systems theory were rejected. They appreciated the opportunity of watching others work but refused to bring their own work for supervision. After about three months, the current group began to bring problems about children on their caseloads. Gradually, they learned how to present a case, what information was required and which questions were useful to ask. Often, it was necessary for the supervisor to digress and teach basic concepts of psychopathology. Trust in one another and the supervisor began to develop. After six months, one of the officers asked if he could present a verbal report of his ongoing work with a family. We were able to follow this family through diagnosis, contract making, working through issues, periods of resistance and, finally, termination. Now, after a year, all are willing to *verbally* share their ongoing family work. Their fears and anxieties about being observed are still unresolved but it is hoped that soon one of them will gain sufficient trust to allow his or her work to be seen.

It might be asked why it has taken so long for observational supervision to begin. After their first weeks on the job when an experienced officer accompanied them on visits, none of the officers had ever subsequently been observed. There is no precedent for ongoing clinical supervision in their field, let alone live supervision. The norm is for each to work on his own.

The administrative supervisors (middle management) frequently have no more clinical skills than the PACOs under them. The priority for them is administrative expertise. They are often ambivalent about their subordinates learning skills that they themselves do not possess. Hence, there is little support for the seminar from middle management or understanding of what the PACOs are trying to learn. PACOs may be told they have to appear in Court or go to a meeting rather than attend sessions. Some have even been told that they cannot bring a family from their caseload for supervision.

Video equipment is not readily available and, although each officer has ready access to audio equipment, most have never thought of taping sessions. All in all, observational supervision is a new experience and one that arouses intense feelings of anxiety, fear and the desire to avoid.

Because the consultant family therapy supervisor is outside the system, she has no direct authority over the officers. This, at times, is an asset but at others a liability. It does make it easier for officers to bring problems, admit their ignorance, and show their ineptitudes without fear of loss of promotion or job. On the other hand, the supervisor cannot force an officer to bring in a family for supervision and has no power, aside from her own credibility, to ensure that directives are followed. If the supervisor is to supervise effectively, she must recognize territorial, competitive and political forces at work. Paradoxically, she must introduce new ideas and ways of working while appearing to maintain the status quo.

The families that the officers must work with are difficult. They have not chosen to be counselled and are often resentful of what they see as an intrusion upon their privacy. Many are multiproblem families that have been rejected as "unworkable". Because officers must work with whomever the Courts send, the question in supervision becomes how to work with the "impossible" family who has no motivation and is openly hostile. All available techniques are taught including admitting that one does not have the slightest idea what to do and so does nothing. It is important for the PACOs to see that the supervisor does not have all the answers and that it can be therapeutic for the family to admit one's limitations and to share one's puzzlement.

Governmental policy fails to clarify whether the officer is to function solely as the legal representative of the Court or whether his job is to be therapeutic, helping individuals and families to grow. The trend, in Ontario, does seem to be toward the latter, with the placing of juvenile correctional services under the umbrella of the Ministry of Community and Social Services. Hence, the officers must make the gigantic leap from thinking along a good/bad legal continuum to a functional/dysfunctional or problem solving frame, and from seeing themselves as authority figures to being comfortable as facilitators of family interaction.

The families have many expectations of the officers but all expect them to have power over their children. When a PACO refuses to accept this mantle and instead expects the parents to assume control of their children albeit with the officer's help, they often respond with anger and frustration. Yet they give the PACOs much power by looking to them for support and leadership. In spite of this, many officers are intimidated by the middle class, verbal families on their case load. Some of them feel poorly educated and inadequate. The task of the supervisor is to help the officers discover their potency while, at the same time, identifying the pain of the families. When working in such situations it is not uncommon to become overly identified with one age versus the other, when one needs to identify with both parents and child to be effective. Also, as some officers are relatively young they may be working with parents who are not too different in age from their own. Some react strongly as if they were being asked to oversee their own parents. The supervision group can help them resolve these and other complex issues. Role playing, feedback from peers, and a focus on developmental tasks, are all useful in resolution of countertransference issues.

Like the psychiatric residents, the PACOs must learn to shift their thinking from an individual and linear model to one of systems and circularity. There is little understanding of, or support for, the systems model outside the seminar.

In the probation service, like other agencies, one is not allowed to open a family chart. Crimes are committed by individuals not families. Therefore, to teach that families have a role in criminal behaviour and that work with the whole family is the optimal approach goes against the norms and practices of the larger system.

Training seminars are usually held in the setting of the supervisor. Most PACOs find this an advantage although it may mean half-an-hour to an hour's travel by car sometimes through bad weather. To be away from the telephone and the stresses of work is important. During the transition from work to seminar they find they can change roles from that of PACO to that of student. The fact that the seminar is in a teaching facility supports this shift, as does the general ambience of the setting with blackboards, observation windows and video equipment. All the PACOs attending the seminar have chosen to be there. This is important for morale as each knows the others have made a commitment.

In summary, because of changes at a senior level of government, the PACOs are being forced to develop ability in family work. This creates real problems for them as not only must they take on a new epistemology and learn new skills but they must also learn to cope with the contradiction of being a therapist to families while at the same time being an extension of the legal system.

Clarke family therapy training programme

The Clarke Family Therapy Training Programme (henceforth referred to as C.F.T.T.P.) is now in its sixth year of operation. It has a three year structured curriculum made up of didactic and experiental components. This programme is one of the few of its kind in Canada and is situated in the University of Toronto, at the Clarke Institute of Psychiatry, Child and Family Studies Centre.

The faculty includes psychiatrists, psychologists and social workers, all of whom are experienced family therapists. Most have university appointments. A number work in other settings within the city. Their orientations cover a broad range. The students, who come from a variety of agencies within a hundred mile radius of the city, are trained mental health professionals with diverse levels of experience and expertise. All are currently engaged in family work. Their high motivation is shown by their readiness to pay a fee for training, attend seminars after a full day's work and, at times, travel long distances.

The supervisors prefer to use both direct observation and videotapes in their sessions. Audio tapes are less acceptable. Students are encouraged to bring in videotapes of their work, or to bring a family that they are working with to the supervisory session. At times, the supervisory group may go to the student's own setting and observe him at work. In spite of the travel time this has proved to be a useful experience, helping both the supervisor and the supervisory group to understand better the circumstances in which the student is working. If a student has difficulty in obtaining material for direct supervision, a family may be provided by the Clarke Institute.

Direct supervision may pose specific problems as the supervisor must balance his responsibility to the family with his commitment to the student. This is generally less of an issue when the student presents his work with a family from his own agency. However, if the student is working with a patient for whom the supervisor is carrying direct clinical responsibility, the supervisor's dual commitments may lead to conflict as in the following example. Recently one of the supervisors was watching a student interview a family who presented with an out of control youngster. After persistent questioning of the mother about how much time she spent away from home, the mother broke down in tears, the child began to act up, while the father ineffectually chastised the child. The supervisor felt compelled to enter the room to redirect the course of the interview. Although the intervention was in the interests of both family and student, the student reacted with a feeling of both inadequacy and relief.

One of the supervisor's primary tasks is to promote the student's feeling of autonomy. The supervisor may decide, during the early phases of learning, to sit in, in order to get the student started. This enables the supervisor to move in quickly, if required, in the interests of both student and family. When the supervisor is present in the room, it may require considerable restraint on his part not to intervene. Whether the supervisor is behind the screen or in the room he must be careful not to foster undue dependency in the student.

Certain faculty members have developed a reputation and following. If a student is denied the opportunity to work with that supervisor he may be upset and angry. These feelings can interfere with the establishment of a strong working alliance with an equally competent but less well-known supervisor.

The formation of a study group for supervisors was a necessary development. Too many were feeling isolated and separated from the programme. Regular meetings have dealt effectively with these feelings and provided a forum for problem solving regarding supervisory issues. Over time, it has led to a greater understanding of how others think and work.

Sometimes two supervisors have worked together. This has worked well when the relationship was compatible. However, when there has been conflict, no matter how well concealed, the students have sensed what has happened and have been affected. When doing live supervision of a group, it is an advantage to have two supervisors as one can take charge of the therapeutic work while the second concentrates on teaching the student observers. Another tactic used is that one supervises the other who works directly with the family. In so doing, the supervisors demonstrate the use of supervision.

The students face the same difficulties as psychiatric residents and PACOs in moving from linear to circular thinking. As they are usually the only one from their home setting, they do not have others to share their discomfort, or to test their new and sometimes novel interpretations of therapeutic events. For these problems, supervision in a group is particularly important in providing mutual support, validating the students' perceptions and allaying the students' uncertainty and anxiety.

The C.F.T.T.P. has regular workshops conducted by well-known visiting family therapists. These workshops have been generally stimulating although, at times, more directly useful to faculty. Furthermore, although it is not necessary for the faculty to follow the visiting workshop leader's approach, it is important for them to have sufficient understanding to be able to explain the concepts to the students. At times, the faculty may require time to assimilate new models. Mostly, the impact of the workshops has been positive. However, early on there was a visitor who strongly advocated his philosophy and by innuendoes criticized the programme which was then new and insecure. The students picked up his tone and roundly complained against the programme, demanding changes in line with the format advocated by the visitor. Unfortunately, the faculty responded defensively and it took considerable discussion to heal the breach. Therefore, it is recommended that programmes be selective in their choice of visiting faculty and also discuss the goals of the workshop carefully in advance.

The C.F.T.T.P. is about to graduate its third class. Its youthful idealism has enabled it to respond to innovative ideas and, when appropriate, to incorporate them into the teaching programme. Its growth has sometimes been painful but always exciting and stimulating.

Discussion

The transition from a linear way of thinking to one of circularity is probably the most difficult step all students must take. There are no short cuts. The transition can only come through reading, continued observation of others, discussion and clinical experience. However, what each student brings to the task from his previous learning can be an additional hurdle. Much of the old and familiar seems to be lost when a new epistemology is espoused. Physicians may feel that they are being forced to abandon their medical model and others their belief in the primacy of intrapsychic forces.

One way of helping residents appreciate the importance of family systems is by showing how such a conceptualization can help them understand their patients' intrapsychic dynamics. On the other hand, when supervising a student committed to a family orientation one may wish to demonstrate the importance of individual psychopathology in understanding the family system. Two vignettes will be given to illustrate these points.

The first was of a resident who felt he understood his adolescent patient but could not fathom the family system. He saw the boy's delinquent behaviour as resulting firstly from an ambivalent identification with his obsessional father and secondly, as a defence against the influence of his mother's depression. The supervisor discussed the homoeostatic balance between the parents' inability to tolerate either closeness or prolonged separations. The boy devoted considerable energy to bringing the parents together so that the father re-entered the home because "his son needed a father to control him". However, the boy also split his parents by, for example, sharing secrets with one and not the other. A discussion of the family system with the supervisor enabled the resident to obtain a clearer picture of the patient's oedipal struggles, which played a key role in his intrapsychic dynamics.

In the second example, the supervisor was sitting in with a female student who was treating the family. At one point, the mother broke down in tears and the supervisor felt compelled to intervene to reduce the level of anxiety. In the discussion which followed, it emerged that mother as a child behaved in an anxious and childlike way in order to get her father to intervene on her behalf, and rescue her from her mother. It was helpful to the student to appreciate the link between her guilt about how she had conducted the session and how the supervisor had also been led to repeat a pattern from mother's past. The discussion of mother's intrapsychic dynamics clarified what had occurred during the session and in an ongoing way in the family.

Problems in supervision may develop if the supervisor becomes too rigid, using the absolutist injunction of "This is *the* way things should be seen and thought about", thus not allowing for the possibility that events may be observed with equal plausibility from a number of different angles and alternative scientific viewpoints (Scheflen, 1978). This was illustrated when a psychiatric resident prefaced his presentation of his work with a family with a brain-damaged child by saying, "I know you like to think in a systems way but . . .". He went on to say that he felt the boy needed help in learning to articulate his feelings and suggested the use of individual psychotherapy. As the discussion continued the supervisor found himself pursuing the details of the family system and how these processes were maintaining the boy's difficulty in speaking. Gradually, the supervisor realized he was getting nowhere and that, in fact, the student's formulation was also valid. The boy in question did need help in learning to articulate and though the family system was reinforcing his difficulties, referral to a speech therapist was indicated along with continuation of the family work. To summarize with a quote, "The relativistic notion that there is no one perspective intrinsically more true, but that each one may be valid within its own frame of reference, is not an easy banner to carry: it undermines the illusion of certainty lent by any one perspective that leaves alternative approaches unrecognized" (Sluzki, 1974).

The Duhls have drawn our attention to the need for supervisors to attend to the different modes of learning of their supervisees (Duhl and Duhl, 1979). Psychiatric residents seem to have an academic style, possibly arising from their need to sit examinations, and the usual format of their training. It appears that the residents must become convinced that the model being taught is theoretically sound, and that there is scientific evidence for its efficacy before trying the new approach. PACOs, on the other hand, seem to learn best from their own practical experience. It is only late in their training that they will turn to the literature to gain the theoretical constructs to explain what they have been doing. Therefore, it is imperative to discover each student's particular style of learning and when it is optimal to introduce theory to facilitate progress.

Conclusion

In all three family therapy training programmes that have been described, the major task is to help the student make the leap from linear to circular (systems) thinking. However, systems theory must be applied not only to families being seen but to other relationships as well. Boundaries must be kept open so that there can be an optimal flow of information leading to greater differentiation and change which in the context of this chapter is equated with learning.

Because of rapid and exciting new developments in the field of family therapy, the supervisor must demonstrate an ability to integrate new ways of thinking, treating and teaching. By avoiding polarization he can provide students with a perspective of the field as a whole and help him to avoid becoming enmeshed in a particular ideology or approach. The supervisee will inevitably be confronted by conflicting ideas about the value of family therapy and which method is best. The task of the supervisee, with the aid of his supervisor, is to find a way through the maze in order to reach the goal of becoming a competent family therapist.

Notes

1. We wish to gratefully acknowledge the help of our colleagues, all our students and Miss Nora Such in the preparation of this chapter.
2. Residents in Canada and the U.S.A. are equivalent to Registrars in the U.K.

References

Alexander, J. F. and Parsons, B. V. (1973). Short-term behavioural intervention with delinquent families. *J. Abnorm. Psychol.* **81**, 219-225.

Barten, H. H. and Barten, S. S. (eds) (1973). *Children and Their Parents in Brief Therapy.* Behavioral Publications, New York.

Broder, E. (1977). The child whose behaviour is antisocial. *Psychological Problems of the*

Child and his Family (P. Steinhauer and Q. Rae-Grant, eds), pp.225-241. Macmillan, Toronto.

The Child Welfare Act (1978). *Statutes of Ontario*, Chapter 85.

The Children's Probation Act (1978). *Statutes of Ontario*, Chapter 41.

Duhl, F. J. and Duhl, B. S. (1979). Structural spontaneity: the thoughtful art of integrative family therapy at B.F.I. *J. Marital Fam. Ther.* **5**, 59-75.

Fisher, L. (1977). On the classification of families. *Arch. Gen. Psychiat.* **34**, 424-433.

Group for the Advancement of Psychiatry, Committee on Child Psychiatry (1966). *Vol. VI, Report 62, Psychopathological Disorders in Childhood: Theoretical Considerations and a Proposed Classification*. Group for the Advancement of Psychiatry, New York.

Gurman, A. S. and Kniskern, D. P. (1978). Deterioration in marital and family therapy: empirical, clinical and conceptual issues. *Family Process* **17**, 275-281.

Haley, J. (1975). Why a mental health clinic should avoid family therapy. *J. Marriage Fam. Counsel.* **1**, 3-13.

Haley, J. (1976). *Problem Solving Therapy*. Jossey-Bass, San Francisco.

The Juvenile Delinquents Act (1970). *Revised Statutes of Canada*, Chapter J-3.

Keeny, B. P. and Cromwell, R. E. (1977). Toward systemic diagnosis. *Family Therapy* **14**, 225-236.

Palazzoli, M. S., Boscolo, L., Cecchin, G. and Prata, G. (1978). *Paradox and Counterparadox*. Aronson, New York.

Scheflen, A. (1978). Susan smiled: on explanation in family therapy. *Family Process* **17**, 39-68.

Sloman, L. (1980). *Inclusive Fitness and Family Group Adaptation*. American Psychiatric Association Annual Meeting, May 3-9, San Francisco, California.

Sluzki, C. E. (1974). On training to "think interactionally". *Soc. Sci. Med.* **8**, 483-485.

Speer, D. E. (1970). Family systems, morphostasis and morphogenesis, or "Is homeostasis enough?" *Family Process* **9**, 259-278.

Stuart, R. B. (1971). Behavioural contracting within the families of delinquents. *J. Behav. Ther. Exp. Psychiat.* **2**, 1-11.

Tseng, W-S. *et al.* (1976). Family diagnosis and classification. *J. Am. Acad. Child Psychiat.* **15**, 15-35.

19. Family Therapy in a Living Context: Training Experience in a Family Day Unit

Alan Cooklin and David Reeves

In this chapter a model of training day care staff to work as conjoint family therapists is described. The family therapy is with families that the therapists "live with" throughout the week in the setting of a specialized day unit. The focus is on supervision of conjoint therapy with individual families, although the design of the unit includes many elements of multi-family group therapy, marital couples therapy, individual therapy and "multiple impact therapy". It is therefore necessary to give some description of the design of the Family Day Unit — the context from which this supervisory model is singled out.

Design of the Day Care Unit

The Family Day Unit has been evolving since October 1976. It began as an attempt to provide for families which had "defeated" multiple agencies or were the subjects of statutory intervention, by devising a programme in which they could "learn by experience". Initially two rooms, which had previously been used as a day unit for autistic children plus two almost derelict rooms in the basement of the hospital were commandeered. Staff sessions were scraped together to provide one, and later two nurses, two teachers, a therapist experienced in work with pre-school children, and a research psychologist, who also participated in the unit's work. There was also an "outside" out-patient or "office" staff group of psychiatrists, psychologists, social workers and child psychotherapists. This latter group did not participate in the day to day work of the unit, although the senior staff members provided consultation, supervision and teaching for the day care group. The reasons for this division are discussed later. By the Summer of 1978 funds had been raised, and a purpose-built unit had been created with space to include kitchen, bathroom, school rooms, playroom, parents room, with observation screens and video, and a garden. The programme which developed was such that up to ten families with children

243

FAMILY THERAPY SUPERVISION
ISBN 0-12-794815-5

whose ages ranged from babyhood to adolescence, would spend their day time week in the unit from 9 a.m. to 3 p.m. from Monday to Friday. The contract was made with the whole nuclear and some of the extended family, although there was often an identified patient at the outset. The decision to admit was shared between the Clinic "outside"[1] Team and the Day Unit Team. The criteria for use of the Day Unit continued to change as the "organism" of the Unit developed. Those admitted however were all families in which the teams judged that:

(1) "Outside" family therapy could not bring about sufficient changes quickly enough for the family to survive without undue harm to one or more members.

(2) Individual residential treatment or "care" would be accompanied by further confirmations of the family's self fulfilling prophesy of incompetence.

Three common categories of presentation were seen by the staff as the Unit's main intake.

Chaotic families

These families usually have many of the characteristics of what Minuchin (1974) has described as enmeshment as well as characteristics of what have been called underorganized families, with diffuse boundaries, particularly between parent/child sub-systems and between various functions of life. They also frequently presented as "united" in relation to the outside world, whilst usually exhibiting serial failure in very basic functions of life; organization of finance, housing, employment and often the physical requirements of child care. Bouts of violence are common, and these families have usually enlisted the simultaneous services of a large number of "helping" agencies. At the same time they have usually made little if any therapeutic progress with these agencies, the staff of which often show evidence of demoralization, frustration or exasperation about them.

Families that had become organized around an "intractable symptom"

These are families with a symptomatic member, sometimes designated as psychotic, around which the whole family structure has become organized. He or she has become their "raison d'etre". Usually they are families who have encountered many different kinds of therapeutic intervention, and almost always without avail.

"Reunion families"

These are families where one or more of the children, or one or more of the parents have been separated from the family for some reason, for instance by hospitalization or being taken into care. Frequently the children have been legally removed from the parents for being "at risk" from physical abuse or neglect. Often, in these cases the family would remain separated during the early part of their attendance at the Day Unit, so that their only experience of "shared life" would be in the Unit. This latter group of families has made up an increasing proportion of the Unit's work, and one with which it has proved particularly effective.

Thus the Unit would actually be composed of a group of parents, a group of pre-school children and babies, a group of school children and the staff.

Not all family members would come full-time. Usually two or three would spend the whole week in the Unit. If a sibling was doing well in school, his or her participation would be planned accordingly. Similarly if the father was a competent bread-winner, he would only be asked to make realistic adjustments so that he could spend an agreed time in the Unit with the rest of his family. The details of and reasons for this arrangement are not the subject of this Chapter.

Design of the Programme

The multiple impact approach of the Unit is reflected in two main goals: (1) Maintaining and sometimes increasing the intensity of family interactions. (2) Providing simultaneous input to different sub-systems.

Many of the families admitted manifested significant failures in organization of day to day events. We viewed these in terms of failure to traverse the boundaries from one event to the next—for example, achieving the transitions from sleep to waking-up, to getting-up, to making breakfast, to getting dressed, to washing up, to going to work or school. Failure to establish boundaries between events, generations or sexual roles for example, was seen as one factor in the failure to make these transitions. This was usually accompanied by failure to differentiate an executive or decision making sub-system within the family to effect such necessary daily changes.

For this reason the programme was structured so that there were many and repeated transitions of this nature included throughout the day. These transitions were not only from one event to the next, but would often include a change from being a member of one sub-group to that of another. For example on a particular day of the programme the families will first meet their own worker, after which the parents might join other parents for some shared activity while the elder children are in school and the younger children are in the playgroup. Later they would all meet for a mid-morning drink, after which they might meet for their session as a family. At some time each day all the families and staff would meet together for a half hour community meeting to integrate the events of the day, and the working of the Unit. The parents would join in a weekly group meeting together, while on other occasions the whole Unit or some part of it would plan and participate in various activities in the Unit such as cooking lunch and a weekly outing such as swimming, visiting the zoo or a museum.

Within a quite short period of time therefore each family has had to make many transitions of organization in different configurations. This also tended to maintain the intensity of interactions. Bringing usually separated functions of life such as those occurring in home, school or work, together under the same roof in a therapeutic setting, maintains the intensity and helps to prevent diffusion and extrusion. For example it becomes harder to see the child as an "angel" at home and the problem entirely located in the school or vice versa.

Within this "hot house" atmosphere, surrogate relationships between the child of one family to the parent of another are actively encouraged. This aims to reverse the self-fulfilling expectations of failure in parent/child relationships by developing surrogate parent/child relationships as a transitional bridge towards the development of greater competence. The staff thus have to resist the enticement to be "better parents" to the children or to their parents, and restrict themselves to policing the boundaries around the various structures which have been developed.

The Unit we have described provides a form of multiple impact therapy. The community meetings modelled on the extended family, were aimed to generate a surrogate extended family, and as such were used by the staff to develop the social matrix of the Unit. Although multi-family therapy was not the explicit goal of these meetings (at the time of writing), within them, similarities and differences between the cultures and communicational patterns of the families became very obvious. The staff were supervised to respond to these differences and counteract the group pressure to achieve "sameness". At the same time the hub of the work for each family was developed from the "one family" session. As a result the strategies worked out in the one-family sessions, had a powerful influence on the shape of the total organization of the Unit, and in turn highlighted differences between families.

This was the context in which the staff were supervised to work as therapists in one family sessions with the families in their care.

Function of the One-family Session

The first goal of the one family sessions is to establish goals for that family, and to initiate the process of change which it is intended to support throughout the week in all the other settings of the Unit's activity.

Realistic boundaries of privacy can be established both for the family as a whole by creating time to talk together and between sub-systems in the family.

For example if questions about the parents sexual relationship come up, they would usually be encouraged to seek a separate marital session or discuss these in the weekly parents group.

Much of the work of the Unit is based on modelling. This seems a particularly appropriate tool for these families in which the analogic elements of communication carry far greater meaning than the literal digital content. An example of the use of modelling as a technique in the wider context of the Unit is the set times when a parent sits behind the one-way mirror with one worker, while they both watch another worker interacting with his or her child, usually an under five-year-old. The parent and worker would then change places and might watch a videotape of either or both events.

In the one family session particular use is made of the modelling potential offered by the very fact that this session is a regular part of the week. It underlines that at a certain time in the week the family meets together with a "third party", that it is different from the other activities of the week, that the worker as the therapist is in a different role and may well behave differently. Lateness or failure to come to the session takes on a different significance from "outside therapy", because it happens in the context of a life shared by therapist and family. Particular use is therefore made of the implied messages: (1) The family can meet together. (2) There can be different or surprising behaviour at this time. (3) What happens one week affects what happens in another — the family suddenly *has* a memory.

Sequences of events presented by the family as random acquire an acknowledged pattern when the week's events are regularly punctuated by the one-family session. The therapist would therefore be directed to stick to a particular symptom, piece of behaviour, or pattern until this gives way to the presentation of new patterns by the family. Thus in the one family session long-term issues of family structure would be attended to, whilst the focus of the rest of the programme would usually be restricted to day to day events.

Model of Therapy

The model of intervention used by the therapists in the one family session has drawn heavily from structural therapy (Minuchin, 1974), although with important differences. Attention is paid to the detail of events in the session with the accent on current rather than past events. Therapist interventions are made on the basis of the overall strategy agreed for the family by the staff group, although the one-family session is the lynch pin for the development of that strategy. Boundary making and the realignment of dysfunctional alliances and coalitions are a common goal of these interventions.

The difference from this model arises out of the fact that the therapist does in reality have much historical and wider contextual information about the family — the effect of rubbing shoulders daily, together with the knowledge which members of one family know and share about another. At certain times therefore the therapist will explore the historical context in which the present family events occur, whilst at the same time maintaining pressure on structural change in the present. The historical and other data is thus used to set in relief the current struggle to change. We have found that this counterpoint of the two elements can serve to potentiate structural change by differentiating history, explanation, or meaning from the sought after change.

This raises the question of why we eventually decided to use the day care staff as the therapists as has been the case for the past two years, rather than involve the outside team. The initial pressure for this arrangement arose from complaints by the day staff that they could not follow or understand the interventions and strategies worked out by the outside staff when the latter were the therapists — despite frequent discussions or observations of videotapes or live sessions. It soon became clear that the complaints had another dimension; namely that the problem was how to follow through in a multi-family community, strategies which had been developed in an outside session. As a result the day care staff often felt devalued or deskilled, feeling that they could not develop a coherent therapeutic strategy. We therefore borrowed from the model which both of us had experienced in another setting (Harrow, 1970) wherein the nursing staff of an adolescent in-patient unit conducted the regular multi-family groups.

The effect of this change was not only that the staff felt and became more competent, more able to think systemically and work to a focused goal, but also that the strategies worked out in the separate session became more congruent to the structure of the Unit as a whole, and the structure of the Unit developed in a way which was more complementary to, and less in rivalry with the one family sessions.

It also had the effect of maintaining and supporting the "pressure cooker" design of the Unit. Fragmentation of information occurred less. In the previous model we often used a form of co-therapy whereby one of the therapists would be from the Day Unit, and one from the outside team. For a number of reasons, including the discouraging effects of co-therapists at different levels of expertise working together, as highlighted by the work of Dowling (1979), we began to move away from co-therapy. This provided a further impetus to make the change.

Lastly, it seemed more congruent to the modelling approach we were using. The day care worker is an intimately familiar person to all members of the family at certain times in the week, and within certain contexts. One assumption of our model was that family members need to acquire the freedom to behave differently within different sub-structures of the family and at different times. In some contexts it may be appropriate for a child to comment on the family's transactions at the meta level. In other contexts such behaviour may be potentially quite dysfunctional and for example be part of a move to avoid bed time. We assumed therefore that the families would benefit if meta communication (usually in the form of comments about what is happening) could become a part of the accepted transactions of family life whilst at the same time bolstering the inherent structure of each family. Thus the family worker, who for much of the week is an intimate "family member", at other times may be in a formalized role—say as teacher—and at this special time of the one family session is in a privileged position with the power to actively intervene in the family's transactions. When these different contextual boundaries are successfully maintained by the staff the one family session becomes invested with great power for change.

Model of Supervision

The use of an analogue of the model of therapy is continued throughout the supervision. Thus as with the model for the family, and the model of therapy, part of the supervisory process is contained in the Day Unit by the day care staff. This has the advantage of being congruent with the model at other levels of the hierarchy, and allowing the external supervision to be carried out by one person, thus maintaining as much congruence as possible in the model. The model was therefore designed to function at two levels:

At the level of on-going therapy:

Each family would have one of the Day Unit staff allocated to them, who would meet them when they arrived each day, be responsible for the overall management of their stay in the Unit and act as their regular family therapist. Another Day Unit staff member, usually the Head of the Unit or one of the more senior members, would be allocated as "front line" supervisor to the conjoint sessions. This person would usually be behind the one-way mirror during the sessions, might telephone in comments, call the therapist out, or enter the session. Although other staff might be observing at these times the families of course knew who this person was, and would be familiar with him or her in other contexts. It could therefore be argued that this is really co-therapy and that the other therapist could as well be in the room. In our experience however, as well as being congruent with our model of maintaining different degrees of distance and proximity in different contexts, by using the mirror the supervisor is able to maintain sufficient distance to help the therapist keep the boundaries of the session.

At the level of therapeutic strategy

The details of the strategy adopted would be worked out with the outside supervisor in a weekly Clinical Review Meeting. At a higher level of abstraction the overall plan would be worked out at an in-depth conference on each family held at approximately three monthly intervals, the average stay in the Unit being nine months.

At the level of generic principles of therapy

Generic principles of therapy would be worked out at a weekly two hour workshop, when all the Unit staff would meet with the outside supervisor. In this time live sessions were restricted to early consultation interviews with the supervisor, crisis situations, or when one of the therapist/supervisor diads needed help to make a radical change in the framing of the problem or in the therapeutic strategy. In the latter case, the live consultation interview would usually be requested by the therapist/supervisor pair, and always mutually agreed. For the rest generic issues would be worked out with the use of videotaped segments of recent interviews, while techniques would usually be "rehearsed" using role plays of simulated sessions. In the workshop the focus was on the therapist's interaction with the interactions in the family. Issues around the use of "self" would only be looked at in the therapeutic context, and specific use of techniques to explore the therapist's own family were not generally used. On the other hand the intimacy of the Unit meant that the Unit staff were usually quite familiar with a number of aspects of each others' families.

Conceptual and theoretical input

All the Unit staff attended a weekly seminar in which they were asked to describe a detailed piece of parent/child interaction which they had observed in the Unit. The goal of this seminar was to develop observational skills of interaction, and was also used as a vehicle to teach relevant aspects of child development. The latter seminar was led by a child psychotherapist who was also an experienced family therapist. Additional theoretical input was provided by reading seminars, although at less frequent intervals. Most of the Day Unit staff had also had some theoretical grounding from the one year introductory course provided by The Institute of Family Therapy.

Working of the Model

The model presented is not ideal. Considering the size of the task taken on by the Day Unit staff the supervisory input is relatively small. On the other hand it seemed to be a realistic arrangement for a service unit, and based on a model which is congruent with our overall philosophy of treatment. The Day Unit front line supervisors would tend to model their interventions on the outside or generic supervisor, and in turn the therapists would tend to model their interventions on the front line supervisors input. The latter were planned to reflect as closely as possible the suggested shifts in the family, as expressed by the staffs' stated goals. The nature of the content and style of behaviour at these four levels (the generic supervisor, the front line supervisor, the therapist and the family) varied greatly, but the perameters of change and the direction of "push" were made as explicitly analogous as possible. This is demonstrated in an example taken from videotaped extracts later.

Supervisory inputs at the case level might be in the form of a message, a statement to the therapist "in front of the family", a piece of advice ("ally closer with the parents"), or a reformulation. At the generic level the supervisory input was commonly aimed: (1) to keep the staff group thinking systemically in the face of the linear pulls exerted by the families, (2) to counteract the tendency to diffuse tension and conflict, a tendency which was often encouraged by the proximity in which the staff "lived with" the families.

A typical example follows of supervisory interventions at these two levels:

The first is taken from a segment of a videotaped transcript of a role-played sequence during the supervisory workshop. The therapist, a nurse, has had some experience of individual psychotherapy and is trying at this point to understand the problem. He apparently becomes interested in the content symbolic significance of the elephant, and has to be helped to recognize that he has been activated to make a structural move to diffuse the tension. In the role play are father, mother and Jean (aged 5).

Staff Role Play Session

Mother: . . . . and it's really left to me most of the time to do something . . . .
Jean: is this an elephant?
Mother: . . . . and she doesn't understand that . . . .
Therapist: She's certainly stopping you from talking now at the moment isn't she . . . .
. . . . do you think you could try and draw me an elephant on the board . . . .
Jean . . . . Do you think you could try and do it for me . . . . oh, well take this elephant over there and try and draw me one on the board . . . . ok.
Therapist: (Begins to say to parents) She seems quite . . .
Supervisor: (enters and asks) Just think now what have you been trying to do so far?
Therapist: Um well, define the problem I suppose
Supervisor: What have you defined it as?
Therapist: Aah, well they come with a problem that the child is uncontrollable, but I see very little evidence initially that she is . . . .

The supervisor assumed that the therapist has returned to an individual diagnostic model; is the child O.K. or not? (and in so doing is siding with the child). His goal is to help the therapist to work with the structural relationships as they exist in the session.

Therapist: Yes it is very theoretical and I can't seem to . . . .
Supervisor: Well, so far you *pointed out* Jean's interruption—which confirms the parents' incompetence, and at the same time you diffused the tension by sending Jean away to "draw nice pictures". If that happens you can only "*discuss*" her. If you want to be able to affect the balance in the relationships you'll need to maintain sufficient intensity—perhaps by them struggling to achieve something you have asked them to do . . . . O.K.? (Supervisor leaves the room).
Therapist: O.K. . . . . shall we start again? Shall we get . . . . (pauses, thinks, and then rephrases) . . . . so would you (to Mother) like to get Jean to sit down so we can all talk together. . . .
Mother: Jean come and sit down . . . . Jean! . . . . Jean!! (and Jean then joins her Mother).

This was a very simple supervisory intervention but at the generic level. Its aim was to help the therapist focus on structure rather than content, move towards enactment of the problem, and the beginning of boundary making.

Following this role play the same team watched a short excerpt of video of the same nurse working with the "T" family. On the tape he is being supervised live by the senior nurse who had played the father in the previous excerpt. It is a "Reunion family"; the three children (Sally aged 14, Ben aged 12 and Sara aged 11) are in the care of a Local Authority Childrens' Home and meet their parents in the Unit. The Father (Nev) is Indian and has recently suffered a fairly severe hemiplegia; the Mother (Jan) is white English, frequently goes on drinking binges, and will disappear from the home for several days at a time, usually staying with other men. One of the goals of the Day Unit admission is to try and interrupt the cycle of promises e.g. "We'll soon have you all home" and the failures to keep these promises in which the parents and children are caught. The therapist has been trying to find an area in which a small decision could be made, and maintained, but is frequently diverted by the rich content of the children's utterances about the parents. The outside supervisor focusses on ways the front line supervisor can help the therapist stay on task.

In the next session with the family the therapist has become diverted by Sally's sullenness and Ben's apparently irrelevant interruptions. The supervisor telephones him and tells him to try and increase the proximity between Sally and her Mother, and suggests he tries to engage the Mother, who is usually defined as the one who "fails" the family, in pinning Sally down. Sara is absent, the others are seated thus:

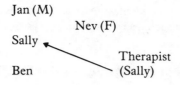

After the telephone call:

Therapist (to Sally): It would be easier if you were to go and sit there . . . . and talk to your Mum . . . .
Sally moves silently as shown above
(M) *Jan:* Well—?
Sally: What . . . .
(F) *Nev:* (to Jan) Here's the ash tray . . . .
Silence.
Therapist: Can you actually sort out Jan when Sally's coming to the hospital, because she says she has exams and doesn't know whether she will be coming. Can you find out and try to make some arrangement with her.
Another long silence.
(M) *Jan:* (to Sally) You have got exams in two weeks?
Sally: (to Mother) and I have got one next week.
(F) *Nev:* Next Wednesday.
Sally: That is why Mr S. (Head of School Year) is coming to see you . . . .
Sally: When I start my options, then I will decide whether it is on a Thursday or Monday I will have to miss next week . . . . cos I don't want to miss my exams.
(M) *Jan:* You've not got one on Thursday tho' anyway . . . .
Sally: Well I'll probably have them on Thursday — English . . . .
Continues for another three minutes or so — therapist limits his participation to giving the mother encouragement.
(M) *Jan:* You could come here Monday and Thursday you have not got an exam on the Monday and if you have an exam on Thursday morning you could come here after.
Sally: Here? . . . .
Sally: After the exam?
(M) *Jan:* Yes, after the exam — you don't have it in the afternoon, you can still come . . . .
Sally: Yes I know I will (gives in with apparent relief).
Therapist: I think you did very well. That was different. You have done extremely well in sorting it out.

In these examples a simple structural approach is being taught at both levels. In the first it is at a generic level, in the second at the level of therapeutic strategy.

The fact that the family worker also shares some authority with the school could have been used by the family to detour the issue of the mother's competence in responding to her daughter. However, the front line supervisor was able to keep him in the position of therapist in relation to the mother/

daughter pair by intervening whenever the parent or child began to activate the
therapist to take a part in such decisions in his role as family worker.

Implications of the Model in the Day Unit Setting

The design of the programme is inherently based on a "hot house" or "pressure
cooker" model. Many commonly separate functions of life are brought together
under one roof. The children will experience a relatively normalized, although
rather intensive classroom situation, albeit for fewer hours than at school. The
parents participate in various activities involved in running the unit, attend a
parents group, and participate in specific activities designed to help them
improve their competence in their own family matters.

This is all based on the assumption that change would be more likely to be
achieved if the pace of family interaction is increased. At the same time the
development of structural boundaries, between time, place, task or role in the
family is seen as a central goal of the approach. Therefore the staff's role is very
often to act as sentries between one function, activity, or role and another,
intervening sufficiently to maintain the safety of the individuals *and* the task in
which they are engaged — while these different functions or tasks are crowded
together.

In the service of these aims use is made of the intrinsic three level hierarchy (or
four level when grandparents are involved); the children, their parents and the
staff. The staff will generally use their authority to try and enhance the parents'
competence, and will encourage the parents to stick to parental rather than
marital issues "in front of the children".

The advantages for the therapeutic process of working in this context are
perhaps obvious. The permeability of the boundary around the family is
increased by the constant daily contact. The form and content of the
communicational patterns in the family are immediately available to the
therapist; the kinds of words they use, the context in which they are used and
their congruence or otherwise to the non-verbal behaviour. The wall around a
family which maintains myths is very soon lowered by the process of admission
to the Unit. For example Alison was a young mother, her husband Tim was a
soldier and they had one child Teddy aged 2. Their admission was prompted by
a combination of serious violence within the marriage together with "hysterical
attacks", which Alison presented each time Tim was stationed away from home.
Both Alison and Tim had maintained the picture of Alison being the innocent
victim. The other parents were soon able to see how she often made provocative
snide comments about Tim from just within his hearing. This example of course
also raises one of the main dangers in the model; namely that the families could
easily feel excessively exposed, not only to the staff but also to each other, and

thus easily experience each other as too painfully critical. This is usually a problem when a new family enters, as with the B's. They had begun to drop out after the first week and on being home visited complained bitterly of feeling judged by another family about their (the parents) method of disciplining their children. This problem presented less often than might be anticipated, partly we think because of the diverse cultural backgrounds of the families in the Unit (Laquer, 1973). The criticisms were often experienced as culturally based, and therefore less personal. As a result each family's method of resolving a particular issue could be more easily added to the different possibilities of solutions which could then be considered in the community meetings, and the parents group.

At all levels the goal for staff supervision is to help them remain in the therapist role and not become "just a member of the family" of families (the community). Whenever the staff experience themselves as in a family position *vis-a-vis* the other families, they will tend to be activated to defend their "family of families" (the Unit), particularly if the Unit is being criticized for being critical. In this case the particular staff member would be encouraged to give a positive connotation to the goal expressed by the parents of being more effective in disciplining their children and exhort them to be more effective still, and by implication use the staff's help.

The success of the model depended on the staff being able to maintain their role as sentries to the various boundaries and not become lost as family members. We assumed, and have felt our experience confirmed the view that providing they could maintain this position their therapeutic effectiveness would otherwise be enhanced by the context. The struggle by the staff to maintain this position was often sorely tested, and nearly always an issue for staff discussions. This occurred particularly when one parent gave a party for all the parents and invited the staff, and when one single parent in the Unit was married and invited the staff to the wedding. It also was particularly tested when the staff and families lived together once per year for a week on the Unit's annual "holiday". Decisions about how and when to accept such invitations and how to manage the boundaries in the climate of greater intimacy experienced during the holiday would take up a fair proportion of supervisory time. The other side of such intimacy is experienced when a staff member for example home visits a family in which one of the children is legally deemed to be "at risk". That is, the child has been officially notified as being in danger of physical damage or neglect. By choice the Unit staff will in some cases agree to take the official responsibility for monitoring the child's safety. In one example a young woman whose baby was considered to be "at risk" was home visited because of her failure to attend for several days. In the course of the visit by her therapist she ran out taking the baby. The therapist had to be helped with the fact that he had a responsibility to stop her, while in his sessions with her and her boyfriend his focus had been to try and help them help each other to be more competent. The central task of supervision in this context is to help the family worker behave differently when wearing different hats in different contexts with the same family. When it is successful this changing of staff roles has proved to be an extremely potent intervention for change in these families. We think this is partly a function of the power of the message which is conveyed when staff change roles as a model for the families. In addition this model maintains a degree of freedom of movement for the staff, and thus helps prevent them from being caught in the family's game.

In many instances the families would be our allies in maintaining relevant boundaries. In the early days one of us (A.C.) had been working as the outside therapist with a single parent family composed of an Irish mother and her two children, while a teacher from the Unit acted as co-therapist. The teacher (from the Day Unit staff) feared that intensely conflict laden and disruptive episodes, with which we worked in the sessions, would be carried over into the classroom. She was surprised to find the family never referred to events in the session at other times in the week. We were equally concerned that if intimate sexual or other matters were faced in a session with a therapist whom they might later meet at lunch, that the members of the family would either be highly inhibited or run out. In our experience this hardly ever occurred. It seemed that the structure allowed a wall to be maintained around such events to a degree which some might regard as pathological, although we felt it was in the service of our stated goals.

In another situation a single mother had activated five different kinds of therapy before her arrival in the Unit. Not surprisingly she had experienced great confusion between these various inputs. She carried similar behaviour into the Unit by confusing different parts of the programme — particularly those that were child centred, from those that were parent-centred, or those that were explicitly parent/child centred. Supervision of the separate family session was geared to help the therapist repeatedly (and sometimes boringly) filter out those elements which were not parent/child focused.

The following two examples demonstrate the use of supervisory input to help the therapist reframe a problem by shifting the therapist's intervention to a higher level of abstraction; that is, to a strategic level aimed to change the rules governing a particular sequence (Gorell Barnes, 1981). Both are examples involving the family sited earlier on p.254; the first at the family level, the second at the community level.

Although the staff were worried about Teddy's poor speech and co-ordination, the ticket for admission was the parents marriage. They would engage in repeated violent rows which nearly always followed a fixed pattern and would usually end with either a social worker, the police, or the army being called. The therapist had felt he must stick explicitly to the problem the couple acknowl- edged that they wished help with, although he was finding that there was little or no change in the severity or frequency of these crises. The supervisor and the workshop had tried to help the therapist use various interventions to interfere with the escalation of the marital conflict from within the frame the therapist had chosen (namely the marriage). The therapist had experienced "violent" resistance to any shift of frame on to one which would include Teddy. The therapist was asked to bring the family for a live consultation during the workshop time. The couple said they would come, but refused to allow themselves to be videoed or the use of the one-way mirror. The supervisor said that this should be accepted, but told the family himself in his role as supervisor, that as this was a regular supervisory session for the staff's benefit all the staff would have to be in the session with them. They agreed to this. Having established some power, the supervisor was then able to challenge the couples' apparent disinterest in improving their management of Teddy (which was usually expressed in threats "if you say anything about Teddy we'll put him in a nursery . . ." or "you'll be responsible if he gets harmed"). The supervisor did this by a direct challenge to the parents about their "self-indulgent" interest in their battles (to one of which an Army Officer had been called the previous night), and then chastised the therapist for his lack of concern about Teddy's welfare. This intervention had been previously discussed with the therapist. The result was that they began to express their loyalty to the therapist who was then able to use their anger with, and wish to discredit the supervisor to engage them on work with Teddy.

In the second example Alison, who was the eldest of thirteen in her own family of origin, had become engaged in a violent physical fight with another mother, Sheena. Sheena was the youngest of a group of five children in a family which had produced another four children eleven years later. Alison's and Sheena's families were both being worked with by the same therapist, and their fight erupted while they were discussing their sessions with each other. We could have considered this episode as the result of the eruption of childhood rivalries, or of sexual rivalries, brought to life by their seeing the same therapist. Our goal however was to increase the differentiation of parent/child boundaries, and such an interpretation would in our view have tended towards sameness or diminution of differentiation. At the same time, while we have frequently found a structural intervention to be the most effective in the family sessions, such moves seemed out of place in the wider community setting of staff, parents and children. In this case a special meeting of the whole Unit was called and a strategic or systemic formulation was handed down by the supervisor after being worked out by the staff group. He announced that the staff group had given very careful consideration to what had happened. We knew that many of them had had difficulty in understanding Sheena's family. (This was a relatively recent admission, and we were thinking here of the fact that she had not resolved the arrival of a new family in her own family of origin). The supervisor continued that we thought that by them all agreeing to have Alison fight Sheena and make it clear that Sheena was therefore not understood, was a helpful way of recreating Sheena's family in the Unit, as it actually was, in order that we could understand it properly. Whilst appreciating their intention to induct Sheena and her present family into the Unit we were concerned lest they were making too great a sacrifice by playing these parts so closely. All the families left without speaking to each other, and the following day Sheena and Alison were to be seen discussing something in private, after which Alison for a few days became Sheena's agent to induct her into the group of mothers.

Comments

So far we have described a model for the supervision of day care staff with relatively little experience of practice in family therapy, to act as the therapists

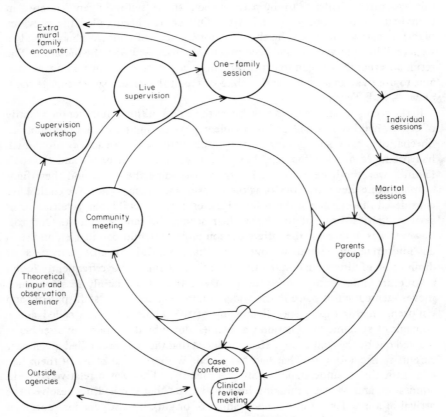

Fig. 1. Information flow in the family day unit.

for the families in their care. The context is complex. Figure 1 is an attempt to represent the information flow. The supervisory arrangements are highly structured. The increase in structure of these was followed by a lowering of resistance to utilizing supervision. Analogously we found that many families who had fled from zealous offers of help, could increasingly use this rich programme as it became more structured.

We have also made relatively little reference to the specific function of multi-family therapy in the Unit. Although we have noted the reports of multi-family therapy since 1963, these have mostly focused on multi-family therapy as an adjunct to in-patient psychiatric treatment (Laqueur and La Burt, 1963; Laqueur *et al.*, 1964; Laqueur, 1973), or as part of an adolescent treatment programme (Harrow, 1970; Van der Lande, 1979).

The model we have described is now achieving some stability, and we are beginning to develop its potential for multi-family therapy.

Notes

1. The term "outside" will be used in this Chapter to denote the function of the out-patient, office or "extramural" team.

References

Dowling, E. (1979). Co-therapy: a clinical researcher's view. In *Family and Marital Psychotherapy: A Critical Approach* (S. Walrond-Skinner, ed.), pp.173-199. Routledge and Kegan Paul, London.

Gorell Barnes, G. (1981). Family bits and pieces: framing a workable reality. *Developments in Family Therapy* (S. Walrond-Skinner, ed.). Routledge and Kegan Paul, London.

Harrow, A. (1970). A Nursing Approach to Multiple Family Group Therapy. *Proceedings of 5th Conference A.P.S.A.*, Edinburgh.

Laquer, H. P. (1973). Multiple family therapy: questions and answers. *Techniques of Family Psychotherapy* (D. Bloch, ed.), pp.75-85. Grune and Stratton, New York.

Laquer, H. P. (1973). Multiple family therapy: questions and answers. *Techniques of Family Psychotherapy* (D. Bloch, ed.), pp.75-85. Grune and Stratton, New York.

Laquer, H. P. and La Burt, H. A. (1963). Conjoint family group therapy: a new approach. developments. *Int. J. Soc. Psychiat., Congress Issue*, 70-80.

Minuchin, S. (1974). *Families and Family Therapy*. Tavistock Publications, London and Harvard University Press, Cambridge, Mass.

Van de Lande, J. (1979). Multiple family therapy in a residential setting for adolescents. *J. Fam. Ther.* **1**, 241-251.

Author Index

Subject Index